PSYCHOLOGY RESEARCH PROGRESS

PANIC DISORDER

ASSESSMENT, MANAGEMENT AND RESEARCH INSIGHTS

PSYCHOLOGY RESEARCH PROGRESS

Additional books in this series can be found on Nova's website under the Series tab.

Additional e-books in this series can be found on Nova's website under the e-Books tab.

PSYCHOLOGY RESEARCH PROGRESS

PANIC DISORDER

ASSESSMENT, MANAGEMENT AND RESEARCH INSIGHTS

YONG-KU KIM
EDITOR

nova
science publishers
New York

Library of Congress Cataloging-in-Publication Data

ISBN: 978-1-53613-001-0

Published by Nova Science Publishers, Inc. † New York

CONTENTS

PREFACE

Patients with panic disorder initially mistake their symptoms for life-threatening medical conditions, and repeatedly seek medical attentions. Clinical management begins by convincing himself that the alarm sign, panic attack, is not caused by medical illness. Although panic disorder may mimic medical conditions, patients with medical conditions, that may pose a real life threat, may be diagnosed when panic attacks, which is not well explained by existing disease, repeatedly appear. It can be more challenging to persuade patient to accept their diagnosis.

After they accept having panic disorder, the most commonly asked question by patients is why they have had panic disorder. For me, even for more than 20 years of clinical experience, it is not easy to satisfy patients with simple answers. An exemplary explanation may be that combination of hereditary, environmental, genetic environmental interactions, neurotransmitter, HPA axis, and life stress affects the onset of panic disorder. Genetic susceptibility obviously affects panic disorder, but does not account for up to 30-40% of occurrence of the disorder. Stressful life event often precedes the onset, and seem to increase the risk of panic disorder, but not all.

In fact, we still do not know the cause of panic disorder. However, we are approaching step by step toward understanding causes and developing new treatments for panic disorder through research on the epidemiological studies, genetics, epigenetic studies, neuroimaging studies, and studies dissecting neural circuits regulating normal fear and anxiety. To date, the most effective treatments for panic disorder are antidepressants and cognitive behavioral therapy. Antidepressants are not disorder-specific, but proven to be effective for long-term treatment of panic disorder. Cognitive behavioral therapy is a specific treatment for panic disorder that corrects dysfunctional thoughts seen in panic disorder. However, it is difficult to apply it to many patients because of low accessibility. In order to overcome this, methods such as internet-based cognitive behavior therapy have appeared recently. There are unmet-medical-demand, treatment-resistant patients who failed to respond the above treatment options. The latest advances in therapy for treatment-resistant patients who do not respond well to therapy have been addressed in this book.

This book is the result of a worldwide collaboration of experts who are outstanding in the research of panic disorder. I hope that this book will give patients, clinicians, and clinical researchers, who have not had a satisfactory answer, latest insights on panic disorder.

Chapter 1 highlights fear network in panic disorder. The authors discuss neurofunctional, neurostructural and neurochemical alterations in panic disorder. They outline an important role of the brain's salience network - mainly composed of the insula, anterior cingulate cortex and amygdala - in the development of panic attacks.

Chapter 2 summarizes genetic, epigenetic and environmental interaction in panic disorder. Determining the genetic, environmental, and epigenetic backgrounds of panic disorder widen our understanding of this disease and potentially help psychiatrists treat patients more effectively.

Chapter 3 focuses imaging genetics in panic disorder. The genes such as serotonergic, COMT, ACCN2, and CRHR1 and their impact on neuronal activity in relevant brain circuits allows better understanding of psychopathology of panic disorder. Imaging genetic studies suggest genetic factors drive a dysfunctional limbic-frontal interaction during emotional processing in panic disorder.

Chapter 4 highlight influence of the sympathetic nervous system on inflammatory responses involving pro-inflammatory cytokines, and neuroinflammation which may ultimately lead to alterations in structure and function of specific brain regions that are involved in etiology of panic disorder.

Chapter 5 describes assessment methods for identifying risk of suicide in panic disorder and interventions for preventing suicide in affected patients.

Chapter 6 reviews various risk factors contributing to development of panic disorder. CBT for anxiety sensitivity, reducing smoking or caffeine intake and treatment of comorbid condition affect the course of panic disorder and may be important to prevent aggravation and recurrence of symptoms of panic disorder.

Chapter 7 focuses application of MRI in the dissection of pathophysiology and alterations of brain functions and structure in panic disorder. From the MRI studies in panic disorder, we can confirm the crucial role of fear network model in the pathophysiology of panic disorder.

Chapter 8 reviews alterations of HPA axis in panic disorder and give an outlook for future studies which should take care into account influencing variables of cortical secretion. Understanding and insight into pathogenesis of panic disorder would be allowed based on involvement of a neural fear network and differentiating between the endocrine and neuronal regulation of HPA axis.

Chapter 9 discusses anomalies encountered in various neurotransmission systems and neuroanatomy of panic disorder. It is suggested that that fear- and anxiety-related responses are mediated by a so-called "fear network" which is centered in amygdala and includes hippocampus, thalamus, hypothalamus, periaqueductal gray region, locus coeruleus and other brainstem sites.

Chapter 10 reviews evidences regarding alternative treatments in treatment-resistant panic disorder. Augmentation of antidepressants, anxiolytics and other drugs with CBT, pindolol, divalproex sodium, aripiprazole, olanzapine, risperidone and sulpiride could be effective in treatment-resistant panic disorder.

Chapter 11 introduces psychological treatment options for panic disorder. CBT is effective when conducted both individually and in a group format. Panic-focused psychodynamic psychotherapy can be indicated as a psychological treatment for panic disorder in specific clinical situations.

Chapter 12 aims to identify evidence based for the effectiveness of internet-based cognitive behavioral therapy (iCBT) and online mindfulness training (OMI) in treatment of panic disorder. Evidence suggests that guided iCBT programs are superior to unguided iCBT programs regarding their effectiveness, acceptability and adherence. Tailored transdiagnostic Internet-delivered programs for comorbid anxiety disorders appear to have some potential for the adjunctive therapy of panic disorder, even as unguided formats.

I wish to give my heartfelt thanks to all chapter authors for their valuable time spent preparing manuscripts. They are leading research scientists with knowledge and expertise in panic disorder. It goes without saying that without their support, this book would not exist. I believe that this book will function as a step on the path toward the ultimate goal of understanding and treating panic disorder.

In: Panic Disorder
Editor: Yong-Ku Kim
ISBN: 978-1-53613-001-0

Chapter 1

FEAR NETWORK IN PANIC DISORDER: EVIDENCE FOR NECESSARY AMENDMENTS

***Thomas Sobanski*[1,*] *and Gerd Wagner*[2]**

[1]Department of Psychiatry, Psychotherapy, and Psychosomatic Medicine Thueringen-Kliniken, Saalfeld, Germany

[2]Department of Psychiatry and Psychotherapy, Jena University Hospital, Psychiatric Brain and Body Research Group, Jena, Germany

ABSTRACT

For explaining the pathogenesis of panic disorder (PD), several cognitive, behavioral and neurobiological theories have been developed, [e.g., 1, 2, 3]. In the year 1989, Gorman et al. introduced a neuroanatomical model that was aimed at integrating the different views of PD as either a biological or a psychological disease [4]. The authors proposed experiments to test their theories. In 2000, Gorman et al. provided a revised version of their model. In this article they suggested that fearful responses and panic attacks are mediated by a "fear network" in the brain that is centered in the amygdala and involves its interaction with the hippocampus and medial prefrontal cortex [5]. Since its inception, this neuroanatomical model has stimulated and greatly

[*] Corresponding author: tsobanski@thueringen-kliniken.de, sobanskit@aol.com.

influenced research in PD – primarily in the field of neuroimaging studies. In this chapter, we will explore the questions if the proposed model of a fear network has been supported or refuted by recent neuroimaging studies or if additional theoretical approaches have to be pursued. Owing to the wide range of this topic, we will only highlight a small selection of the studies performed. For a more comprehensive overview, we refer to previously published review articles [e.g., 6, 7-10].

1. THE "FEAR NETWORK" PROPOSED BY GORMAN ET AL.

According to Gorman et al. [4], three components of PD (1) acute panic attacks, (2) anticipatory anxiety, and (3) phobic avoidance are located in three specific sites of the CNS: the brainstem, limbic system, and prefrontal cortex. These three neural systems were suggested to be structurally and functionally closely connected, reflecting manifold interactions of the three mentioned clinical features. Hence, according to Gorman et al. [4] different treatments for panic disorder and agoraphobia not only affect different symptoms of the illness but also different parts of the brain. Thus, according to the authors, antipanic drugs like tricyclic antidepressants (TCA) or MAO inhibitors block brainstem-provoked panic attacks; benzodiazepines and relaxation training reduce anticipatory anxiety via the limbic system, and desensitization and cognitive therapies relieve phobic avoidance by influencing functions of the prefrontal cortex. In our opinion it is notable that both psychopharmacological and psychotherapeutic treatments are put on the same level by being conceptualized to act directly on specific neural networks. Therefore the neuroanatomical model proposed by Gorman et al. [4] successfully integrates biological and psychological facets of PD.

In the revised version of their hypothesis, Gorman et al. [5] suggest that the behavioral symptoms of panic disorder are mediated by a "fear network" in the brain, which is centered in the amygdala and includes the hippocampus, thalamus, hypothalamus, the periaqueductal gray (PAG) region, locus coeruleus, and other brainstem sites. This theory states that patients with PD have a decreased threshold for the activation of the fear network. Excessive activity in this network leads to autonomic and neuroendocrine activation through projections from the amygdala to the brainstem and hypothalamus, resulting in typical PD symptoms. The lateral nucleus of the amygdala receives afferents from cortical regions involved in processing and evaluating sensory information. According to Gorman et al. [5] abnormal functioning in these cortical areas could potentially result in the misinterpretation of sensory information (bodily cues), leading to an inappropriate activation of the fear network via misguided excitatory input to the amygdala. The authors propose that activation of the fear network as a result of cognitive misinterpretations could lead to the release of certain neurotransmitters that can cause autonomic behavioral responses related to panic disorder. These responses include an increase in respiratory rate, increases in blood pressure, heart rate, defensive behaviors and postural freezing. Thus, processes at the biological level can directly lead to behavioral symptoms [5]. With regards to drug therapy in PD, Gorman et al. [5] not only stated that antidepressants exhibit their antipanic effects via the brainstem, as proposed in their original model [4], but also that therapy with SSRIs might act directly on the limbic system - in particular via the central and lateral nuclei of the amygdala [5].

2. The Role of Serotonin

It is well established that PD responds to drugs that increase serotonergic function, such as certain tricyclic antidepressants (TCA), inhibitors of monoamine oxidase (classical MAOIs), selective serotonin reuptake inhibitors (SSRIs), and serotonin-norepinephrine reuptake inhibitors [SNRIs; 11]. The serotonin reuptake inhibitors (SSRIs) are now generally accepted as the first-line pharmacological treatment for PD [12]. Therefore, there is clear evidence for an important role of serotonin in the pathophysiology of PD that has led to extensive research – predominantly in neuroimaging and animal studies. According to Gorman et al. [5] the anxiolytic effect of SSRIs is mediated by at least three mechanisms: (1)

Inhibitory serotonergic projections from the raphe nuclei downregulate the activity of noradrenergic neurons in the locus coeruleus [13]. The authors concluded that SSRIs, by increasing serotonergic activity in the brain, have a secondary effect of decreasing noradrenergic activity. This would lead to an amelioration of the somatic symptoms of panic attacks. (2) The projection of the dorsal raphe (DRN) neurons to the PAG is thought to modify defense/escape behaviors. As derived from animal studies, stimulation of the DRN markedly increases serotonin release in the dorsal PAG region, resulting in diminished activity in this brain area [14] associated with reduced defense/escape responses, i.e., reduced propensity for panic-like reactions. (3) As a third point, Gorman et al. [5] state that long-term treatment with SSRIs may reduce hypothalamic release of corticotropin-releasing factor [CRF; 15]. CRF, which leads to adrenal cortical production of cortisol, is also a neurotransmitter in the CNS and has been shown to increase fear in preclinical models [16]. CRF enhances activity of the LC, when directly administered into the brain [17]. Furthermore, as stated by Gorman et al. [5] SSRIs seem to have an effect on the central nucleus of the amygdala itself. Serotonergic neurons originating in the dorsal and medial raphe nuclei project directly to the amygdala via the medial forebrain bundle [18]. Moreover, serotonergic neurons modulate sensory input at the lateral nucleus of the amygdala, inhibiting excitatory inputs from glutamatergic thalamic and cortical pathways [19]. According to Gorman et al. [5] this might be one of the major mechanisms for the anxiolytic action of the SSRIs.

Deakin and Graeff [2] proposed a hypothesis suggesting that different subpopulations of serotonergic neurons in the dorsal and median raphe nucleus through topographically organized projections to different brain regions are involved in the pathophysiology of anxiety and affective disorders. These different subpopulations of serotonergic neurons included (1) serotonergic neurons within the DNR projecting to the dorsal periaqueductal gray that inhibit innate panic-/escape-like physiological and behavioral responses, (2) serotonergic neurons within the dorsal raphe nucleus projecting to the amygdala, that facilitate conditioned fear and conflict anxiety-like responses, and (3) serotonergic neurons within the median raphe nucleus that increase stress resilience and mediate antidepressant-like effects. This concept partly overlaps with the model developed by Gorman et al. [5]. The Deakin/Graeff hypothesis still is a cornerstone that stimulates most recent research in panic disorder.

Spiacci et al. [20] investigated whether or not the enhancement of 5-HT-mediated neurotransmission within the dorsal PAG affects panic-like defensive reactions in rats submitted to a hypoxia challenge. Intra-dorsal-PAG injection of serotonin, a 5-HT1A receptor agonist or a 5-HT2A agonist reduced the number of upward jumps during hypoxia, interpreted as escape attempts. These effects were similar to those caused by chronic, but not acute, intraperitoneal administration of the antidepressant fluoxetine, or acute systemic administration of the benzodiazepine receptor agonist alprazolam. These observations confirm that the dorsal PAG is a key region involved in panic-like defensive behaviors. In a subsequent study, the authors demonstrated that serotonergic neurons of the lateral wings of the DRN (one of the five subnuclei of the DRN) are primarily involved in the mediation of PD-associated responses [21].

While the function of the DRN in the regulation of panic-like defense behaviors is well understood, the median raphe nucleus has received less attention. Generally, evidence derived from animal studies points to a relevant role of this raphe nucleus in the regulation of anxiety, but not of panic. This can be achieved through the serotonergic pathway that rises from the MRN to the dorsal hippocampus [22]. Alternatively, the DRN seems to participate in both anxiety and panic. Interestingly, the regulation of anxiety by the dorsal and median raphe serotonergic pathway is carried out through different target structures – the amygdala, dorsal PAG and ventral hippocampus in the case of the DRN, and the dorsal hippocampus in the case of the median raphe nucleus. Because these structures have different functional profiles, it is conceivable that different aspects of anxiety are underpinned by each of them. In this regard, Gray and McNaughton [23] have argued that the amygdala may underpin the neurovegetative arousal and affective components of anxiety, whereas the dorsal hippocampus (posterior part in humans) may regulate cognitive manifestations, such as worry. This suggestion is supported by the reported interaction between the dorsal hippocampus and the prefrontal cortex underpinning fear learning and memory [22, 24]. According to a recent study by Ohmura et al. [25] the ventral (anterior part in humans) hippocampus may be involved in inappropriate retrieval of fear memory in PD. By microinjection of a 5-HT7 receptor antagonist into a rat`s ventral hippocampus, the expression of freezing behavior - an index of fear memory retrieval - was significantly suppressed. The authors argued that the 5-HT7 receptor might be a target of drug development for the treatment of PD.

3. Recent Neurostructural, Neurofunctional, and Neurochemical Studies

One of the most important approaches to elucidate the neurobiological foundation of PD is to perform neuroimaging studies investigating the function as well as the structure of specific brain regions that are supposedly related to this disease. Today, there are numerous neurofunctional, neurostructural, and neurochemical studies that have demonstrated the significant role of certain structures in the fear network [6-10].

Functional neuroimaging studies have frequently used functional magnetic resonance imaging (fMRI) to investigate the neurobiological correlates of panic symptoms. Such studies often employed paradigms focusing on stimuli directly related to PD, but also paradigms, which investigated brain activation during experimental panic provocation. A few further studies investigated brain functioning in PD during the resting-state. For example, Engel et al. [26] used pictures showing characteristic panic/agoraphobia situations to investigate activation differences in PD patients in the predefined regions of interest (ROIs), i.e., prefrontal, cingulate, and insular cortex, and the amygdalo-hippocampal complex. Greater activation in PD patients than in controls was detected in the insula, left inferior frontal gyrus (IFG), dorsomedial prefrontal cortex

(DMPFC), the left hippocampal formation, and left caudate nucleus, when panic-related and neutral scenes were compared. In a very recent fMRI study, Feldker et al. [27] presented panic-related and neutral visual scenes to PD patients to study the neural underpinnings of threat processing. Similar to the results found by Engel et al. [26], patients showed hyperactivation in a fear network proposed by Gorman et al. [5] comprising the brainstem and the thalamus, but also in the insula, anterior cingulate cortex (ACC), midcingulate cortex (MCC), and DMPFC for disorder-related versus neutral scenes, compared to healthy controls. No significant amygdala differences between groups could be found. Subjective levels of anxiety significantly correlated with brainstem activation in PD patients. In contrast to these studies, which did not find the amygdala to be abnormally activated, very recently Liebscher et al. [28] showed that successful cognitive-behavioral therapy (CBT) led to a greater decrease in anxiety symptoms going along with a reduction in bilateral amygdala activation during processing of agoraphobia-related pictures, compared to patients receiving antidepressants and a wait-list control group. This study impressively demonstrates the habituation of amygdala activity after repeatedly facing panic-provoking stimuli duringCBT.

FMRI studies which investigated neural activation patterns in patients with PD during a fear conditioning task showed differential conditioning to be related to enhanced activation of the bilateral IFG, whereas simple conditioning and safety signal processing were related to increased midbrain activation in patients with PD compared to healthy controls [29]. Kircher et al. [30] investigated the effects of CBT on brain activation during fear conditioning and showed that after CBT medication-free patients with panic disorder and agoraphobia revealed reduced activation for the conditioned response (CS+ > CS-) in the left IFG compared to control subjects. This activation decrease was related to reduction in agoraphobic symptoms.

Increased functional connectivity between the IFG and amygdala, insula, as well as ACC was found in patients after CBT. Thus, this result may indicate increased top-down control of the extended fear network by prefrontal cortex, going along with increased control at the emotional and behavioral level.

Similarly to the studies cited above, the most consistent differences between patients with PD and healthy controls yielded by provocation studies were found in the cingular, insular, frontal and brain stem areas [6]. Recently, Goossens et al. [31] studied the effects of hypercapnia on the brainstem BOLD signal in patients with PD using fMRI. Three brainstem regions were defined as ROIs (regions of interest) due to their putative involvement in panic and chemosensitivity: the peri-aqueductal gray (PAG), the raphe nuclei and the locus coeruleus (LC). The authors demonstrated increased brainstem activation in patients, i.e., located in the rostral raphe ROI in response to hypercapnia compared to healthy controls and healthy divers. Despite low spatial resolution, this study provides further support for the significant role of specific brainstem nuclei in triggering panic attacks.

The few resting-state fMRI (rs-fMRI) studies, which investigated neural functional connectivity patterns in patients with PD found an increased resting-state functional connectivity (RSFC) between the amygdala and the bilateral precuneus as well as altered RSFC between dACC and frontal, parietal as well as occipital areas [32]. The RSFC is a parameter that indicates how coherent the BOLD signal fluctuates in two specific regions. Lai and Wu [33-35] reported abnormalities in the occipital cortex, putamen and thalamus in first-episode medication-naive patients with PD compared to matched controls using different rs-fMRI parameters.

To sum up, functional studies suggest abnormal activation in the originally proposed fear network [5], comprising brainstem, especially LC and thalamus, but additionally in the insula, anterior and midcingulate cortex and lateral as well as medial parts of the prefrontal cortex. Thus, the recent functional neuroimaging data point toward the necessity of an extension of the "fear network." Interestingly, differences in amygdala activation were not as consistently reported as one would predict from the hypothesis of Gorman et al. [5].

With regard to structural neuroimaging studies investigating volumetric or morphometric changes in PD, limbic structures, frontal and temporal cortical areas, the basal ganglia, the pituitary gland and hypothalamus as well as the midbrain and brainstem structures were found to exhibit abnormalities [6, 36-39]. However, a relatively large heterogeneity with regard to structural abnormalities exists between these studies, which makes it difficult to relate abnormal volume or gray matter (GM) to a specific brain region to PD. The reasons for this inconsistency are manifold. Many of these studies had relatively small sample sizes. Moreover, the presence of comorbid depression or other psychiatric disorders among patients might also have had an impact on the GM volume estimation in some of these studies. Considering the white matter (WM) abnormalities in PD, the few studies that specifically investigated the WM integrity by applying the diffusion tensor imaging (DTI) technique revealed higher structural integrity in terms of greater fractional anisotropy (FA) values in the cingulum bundle [40]. Recently, Lai et al. [41] showed reduced integrity in WM tracts of the right inferior fronto-occipital fasciculus (IFOF), left body of corpus callosum and left superior longitudinal fasciculus (SLF) in first-episode, medication-naive and late-onset PD patients, when compared to healthy controls. Kim et al. [42] reported decreased FA in frontal white matter and the genu of the corpus callosum in medicated patients with PD. To sum up, the few studies on white matter in PD also revealed significant abnormalities in the structural connectivity between the regions of the extended fear network, which has been recently shown to exhibit abnormal function.

A major role of serotonin in the pathophysiology of PD has been deduced from the therapeutic effects of serotonergic drugs [11, 12]. In accordance with this hypothesis, studies on 5-HT1AR and SERT binding performed by single-photon emission computed tomography (SPECT) and positron emission tomography (PET) have revealed altered and mostly reduced serotonergic activity in the raphe nuclei, orbitofrontal cortex, temporal lobes, anterior and posterior cingulate cortex, amygdala, and hypothalamus in patients with PD [43-46]. In the course of therapy with SSRIs, postsynaptic alterations seem to decline while the presynaptic changes persist [44]. In addition to these functional alterations, structural abnormalities, e.g., disintegration of the raphe nuclei in the brainstem, have also been described [47]. Ascending serotonergic projections to cortical and subcortical brain regions have their origin mainly in the dorsal and median raphe nucleus. There is evidence from current animal studies, that efferent inputs of dorsal raphe neurons may moderate panic-like defensive behaviors by controlling the activity of the dorsal periaqueductal gray [20, 21], thus confirming the earlier hypotheses of Deakin and Graeff [2, 9] as well as of Gorman et al. [5] on this point.

4. Necessary Amendments of the "Fear Network" as Deduced From Recent Research

As described in detail at the beginning of this chapter, the "fear network" proposed by Gorman et al. [5] includes the amygdala, the hippocampus, thalamus, hypothalamus, the periaqueductal gray region, locus coeruleus, and other brainstem sites. Prior neuroimaging studies have reinforced the role of these regions in the pathophysiology of panic disorder. Furthermore, recent functional and structural neuroimaging studies additionally showed alterations in the anterior and mid-cingulate cortex, inferior and dorsomedial frontal cortex, as well as in the insula [6, 7, 48], suggesting the necessity for the extension of the originally proposed "fear network." Interestingly, differences in the amygdala activation were not as consistently reported as one would predict from the hypothesis of Gorman et al. [5]. Regarding this issue, Feldker et al. [27] stated that, given the role of the amygdala proposed for the pathophysiology of PD, it seems surprising that amygdala hyperactivation only reached marginal significance. In the same tenor, Etkin and Wager [49] come to the conclusion that "in panic disorder, amygdala hyperactivity appears to be the exception, rather than the rule." At present, it remains unclear whether aberrant amygdala activation is simply not as characteristic of PD as proposed earlier, whether it is too weak to be detected with common thresholds, or whether specific methodological limitations make it difficult to detect. Indeed, amygdala hyperactivation seems to strongly depend on stimuli and experimental paradigms, sample heterogeneity and size, as well as on limitations of neuroimaging techniques [7, 50, 51]. However, in our view, it is notable that the amygdala is strongly involved in salience and significance detection in the information stream [52]. Since paradigms with specific fear-evoking stimuli are more difficult to develop for PD patients in contrast to patients with specific phobias, we can speculate that the often observed lack of amygdala hyperactivation in PD might be based on such methodological issues, e.g., using appropriate stimuli and experimental paradigms.

In summary, the alterations of neural activation in patients with PD as reported in past and present studies remain somewhat inconsistent. Interestingly, two very recent studies using clear panic-related pictorial stimuli and relatively large sample sizes have put strong emphasis on a specific role of the insula and dorsal anterior cingulate cortex in the pathophysiology of panic disorder [26, 27]. There is growing evidence that the insula, the dorsal anterior cingulate cortex as well as subcortical structures, such as the amygdala as well as ventral striatum and brainstem/midbrain structures, i.e., the substantia nigra and ventral tegmental area, play a crucial role in salience processing across multiple sensory and cognitive domains by integrating external sensory information with internal emotional and bodily state signals [53].

These regions are typically considered to constitute the so-called salience network (SN), an intrinsically strongly interconnected large-scale brain network, which represents the core brain systems involved in identification of biologically and cognitively relevant events in order to adapt behavior to changing environmental conditions [54]. Thus, the SN contributes to several complex brain functions by integrating cognitive, affective, sensory information and bodily state signals.

The latter can be paraphrased with the term interoception, which refers to conscious awareness, emotional processes and behavior related to physiological information arising from the body. This includes processing of proprioceptive and visceroceptive processes such as heart rate, respiration, and blood pressure. Abnormal interoception has been suggested to play a key role in the etiology and maintenance of anxiety disorders [55] in terms of oversensitive perception of somatic sensations and subsequent catastrophizing interpretations. There is evidence to assume that ascending inputs providing information about interoceptive and visceromotor signals related to the current bodily state converge in the insular cortices [56]. In close cooperation with the amygdala, insular activity seems to represent a specific subjective emotional state and the emotive value of external stimuli in terms of salience [57]. Thus, this observation may explain differences between studies on PD patients regarding the amygdala or insula activation, which might be attributed to different subjective emotive values of presented stimuli. Another source of variability that induces potentially different insula/amygdala activation in patients with PD, as well as in control subjects, is the subject-specific state of physiological arousal. Thus, simultaneous acquisition of physiological signals, e.g., heart or respiratory rate in the MR scanner, may potentially explain some part of activation variance in these brain structures.

In addition, the ACC is another brain structure considered to be a key node within the salience network [53] and which has often been observed to show abnormal functioning in PD. It is involved in automatic attentional control as well as in response selection and conflict monitoring [58], thus enabling rapid access to the motor system, comprising the basal ganglia, primary motor cortex, supplementary motor areas, including the DMPFC, which was also found to show abnormal activation in panic disorder.

Moreover, the salience network recruits the ventral fronto-parietal network, mainly consisting of the temporo-parietal junction and inferior frontal gyrus [59], which is typically activated by infrequent or unexpected behaviorally relevant (salient) events. This recruits additional executive resources to ensure focused attention on task-relevant goals, e.g., to cope with panic-relevant stimuli [60]. This may explain the often observed abnormal activation of the inferior frontal gyrus in patients in PD. In summary, besides the brainstem/midbrain, amygdala and prefrontal cortex, further brain areas such as the insula and the ACC are emerging from recent imaging studies in PD and seem to be of greater importance than originally proposed.

Interestingly, recent studies applying the diffusion tensor imaging to investigate the white matter connectivity in PD reported abnormal white matter integrity in the cingulum bundle as well as in the major fiber tracts, which connect frontal with temporal, parietal and occipital brain regions: the inferior and superior longitudinal fasciculi [61]. This finding is in accordance with the observation of abnormal functional activation in regions of the salience network and of the ventral fronto-parietal network. However, to date only few studies have investigated the integrity of specific white matter tracts in patients with PD. Therefore, more studies are required to elucidate the abnormal structural connectivity in PD.

5. SUMMARY – "FEAR NETWORK" AND AMENDMENTS

In this chapter we discuss the recently published neurofunctional, neurostructural and neurochemical alterations in panic disorder. As described above, the "fear network" proposed by Gorman et al. [5] includes the amygdala, the hippocampus, thalamus, hypothalamus, the periaqueductal gray region, locus coeruleus, and other brainstem sites. While many neuroimaging studies have reinforced the role of these regions in the pathophysiology of PD, it is noteworthy that several recent functional and structural neuroimaging studies also reported alterations in the anterior and mid-cingulate cortex, inferior and dorsomedial frontal cortex, as well as in the insula [6, 7, 48]. In this chapter we try to elucidate the background of these findings. We outline the important role of the brain's salience network - mainly composed of the insula, anterior cingulate cortex and amygdala - in the development of panic attacks and we substantiate the necessity for an extension of the originally proposed "fear network."

References

[1] Beck, AT; Emery, G; Greenberg, RL. 1985. *Anxiety disorders and phobias: a cognitive perspective.* New York: Basic Books.

[2] Deakin, JF; Graeff, FG. 5-HT and mechanisms of defence. *Journal of Psychopharmacology*. 1991, 5(4), 305-15.

[3] Klein, DF. False suffocation alarms, spontaneous panics, and related conditions. An integrative hypothesis. *Archives of General Psychiatry.* 1993, 50(4), 306-17.

[4] Gorman, JM; Liebowitz, MR; Fyer, AJ; Stein, J. A neuroanatomical hypothesis for panic disorder. *American Journal of Psychiatry.* 1989, 146(2), 148-61.

[5] Gorman, JM; Kent, JM; Sullivan, GM; Coplan, JD. Neuroanatomical hypothesis of panic disorder, revised. *American Journal of Psychiatry*. 2000, 157(4), 493-505.

[6] Dresler, T; Guhn, A; Tupak, SV; Ehlis, AC; Herrmann, MJ; Fallgatter, AJ; et al. Revise the revised? New dimensions of the neuroanatomical hypothesis of panic disorder. *Journal of Neural Transmission (Vienna).* 2013, 120(1), 3-29.

[7] Holzschneider, K; Mulert, C. Neuroimaging in anxiety disorders. *Dialogues in Clinical Neuroscience.* 2011, 13(4), 453-61.

[8] Pannekoek, JN; van der Werff, SJ; Stein, DJ; van der Wee, NJ. Advances in the neuroimaging of panic disorder. *Human Psychopharmacology.* 2013, 28(6), 608-11.

[9] Paul, ED; Johnson, PL; Shekhar, A; Lowry, CA. The Deakin/Graeff hypothesis: focus on serotonergic inhibition of panic. *Neuroscience and Biobehavioral Reviews.* 2014, 46 Pt 3, 379-96.

[10] Sobanski, T; Wagner, G. Functional neuroanatomy in panic disorder: Status quo of the research. *World Journal of Psychiatry.* 2017, 7(1), 12-33.

[11] Nash, JR; Nutt, D. Psychopharmacology of anxiety. *Psychiatry.* 2007, 6(4), 143-8.

[12] Baldwin, DS; Anderson, IM; Nutt, DJ; Allgulander, C; Bandelow, B; den Boer, JA; et al. Evidence-based pharmacological treatment of

anxiety disorders, post-traumatic stress disorder and obsessive-compulsive disorder: a revision of the 2005 guidelines from the British Association for Psychopharmacology. *Journal of Psychopharmacol*ogy. 2014, 28(5), 403-39.

[13] Aston-Jones, G; Akaoka, H; Charlety, P; Chouvet, G. Serotonin selectively attenuates glutamate-evoked activation of noradrenergic locus coeruleus neurons. *Journal of Neuroscience.* 1991, 11(3), 760-9.

[14] Viana, MB; Graeff, FG; Loschmann, PA. Kainate microinjection into the dorsal raphe nucleus induces 5-HT release in the amygdala and periaqueductal gray. *Pharmacology, Biochemistry and Behavior.* 1997, 58(1), 167-72.

[15] Brady, LS; Gold, PW; Herkenham, M; Lynn, AB; Whitfield, HJ Jr. The antidepressants fluoxetine, idazoxan and phenelzine alter corticotropin-releasing hormone and tyrosine hydroxylase mRNA levels in rat brain: therapeutic implications. *Brain Research.* 1992, 572(1-2), 117-25.

[16] Elkabir, DR; Wyatt, ME; Vellucci, SV; Herbert, J. The effects of separate or combined infusions of corticotrophin-releasing factor and vasopressin either intraventricularly or into the amygdala on aggressive and investigative behaviour in the rat. *Regulatory Peptides.* 1990, 28(2), 199-214.

[17] Butler, PD; Weiss, JM; Stout, JC; Nemeroff, CB. Corticotropin-releasing factor produces fear-enhancing and behavioral activating effects following infusion into the locus coeruleus. *Journal of Neuroscience.* 1990, 10(1), 176-83.

[18] Tork, I; Hornung, JP. 1990. *Raphe nuclei and the serotonergic system in the human nervous system.* San Diego: Academic Press.

[19] Stutzmann, GE; LeDoux, JE. GABAergic antagonists block the inhibitory effects of serotonin in the lateral amygdala: a mechanism for modulation of sensory inputs related to fear conditioning. *Journal of Neuroscience.* 1999, 19(11), RC8.

[20] Spiacci, A Jr.; Sergio, Tde O; da Silva, GS; Glass, ML; Schenberg, LC; Garcia-Cairasco, N; et al. Serotonin in the dorsal periaqueductal

gray inhibits panic-like defensive behaviors in rats exposed to acute hypoxia. *Neuroscience.* 2015, 307, 191-8.

[21] Spiacci, A Jr.; Pobbe, RL; Matthiesen, M; Zangrossi, H Jr. 5-HT1A receptors of the rat dorsal raphe lateral wings and dorsomedial subnuclei differentially control anxiety- and panic-related defensive responses. *Neuropharmacology.* 2016, 107, 471-9.

[22] Andrade, TG; Zangrossi, H Jr.; Graeff, FG. The median raphe nucleus in anxiety revisited. *Journal of Psychopharmacology.* 2013, 27(12), 1107-15.

[23] Gray, JA; McNaughton, N. 2000. *The neuropsychology of anxiety.* 2nd edition ed. Oxford: University Press.

[24] Zelikowsky, M; Bissiere, S; Hast, TA; Bennett, RZ; Abdipranoto, A; Vissel, B; et al. Prefrontal microcircuit underlies contextual learning after hippocampal loss. *Proceedings of the National Academy of Sciences of the United States of America.* 2013, 110(24), 9938-43.

[25] Ohmura, Y; Konno, K; Minami, M; Watanabe, M; Yoshioka, M. Serotonin 5-HT7 receptor in the ventral hippocampus modulates the retrieval of fear memory and stress-induced defecation. *International Journal of Neuropsychopharmacology.* 2016, (1), 1-12.

[26] Engel, KR; Obst, K; Bandelow, B; Dechent, P; Gruber, O; Zerr I; et al. Functional MRI activation in response to panic-specific, non-panic aversive, and neutral pictures in patients with panic disorder and healthy controls. *European Archives of Psychiatry and Clinical Neuroscience.* 2016, 266(6), 557-66.

[27] Feldker, K; Heitmann, CY; Neumeister, P; Bruchmann, M; Vibrans, L; Zwitserlood, P; et al. Brain responses to disorder-related visual threat in panic disorder. *Human Brain Mapping.* 2016, 37(12), 4439-53.

[28] Liebscher, C; Wittmann, A; Gechter, J; Schlagenhauf, F; Lueken, U; Plag, J; et al. Facing the fear--clinical and neural effects of cognitive behavioural and pharmacotherapy in panic disorder with agoraphobia. *European Neuropsychopharmacology.* 2016, 26(3), 431-44.

[29] Lueken, U; Straube, B; Reinhardt, I; Maslowski, NI; Wittchen, HU; Strohle, A; et al. Altered top-down and bottom-up processing of fear conditioning in panic disorder with agoraphobia. *Psychological Medicine.* 2014, 44(2), 381-94.

[30] Kircher, T; Arolt, V; Jansen, A; Pyka, M; Reinhardt, I; Kellermann, T; et al. Effect of cognitive-behavioral therapy on neural correlates of fear conditioning in panic disorder. *Biological Psychiatry.* 2013, 73(1), 93-101.

[31] Goossens, L; Leibold, N; Peeters, R; Esquivel, G; Knuts, I; Backes W; et al. Brainstem response to hypercapnia: A symptom provocation study into the pathophysiology of panic disorder. *Journal of Psychopharmacology.* 2014, 28(5), 449-56.

[32] Pannekoek, JN; Veer, IM; van Tol, MJ; van der Werff, SJA; Demenescu, LR; Aleman, A; et al. Aberrant limbic and salience network resting-state functional connectivity in panic disorder without comorbidity. *Journal of Affective Disorders.* 2013, 145(1), 29-35.

[33] Lai, CH; Wu, YT. Patterns of fractional amplitude of low-frequency oscillations in occipito-striato-thalamic regions of first-episode drug-naive panic disorder. *Journal of Affective Disorders.* 2012, 142(1-3), 180-5.

[34] Lai, CH; Wu, YT. Decreased regional homogeneity in lingual gyrus, increased regional homogeneity in cuneus and correlations with panic symptom severity of first-episode, medication-naive and late-onset panic disorder patients. *Psychiatry Research-Neuroimaging.* 2013, 211(2), 127-31.

[35] Lai, CH; Wu, YT. The alterations in inter-hemispheric functional coordination of patients with panic disorder: the findings in the posterior sub-network of default mode network. *Journal of Affective Disorders.* 2014, 166, 279-84.

[36] Del Casale, A; Serata, D; Rapinesi, C; Kotzalidis, GD; Angeletti, G; Tatarelli, R; et al. Structural neuroimaging in patients with panic disorder: findings and limitations of recent studies. *Psychiatria Danubina.* 2013, 25(2), 108-14.

[37] Sobanski, T; Wagner, G; Peikert, G; Gruhn, U; Schluttig, K; Sauer, H; et al. Temporal and right frontal lobe alterations in panic disorder: a quantitative volumetric and voxel-based morphometric MRI study. *Psychological Medicine*. 2010, 40(11), 1879-86.

[38] Vythilingam, M; Anderson, ER; Goddard, A; Woods, SW; Staib, LH; Charney, DS; et al. Temporal lobe volume in panic disorder--a quantitative magnetic resonance imaging study. *Psychiatry Research*. 2000, 99(2), 75-82.

[39] Uchida, RR; Del-Ben, CM; Santos, AC; Araujo, D; Crippa, JA; Guimaraes, FS; et al. Decreased left temporal lobe volume of panic patients measured by magnetic resonance imaging. *Brazilian Journal of Medical and Biological Research*. 2003, 36(7), 925-9.

[40] Han, DH; Renshaw, PF; Dager, SR; Chung, A; Hwang, J; Daniels, MA; et al. Altered cingulate white matter connectivity in panic disorder patients. *Journal of Psychiatric Research*. 2008, 42(5), 399-407.

[41] Lai, CH; Wu, YT. Fronto-occipital fasciculus, corpus callosum and superior longitudinal fasciculus tract alterations of first-episode, medication-naive and late-onset panic disorder patients. *Journal of Affective Disorders*. 2013, 146(3), 378-82.

[42] Kim, B; Kim, JH; Kim, MK; Lee, KS; Kim, Y; Choi, TK; et al. Frontal white matter alterations in short-term medicated panic disorder patients without comorbid conditions: a diffusion tensor imaging study. *Public Library of Science One*. 2014, 9(4), e95279.

[43] Neumeister, A; Bain, E; Nugent, AC; Carson, RE; Bonne, O; Luckenbaugh, DA; et al. Reduced serotonin type 1A receptor binding in panic disorder. *Journal of Neuroscience*. 2004, 24(3), 589-91.

[44] Nash, JR; Sargent, PA; Rabiner, EA; Hood, SD; Argyropoulos, SV; Potokar, JP; et al. Serotonin 5-HT1A receptor binding in people with panic disorder: positron emission tomography study. *British Journal of Psychiatry*. 2008, 193(3), 229-34.

[45] Maron, E; Kuikka, JT; Shlik, J; Vasar, V; Vanninen, E; Tiihonen, J. Reduced brain serotonin transporter binding in patients with panic disorder. *Psychiatry Research*. 2004, 132(2), 173-81.

[46] Maron, E; Toru, I; Hirvonen, J; Tuominen, L; Lumme, V; Vasar, V; et al. Gender differences in brain serotonin transporter availability in panic disorder. *Journal of Psychopharmacology*. 2011, 25(7), 952-9.
[47] Silhan, P; Jelinkova, M; Walter, U; Pavlov Prasko, J; Herzig, R; Langova, K; et al. Transcranial sonography of brainstem structures in panic disorder. *Psychiatry Research*. 2015, 234(1), 137-43.
[48] Chen, J; Shi, S. A review of neuroimaging studies of anxiety disorders in China. *Neuropsychiatric Disease and Treatment*. 2011, 7, 241-9.
[49] Etkin, A; Wager, TD. Functional neuroimaging of anxiety: a meta-analysis of emotional processing in PTSD, social anxiety disorder, and specific phobia. *American Journal of Psychiatry*. 2007, 164(10), 1476-88.
[50] Kim, JE; Dager, SR; Lyoo, IK. The role of the amygdala in the pathophysiology of panic disorder: evidence from neuroimaging studies. *Biology of Mood and Anxiety Disorders*. 2012, 2, 20.
[51] Shin, LM; Liberzon, I. The neurocircuitry of fear, stress, and anxiety disorders. *Neuropsychopharmacology*. 2010, 35(1), 169-91.
[52] Pessoa, L; Adolphs, R. Emotion processing and the amygdala: from a 'low road' to 'many roads' of evaluating biological significance. *Nature Reviews Neuroscience*. 2010, 11(11), 773-83.
[53] Seeley, WW; Menon, V; Schatzberg, AF; Keller, J; Glover, GH; Kenna, H; et al. Dissociable intrinsic connectivity networks for salience processing and executive control. *Journal of Neuroscience*. 2007, 27(9), 2349-56.
[54] Menon, V. Large-scale brain networks and psychopathology: a unifying triple network model. *Trends in Cognitive Sciences*. 2011, 15(10), 483-506.
[55] Olatunji, BO; Deacon, BJ; Abramowitz, JS; Valentiner, DP. Body vigilance in nonclinical and anxiety disorder samples: structure, correlates, and prediction of health concerns. *Behavior Therapy*. 2007, 38(4), 392-401.
[56] Uddin, LQ. Salience processing and insular cortical function and dysfunction. *Nat Rev Neurosci*. 2015, 16(1), 55-61.

[57] Critchley, HD. The human cortex responds to an interoceptive challenge. *Proceedings of the National Academy of Sciences of the United States of America.* 2004, 101(17), 6333-4.

[58] Mansouri, FA; Tanaka, K; Buckley, MJ. Conflict-induced behavioural adjustment: a clue to the executive functions of the prefrontal cortex. *Nature Reviews Neuroscience.* 2009, 10(2), 141-52.

[59] Corbetta, M; Patel, G; Shulman, GL. The reorienting system of the human brain: from environment to theory of mind. *Neuron.* 2008, 58(3), 306-24.

[60] Bressler, SL; Menon, V. Large-scale brain networks in cognition: emerging methods and principles. *Trends in Cognitive Sciences.* 2010, 14(6), 277-90.

[61] Schmahmann, JD; Sherman, JC. The cerebellar cognitive affective syndrome. *Brain.* 1998, 121 (Pt 4), 561-79.

In: Panic Disorder
Editor: Yong-Ku Kim
ISBN: 978-1-53613-001-0

Chapter 2

GENETIC, EPIGENETIC AND ENVIRONMENTAL INTERACTION IN PANIC DISORDER

Eun-Jeong Kim, Han-Joon Kim and Yong-Ku Kim*
Department of Psychiatry, College of Medicine, Korea University, Ansan Hospital, Republic of Korea

ABSTRACT

Panic disorder (PD) is the most common heritable anxiety disorder; there is a three- to eight-fold increased risk of panic disorder among relatives of panic disorder patients versus relatives of non-affected individuals. Family studies, twin studies, and combined models have revealed that the heritability estimate for panic disorder is 0.48. Linkage analyses and genetic association studies have made progress in identifying genetic risk factors for panic disorder. However, the remaining 52% of risk for developing PD is attributable to individual environmental factors, highlighting the complex genetic nature of panic disorder. Psychosocial factors have been explored using cognitive behavioral theories and classic conditioning approaches. Epigenetic

* Corresponding author. yongku@korea.ac.kr, yongku0304@gmail.com.

processes have also been shown to critically influence gene regulation and mediate the impact of environmental factors in mental disorders and thus have been suggested as a necessary complement to genetic analyses of complex-genetic disorders. DNA hypomethylation of glutamate decarboxylase 1 (*GAD1*) or the monoamine oxidase A (*MAOA*) gene might play a role in the manifestation of panic disorder based on gene-environment interactions.

INTRODUCTION

Pathogenesis of panic disorder (PD) is complex. Psychiatrists have investigated the development of PD using psychological, cognitive, neurobiological, and genetic approaches. Nevertheless, our understanding of the pathogenesis and background of PD, even only its genetic aspects, is limited despite significant advances over the last few decades. Like many other psychiatric disorders, PD does not seem to be caused by a single genetic or environmental factor, but by multiple genetic, epigenetic, and environmental factors and their interactions. Candidate genes have been identified based on numerous chromosomal studies and genome-wide association studies (GWAS). So-called candidate stressors involved in the pathogenesis of PD have also been identified. The aim of this chapter is to review the genetic, environmental, and epigenetic factors associated with PD and to propose directions for future research.

1. GENETIC ETIOLOGY OF PANIC DISORDER

PD is well known to be highly heritable, indicating a significant genetic contribution to development of this disorder. The incidence of PD is about three- to eight-fold higher in patients with a familial history of panic disorder than patients without familial loading [1, 2]. The relative risk of PD in first degree relatives of patients with PD ranges from 2.8 to 14.7.

Twin studies have revealed the very high heritability of panic disorder - 30 to 48% based on a genetic heritability rate of 45% in monozygotic twins [3, 4] and 15% in dizygotic twins [5]. As for other twin studies of diseases, shared and non-shared environmental risk factors should be considered when interpreting these numbers. Shared environmental risk factors include poverty and parental separation, whereas non-shared environmental risk factors include stress, perinatal factors, and history of substance misuse.

Linkage analysis and genome-wide association studies (GWASs) have provided insight into the genes associated with PD. Four chromosomal regions (4q31-q34 from the Yale study of 19 US pedigrees of panic disorder patients [6, 7], 15q21 from the Columbia study of 120 US pedigrees [8], 9q from the Iceland study of 25 pedigrees [7, 9], and 13q of 60 pedigrees [7, 10]) were significantly associated with PD, while 1q [11], 2q [8], 7p [12, 13], 12q [14], 14q [7, 15], 22q [7, 16, 17] regions have also been identified as chromosomal areas associated with panic disorder.

Nineteen extended American pedigrees, which were probands with PD, were studied in a follow-up study from the Yale group. Among many regions, 4q31-q34 showed the strongest association with PD [18]. Consistent results were found in later studies; within this region, the NPY5R gene, encoding neuropeptide Y receptor 5, was identified as a candidate gene [19]. The region 15q21 was also shown to have a strong association with PD with an LOD score of 2.56 [20]. This region contains GABA-A receptor subunit genes. An Icelandic study analyzed 25 families that contained at least one PD patient and found that 9q31 had the highest LOD score [21]. Chromosome 9 had several locations with high LOD scores, including 9p22, 9q32, 9q34.3 [22]. The Columbia group also found that 13q had a high LOD score of 3.57 [17]. In particular, this chromosomal region was associated with PD and other related problems such as bladder issues, headaches, and thyroid conditions. The 13q region contains genes encoding D-amino acid oxidase activator LG30 and serotonin receptor 2A. The clinical significance of these genes need to be determined in future studies.

Meta-analysis of these linkage results, however, has not been performed, and it is unclear why the findings of the different studies are inconsistent. It might be that genetic variants associated with panic disorder have incomplete penetrance, and that various risk genes and their variants are related to the etiology of panic disorder, rather than there being one unique risk gene or variant [23].

Since segregation analyses showed that panic disorder is not a Mendelian disorder, many association studies to find genes related to panic disorder have been performed. The genes identified as being associated with PD encode proteins involved in fear and alarm responses, neurotransmitters known to be related to these actions, and neuronal pathways. Neurotransmitters include serotonin (5-hydroxytryptamine, 5-HT), norepinephrine, gamma-aminobutyric acid (GABA), and others. The most widely known genes related to panic disorder are adenosine 2A receptor (*ADORA2A*) [24, 25], catechol-O-methyltransferase (*COMT*) [16, 26-28], monoamine oxidase A (*MAOA*) [29-31], serotonin receptor 1A (*5-HT$_{1A}$*) [32], serotonin 2A receptor (*5-HT$_{2A}$*) gene [33, 34], transmembrane-protein-132D (*TMEM132D*) gene [35], tryptophan hydroxylase 2 (*TPH2*) [36], cholecystokinin B (CCKB) receptor [37, 38], neuropeptide S receptor (*NPSR1*) [39], and brain-derived neurotrophic factor (*BDNF*) [40]. Within the context of the limitations of small sample sizes, different study designs, and heterogeneous diagnostic criteria, alleles of the *COMT, MAOA, NPSR,* and *TMEM* genes have been confirmed to be associated with PD in independent samples by meta-analyses, but none of these have proven to be consistent risk alleles for panic disorder [41, 42] and were not identified in a genome-wide association study [43].

Although larger sample sizes and controlled studies might provide more insight, the discrepancies among studies could be due to the confounding effects of gene-gene interactions and gene-environmental interactions. For example, interactions between *5-HTR1A* 1019C/G and *COMT* (472G/A = V158M) [44] as well as between caffeine and *ADORA2A* polymorphism [45] have been demonstrated.

Caffeine-induced anxiety and associations with multiple gene polymorphisms have been investigated by several research groups.

Caffeine has an anxiogenic effect by antagonizing adenosine A1 and A2A receptors and dopamine receptors. Alsene et al. found that adenosine A2a receptor gene variations were associated with differences in caffeine-induced anxiety level. The gene polymorphism 1976T > C A2A was also found in panic disorder patients [46]. Caffeine also provokes greater anxiety in panic disorder patients than in healthy controls. Panic disorder patients appear to have particular dopamine receptor DRD2 gene polymorphisms. Childs et al. found that individuals with the G/- genotype for rs1110976 intron 6 of *DRD2* showed higher anxiety than G/G individuals [47]. However, this result is not consistent among studies, and further research is required. Nevertheless, caffeine-induced anxiety is related to panic disorder and can worsen panic disorder, indicating a meaningful relationship. Caffeine-induced anxiety should therefore be a future research topic.

Similar to other anxiety disorders, panic disorder also occurs more frequently in women than men, with a female: male ratio of 2.5 [48]. The Val158Met polymorphism in *COMT* is a prominent factor associated with the higher susceptibility of females than males to PD [16, 26, 27, 32]. Variable number tandem repeat polymorphisms (VNTRs) in the *MAOA* gene [49, 50] and polymorphisms of tryptophan hydroxylase 2 (*TPH2*) [50], neuropeptide S receptor (*NPSR1*) [39], neuropeptide Y5 receptor (*NPYY5*) [51], serotonin transporter (5-HTT) binding potential (BPND) [52], glutamate decarboxylase 1 (*GAD1*) [53], and hypocretin receptor 2 (*HCRTR2*) [54] genes also appear to contribute to the female susceptibility to panic attack. Another study recently proposed that a particular IL-10 variant was associated with lower risk of panic disorder [55].

2. Environmental Etiology of Panic Disorder

Along with genetic studies, environmental factors impacting PD progression have been studied. Although these research studies have not identified as many environmental factors affecting anxiety disorder as those found for depressive disorder, the finding that emotional and/or physical abuse in childhood had different effect according to the serotonin transporter *5-HTTLPR* genotype, thereby increasing anxiety susceptibility [56], has prompted further research into this transporter gene.

Panic disorder patients show extreme anxiety reactions, followed by avoidance and anticipatory anxiety. From a developmental perspective, panic disorder develops in the context of adversity, especially sexual abuse [57]. An attempt has therefore been made to explain the susceptibility of females to panic disorder from a psychosocial perspective [58]. The physical weakness of women compared to men was hypothesized to make women more susceptible to anxiety. For instance, chronic stressors such as housework, working outside the home, relatively low wages, and difficulty in gaining promotion might increase the anxiety sensitivity of females [59]. Although these environmental factors were not confirmed in a twin study [60], another study revealed that important life events, such as interpersonal relationships and health problems, play an important role in the manifestation of panic disorder, especially in females [61]. Another study demonstrated that the high incidence of sexual abuse in females was a reason for their high panic disorder sensitivity [62], but many variables still need to be examined [58].

A recent study looked at so-called "candidate stressors" [58] and showed that preceding events affected the emergence of the disease, and that these events were not only cumulative, but also specific [58]. Specific events include threat [63], interpersonal and health-related events during adulthood, and abuse, loss, or separation during childhood [64, 65].

Horesh et al. explored 44 PD patients and a matched control group [64] and found that the PD group experienced more life events than the control group during childhood and adolescence. During the year preceding disease emergence, however, there was no difference in stressful life events between the PD group and control group. These results are consistent with those from previous studies.

Another study of 51 panic disorder patients examined the existence of interpersonal loss events immediately preceding the onset of panic disorder [66]. The authors of that study reported that 47% of patients experienced a significant interpersonal loss 6 weeks before the emergence of panic disorder. This study did not include a healthy control group, making it difficult to determine the importance of an interpersonal loss event as a direct precipitating factor of panic disorder. It is, however, important to investigate panic as an outcome of loss or form of complicated bereavement in future studies.

One large-scale community-based study including more than 3000 American Indians reported results consistent with those described above. The study included participants from two tribes, one from the southwest and one from the northern plains of the USA, and 7% of participants from each tribe reported physical abuse in childhood [67]. Childhood physical abuse has been shown to be a significant factor in the emergence of anxiety disorders as well as depressive disorders and posttraumatic stress disorder (PTSD). Adult physical or sexual victimization, chronic illness, and lifetime alcohol or drug disorder have also been suggested to be covariates associated with development of anxiety disorders [67].

An association between PD and CO_2 sensitivity was proposed by one study group in 2010. This study analyzed histories of the patients' early life and had the participants inhale a gas mixture (35% CO_2/65% O_2 and air) [68]. The study also measured scales related to anxiety and panic symptoms, including the Visual Analogue Scale for Anxiety (VASA), and performed clinical interviews. The authors of that study found that early life events changed chemoreception via genetic-environmental mechanisms, and that this change could persist through maturity. The study partially explained the importance of early life events in the pathogenesis of PD.

Gene-environment interactions in PD have not been well studied. Anxiety sensitivity is fear of anxiety-related sensation and is a well-established risk factor for development of panic attacks [56]. Stein et al. found that childhood emotional (or physical) maltreatment and a particular serotonin transporter gene (*SLC6A4*) promoter polymorphism (*5-HTTLPR*) showed statistically significant associations with anxiety sensitivity. Individuals with the S/S genotype and higher levels of maltreatment showed higher levels of anxiety sensitivity than individuals with other genotypes and levels of maltreatment.

Two recent studies found associations in gene-environment interactions between specific genes and caffeine. Childs et al. studied 102 individuals and their subjective anxiety after administering oral capsules containing various doses of caffeine. They found a significant association among a dose of 150 mg of caffeine, caffeine-induced anxiety, and *ADORA2A* and *DRD2* polymorphisms [47]. Alsene et al. studied the adenosine receptor system and caffeine. They enrolled 94 individuals, administered 150 mg oral caffeine, recorded subjective mood states, and found a significant association between self-reported anxiety after caffeine administration in healthy controls and a specific polymorphism of the adenosine A2a receptor gene [46]. These studies support the hypothesis that patients with certain risk alleles that confer sensitivity to particular environmental factors are vulnerable to anxiety.

3. Epigenetic Etiology of Panic Disorder

Recently, epigenetic mechanisms such as DNA methylation have received attention for their role in mediating the relationship between genetic and environmental factors. Two important epigenetic studies have been published; one investigated DNA hypomethylation of the monoamine oxidase A (*MAOA*) gene and found that it conferred susceptibility to panic disorder (31). The other studied the relationship of epigenetic modification of the *GAD1* gene to panic disorder.

The protein encoded by the *MAOA* gene plays a role in degrading biogenic amines including epinephrine, norepinephrine, and serotonin via oxidative deamination [69]. Considering their mechanism of action, MAO inhibitors have been used to treat panic disorder in some populations. Altered methylation of the *MAOA* gene was found to correlate with panic disorder [70]. Among 42 studied CpG (cytosine/guanine) sites, relative hypomethylation in patients relative to controls was observed at 10 CpG sites. Hypomethylation of MAOA can result in decreased availability of epinephrine and norepinephrine. Furthermore, negative and positive life events were found to correspond to DNA hypomethylation and hypermethylation, respectively [31]. A higher ratio of negative life events and a lower ratio of positive life events during the previous 6 months were found in PD patients compared to healthy controls. These results highlight the epigenetic importance of positive and negative environmental stressors on development of PD.

A recent study reported hypermethylation of the *MAOA* gene in patients who underwent psychotherapy such as cognitive behavioral therapy (CBT), implying the reversibility of these mechanisms [71]. The study enrolled 28 PD patients and 28 healthy controls. *MAOA* methylation was analyzed at baseline and after a 6-week CBT session. *MAOA* methylation was significantly lower in the patient group than in healthy controls at baseline; however, after CBT, *MAOA* methylation was found to have increased while non-responders still had a low methylation ratio. This recent study suggests that psychotherapeutic interventions can affect epigenetic patterns and provides insight into how the environment can influence gene expression.

Another pilot study showed that the degree of DNA hypomethylation of the glutamate decarboxylase (*GAD1*) gene differed among patient and control groups. The study enrolled 65 patients and matched controls and analyzed 38 *GAD1* CpG sites and 10 GD2 CpG sites. Patients showed lower methylation levels than controls [72]. Negative life events were found to be related with lower average methylation, especially in females. Decreased *GAD1* DNA methylation can lead to increased *GAD67* gene expression, which in turn can result in an increased level of GABA. This can be interpreted as a compensatory response to stressful events and is consistent with the results of a previous study that reported an increased level of amygdalar *GAD67* mRNA during stressful events. These results suggest that epigenetic modification of GAD1 can mediate the negative influences of life events on PD.

Females have been shown to have a great tendency to develop PD than males in numerous studies. In previous genetic studies, women were found to be more susceptible to PD emergence because of anxiety sensitivity. In addition, candidate genes have also shown female-specific associations.

This tendency has also been observed in epigenetic studies, suggesting a gender-specific pathogenetic mechanism of panic disorder.

As epigenetic features can influence genetic regulation in panic disorder patients, further evaluation and replication of results are required [72]. The identification of epigenetic features could affect disease diagnosis and might have possible therapeutic implications.

4. Summary of Genetic, Epigenetic and Environmental Interaction in Panic Disorder

In this chapter, we summarized genetic, epigenetic, and environmental interactions in PD. PD shows considerable heritability compared to other psychiatric disorders, and several chromosomal regions associated with PD, including 4q, 15q, 9q and 13q, have been discovered. These regions generally contain genes encoding neurotransmitters and their receptors, GABA-A receptors, or serotonin 2A receptors. The exact clinical meaning of these regions and the roles of specific genes and variants in these regions remain unknown. Genes such as *ADORA2A, COMT, and MAOA* have been shown to be associated with panic disorder. The higher prevalence of PD in females is partially explained by genetic background.

Environmental etiology includes adversity during childhood, which is related to anxiety reactions and avoidance. Other adversity events include threat and interpersonal and health-related events during childhood. Empirical studies have confirmed the contribution of gene-environment interactions to panic disorder. Childhood maltreatment, for example, showed a statistical association with a specific gene polymorphism.

Two studies showed a link among methylation pattern of MAOA, the GAD promoter, and PD. Each study reported a different ratio of methylation between the patient group and control group. Clinical variables, such as history of negative or positive life events, also showed a relationship to methylation levels. These studies suggest that epigenetic factors affect the development of PD. Gender differences consistent with those found in earlier classic genetic studies were also found in these epigenetic studies.

Determining the genetic, environmental, and epigenetic backgrounds of panic disorder will widen our understanding of this disease and potentially help psychiatrists treat patients more effectively. Promisingly, a recent study showed that psychotherapeutic intervention affected methylation patterns. Further studies should investigate the epigenetic changes associated with PD and the effects of interventions on these epigenetic patterns.

REFERENCES

[1] Maier W, Lichtermann D, Minges J, Oehrlein A, Franke P. A controlled family study in panic disorder. *J Psychiatr Res*. 1993;27 Suppl 1:79-87.

[2] Nocon A, Wittchen HU, Beesdo K, Bruckl T, Hofler M, Pfister H, et al. Differential familial liability of panic disorder and agoraphobia. *Depress Anxiety*. 2008;25 (5):422-34.

[3] Hettema JM, Neale MC, Kendler KS. A review and meta-analysis of the genetic epidemiology of anxiety disorders. *Am J Psychiatry*. 2001;158 (10):1568-78.

[4] Kessler RC, Berglund P, Demler O, Jin R, Merikangas KR, Walters EE. Lifetime prevalence and age-of-onset distributions of DSM-IV disorders in the National Comorbidity Survey Replication. *Arch Gen Psychiatry*. 2005;62 (6):593-602.

[5] Skre I, Onstad S, Torgersen S, Lygren S, Kringlen E. A twin study of DSM-III-R anxiety disorders. *Acta Psychiatr Scand*. 1993;88 (2):85-92.

[6] Kaabi B, Gelernter J, Woods SW, Goddard A, Page GP, Elston RC. Genome scan for loci predisposing to anxiety disorders using a novel multivariate approach: strong evidence for a chromosome 4 risk locus. *Am J Hum Genet*. 2006;78 (4):543-53.

[7] Maron E, Hettema JM, Shlik J. Advances in molecular genetics of panic disorder. *Mol Psychiatry*. 2010;15 (7):681-701.

[8] Fyer AJ, Hamilton SP, Durner M, Haghighi F, Heiman GA, Costa R, et al. A third-pass genome scan in panic disorder: evidence for multiple susceptibility loci. *Biol Psychiatry*. 2006;60 (4):388-401.

[9] Thorgeirsson TE, Oskarsson H, Desnica N, Kostic JP, Stefansson JG, Kolbeinsson H, et al. Anxiety with panic disorder linked to chromosome 9q in Iceland. *Am J Hum Genet*. 2003;72 (5):1221-30.

[10] Weissman MM, Fyer AJ, Haghighi F, Heiman G, Deng Z, Hen R, et al. Potential panic disorder syndrome: clinical and genetic linkage evidence. *Am J Med Genet*. 2000;96 (1):24-35.

[11] Gelernter J, Bonvicini K, Page G, Woods SW, Goddard AW, Kruger S, et al. Linkage genome scan for loci predisposing to panic disorder or agoraphobia. *Am J Med Genet*. 2001;105 (6):548-57.

[12] Crowe RR, Goedken R, Samuelson S, Wilson R, Nelson J, Noyes R, Jr. Genomewide survey of panic disorder. *Am J Med Genet*. 2001;105 (1):105-9.

[13] Knowles JA, Fyer AJ, Vieland VJ, Weissman MM, Hodge SE, Heiman GA, et al. Results of a genome-wide genetic screen for panic disorder. *Am J Med Genet*. 1998;81 (2):139-47.

[14] Smoller JW, Acierno JS, Jr., Rosenbaum JF, Biederman J, Pollack MH, Meminger S, et al. Targeted genome screen of panic disorder and anxiety disorder proneness using homology to murine QTL regions. *Am J Med Genet*. 2001;105 (2):195-206.

[15] Middeldorp CM, Hottenga JJ, Slagboom PE, Sullivan PF, de Geus EJ, Posthuma D, et al. Linkage on chromosome 14 in a genome-wide linkage study of a broad anxiety phenotype. *Mol Psychiatry*. 2008;13 (1):84-9.

[16] Domschke K, Deckert J, O'Donovan M C, Glatt SJ. Meta-analysis of COMT val158met in panic disorder: ethnic heterogeneity and gender specificity. *Am J Med Genet B Neuropsychiatr Genet*. 2007;144B (5):667-73.

[17] Hamilton SP, Fyer AJ, Durner M, Heiman GA, Baisre de Leon A, Hodge SE, et al. Further genetic evidence for a panic disorder

syndrome mapping to chromosome 13q. *Proc Natl Acad Sci US.* 2003;100 (5):2550-5.

[18] Kaabi B, Gelernter J, Woods SW, Goddard A, Page GP, Elston RC. Genome scan for loci predisposing to anxiety disorders using a novel multivariate approach: strong evidence for a chromosome 4 risk locus. *The American Journal of Human Genetics*. 2006;78 (4):543-53.

[19] Domschke K, Hohoff C, Jacob C, Maier W, Fritze J, Bandelow B, et al. Chromosome 4q31-34 panic disorder risk locus: Association of neuropeptide Y Y5 receptor variants. *American Journal of Medical Genetics Part B: Neuropsychiatric Genetics*. 2008;147 (4):510-6.

[20] Fyer AJ, Hamilton SP, Durner M, Haghighi F, Heiman GA, Costa R, et al. A third-pass genome scan in panic disorder: evidence for multiple susceptibility loci. *Biological psychiatry*. 2006;60 (4):388-401.

[21] Thorgeirsson TE, Oskarsson H, Desnica N, Kostic JP, Stefansson JG, Kolbeinsson H, et al. Anxiety with panic disorder linked to chromosome 9q in Iceland. *The American Journal of Human Genetics.* 2003;72 (5):1221-30.

[22] Donner J, Pirkola S, Silander K, Kananen L, Terwilliger JD, Lönnqvist J, et al. An association analysis of murine anxiety genes in humans implicates novel candidate genes for anxiety disorders. *Biological psychiatry*. 2008;64 (8):672-80.

[23] Vieland VJ, Goodman DW, Chapman T, Fyer AJ. New segregation analysis of panic disorder. *Am J Med Genet*. 1996;67 (2):147-53.

[24] Deckert J, Nothen MM, Franke P, Delmo C, Fritze J, Knapp M, et al. Systematic mutation screening and association study of the A1 and A2a adenosine receptor genes in panic disorder suggest a contribution of the A2a gene to the development of disease. *Mol Psychiatry.* 1998;3 (1):81-5.

[25] Hamilton SP, Slager SL, De Leon AB, Heiman GA, Klein DF, Hodge SE, et al. Evidence for genetic linkage between a polymorphism in the adenosine 2A receptor and panic disorder. *Neuropsychopharmacology.* 2004;29 (3):558-65.

[26] Domschke K, Freitag CM, Kuhlenbaumer G, Schirmacher A, Sand P, Nyhuis P, et al. Association of the functional V158M catechol-O-methyl-transferase polymorphism with panic disorder in women. Int *J Neuropsychopharmacol*. 2004;7 (2):183-8.

[27] Hamilton SP, Slager SL, Heiman GA, Deng Z, Haghighi F, Klein DF, et al. Evidence for a susceptibility locus for panic disorder near the catechol-O-methyltransferase gene on chromosome 22. *Biol Psychiatry*. 2002;51 (7):591-601.

[28] Rothe C, Koszycki D, Bradwejn J, King N, Deluca V, Tharmalingam S, et al. Association of the Val158Met catechol O-methyltransferase genetic polymorphism with panic disorder. *Neuropsychopharmacology*. 2006;31 (10):2237-42.

[29] Deckert J, Catalano M, Syagailo YV, Bosi M, Okladnova O, Di Bella D, et al. Excess of high activity monoamine oxidase A gene promoter alleles in female patients with panic disorder. *Hum Mol Genet*. 1999;8 (4):621-4.

[30] Reif A, Weber H, Domschke K, Klauke B, Baumann C, Jacob CP, et al. Meta-analysis argues for a female-specific role of MAOA-uVNTR in panic disorder in four European populations. *Am J Med Genet B Neuropsychiatr Genet. 2012*;159B (7):786-93.

[31] Domschke K, Tidow N, Kuithan H, Schwarte K, Klauke B, Ambree O, et al. Monoamine oxidase A gene DNA hypomethylation - a risk factor for panic disorder? *Int J Neuropsychopharmacol*. 2012;15 (9):1217-28.

[32] Samochowiec J, Hajduk A, Samochowiec A, Horodnicki J, Stepien G, Grzywacz A, et al. Association studies of MAO-A, COMT, and 5-HTT genes polymorphisms in patients with anxiety disorders of the phobic spectrum. *Psychiatry Res*. 2004;128 (1):21-6.

[33] Yoon HK, Yang JC, Lee HJ, Kim YK. The association between serotonin-related gene polymorphisms and panic disorder. *J Anxiety Disord*. 2008;22 (8):1529-34.

[34] Inada Y, Yoneda H, Koh J, Sakai J, Himei A, Kinoshita Y, et al. Positive association between panic disorder and polymorphism of the serotonin 2A receptor gene. *Psychiatry Res*. 2003;118 (1):25-31.

[35] Erhardt A, Czibere L, Roeske D, Lucae S, Unschuld PG, Ripke S, et al. TMEM132D, a new candidate for anxiety phenotypes: evidence from human and mouse studies. *Mol Psychiatry*. 2011;16 (6):647-63.

[36] Kim YK, Lee HJ, Yang JC, Hwang JA, Yoon HK. A tryptophan hydroxylase 2 gene polymorphism is associated with panic disorder. *Behav Genet*. 2009;39 (2):170-5.

[37] Hosing VG, Schirmacher A, Kuhlenbaumer G, Freitag C, Sand P, Schlesiger C, et al. Cholecystokinin- and cholecystokinin-B-receptor gene polymorphisms in panic disorder. *J Neural Transm Suppl*. 2004 (68):147-56.

[38] Kennedy JL, Bradwejn J, Koszycki D, King N, Crowe R, Vincent J, et al. Investigation of cholecystokinin system genes in panic disorder. *Mol Psychiatry*. 1999;4 (3):284-5.

[39] Domschke K, Reif A, Weber H, Richter J, Hohoff C, Ohrmann P, et al. Neuropeptide S receptor gene -- converging evidence for a role in panic disorder. *Mol Psychiatry*. 2011;16 (9):938-48.

[40] Han EJ, Kim YK, Hwang JA, Kim SH, Lee HJ, Yoon HK, et al. Evidence for Association between the Brain-Derived Neurotrophic Factor Gene and Panic Disorder: A Novel Haplotype Analysis. *Psychiatry Investig*. 2015;12 (1):112-7.

[41] Howe AS, Buttenschon HN, Bani-Fatemi A, Maron E, Otowa T, Erhardt A, et al. Candidate genes in panic disorder: meta-analyses of 23 common variants in major anxiogenic pathways. *Mol Psychiatry*. 2016;21 (5):665-79.

[42] Erhardt A, Akula N, Schumacher J, Czamara D, Karbalai N, Muller-Myhsok B, et al. Replication and meta-analysis of TMEM132D gene variants in panic disorder. *Transl Psychiatry*. 2012;2:e156.

[43] Roy-Byrne PP, Craske MG, Stein MB. *Panic disorder. Lancet*. 2006;368 (9540):1023-32.

[44] Freitag CM, Domschke K, Rothe C, Lee YJ, Hohoff C, Gutknecht L, et al. Interaction of serotonergic and noradrenergic gene variants in panic disorder. *Psychiatr Genet*. 2006;16 (2):59-65.

[45] Rogers PJ, Hohoff C, Heatherley SV, Mullings EL, Maxfield PJ, Evershed RP, et al. Association of the anxiogenic and alerting effects of caffeine with ADORA2A and ADORA1 polymorphisms and habitual level of caffeine consumption. *Neuropsychopharmacology*. 2010;35 (9):1973-83.

[46] Alsene K, Deckert J, Sand P, de Wit H. Association between A2a receptor gene polymorphisms and caffeine-induced anxiety. *Neuropsychopharmacology: official publication of the American College of Neuropsychopharmacology*. 2003;28 (9):1694-702.

[47] Childs E, Hohoff C, Deckert J, Xu K, Badner J, de Wit H. Association between ADORA2A and DRD2 polymorphisms and caffeine-induced anxiety. *Neuropsychopharmacology: official publication of the American College of Neuropsychopharmacology*. 2008;33 (12):2791-800.

[48] Wittchen HU, Jacobi F, Rehm J, Gustavsson A, Svensson M, Jonsson B, et al. The size and burden of mental disorders and other disorders of the brain in Europe 2010. *Eur Neuropsychopharmacol*. 2011;21 (9):655-79.

[49] Maron E, Tasa G, Toru I, Lang A, Vasar V, Shlik J. Association between serotonin-related genetic polymorphisms and CCK-4-induced panic attacks with or without 5-hydroxytryptophan pretreatment in healthy volunteers. *World J Biol Psychiatry*. 2004;5 (3):149-54.

[50] Maron E, Toru I, Must A, Tasa G, Toover E, Vasar V, et al. Association study of tryptophan hydroxylase 2 gene polymorphisms in panic disorder. *Neurosci Lett*. 2007;411 (3):180-4.

[51] Domschke K, Hohoff C, Jacob C, Maier W, Fritze J, Bandelow B, et al. Chromosome 4q31-34 panic disorder risk locus: association of neuropeptide Y Y5 receptor variants. *Am J Med Genet B Neuropsychiatr Genet*. 2008;147B (4):510-6.

[52] Cannon DM, Klaver JM, Klug SA, Carlson PJ, Luckenbaugh DA, Ichise M, et al. Gender-specific abnormalities in the serotonin transporter system in panic disorder. *Int J Neuropsychopharmacol*. 2013;16 (4):733-43.

[53] Weber H, Scholz CJ, Domschke K, Baumann C, Klauke B, Jacob CP, et al. Gender differences in associations of glutamate decarboxylase 1 gene (GAD1) variants with panic disorder. *PLoS One.* 2012;7 (5):e37651.

[54] Annerbrink K, Westberg L, Olsson M, Andersch S, Sjodin I, Holm G, et al. Panic disorder is associated with the Val308Iso polymorphism in the hypocretin receptor gene. *Psychiatr Genet.* 2011;21 (2):85-9.

[55] Kim HJ, Kim YK. The G allele in IL-10-1082 G/A may have a role in lowering the susceptibility to panic disorder in female patients. *Acta Neuropsychiatr*. 2016:1-5.

[56] Stein MB, Schork NJ, Gelernter J. Gene-by-environment (serotonin transporter and childhood maltreatment) interaction for anxiety sensitivity, an intermediate phenotype for anxiety disorders. *Neuropsychopharmacology: official publication of the American College of Neuropsychopharmacology*. 2008;33 (2):312-9.

[57] Dinwiddie S, Heath AC, Dunne MP, Bucholz KK, Madden PA, Slutske WS, et al. Early sexual abuse and lifetime psychopathology: a co-twin-control study. *Psychol Med.* 2000;30 (1):41-52.

[58] Klauke B, Deckert J, Reif A, Pauli P, Domschke K. Life events in panic disorder-an update on "candidate stressors." *Depress Anxiety.* 2010;27 (8):716-30.

[59] Deborah JBD. Poverty, Inequality, And Discrimination As Sources Of Depression Among U. S. Women. *Psychology of women quarterly*. 2003;27 (2):101-13.

[60] Hettema JM, Prescott CA, Myers JM, Neale MC, Kendler KS. The structure of genetic and environmental risk factors for anxiety disorders in men and women. *Arch Gen Psychiatry*. 2005;62 (2):182-9.

[61] Barzega G, Maina G, Venturello S, Bogetto F. Gender-related differences in the onset of panic disorder. *Acta Psychiatr Scand.* 2001;103 (3):189-95.

[62] Kessler RC, Sonnega A, Bromet E, Hughes M, Nelson CB. Posttraumatic stress disorder in the National Comorbidity Survey. *Arch Gen Psychiatry*. 1995;52 (12):1048-60.

[63] Faravelli C. Life events preceding the onset of panic disorder. *Journal of affective disorders*. 1985;9 (1):103-5.

[64] Horesh N, Amir M, Kedem P, Goldberger Y, Kotler M. Life events in childhood, adolescence and adulthood and the relationship to panic disorder. *Acta Psychiatrica Scandinavica*. 1997;96 (5):373-8.

[65] Roy-Byrne P, Geraci M, Uhde T. Life events and course of illness in patients with panic disorder. *American Journal of Psychiatry*. 1986;143 (8):1033-5.

[66] Milrod B, Leon AC, Shear MK. Can interpersonal loss precipitate panic disorder? *The American journal of psychiatry*. 2004;161 (4):758-9.

[67] Libby AM, Orton HD, Novins DK, Beals J, Manson SM. Childhood physical and sexual abuse and subsequent depressive and anxiety disorders for two American Indian tribes. *Psychological medicine*. 2005;35 (3):329-40.

[68] Spatola CA, Scaini S, Pesenti-Gritti P, Medland SE, Moruzzi S, Ogliari A, et al. Gene-environment interactions in panic disorder and CO (2) sensitivity: Effects of events occurring early in life. American journal of medical genetics Part B, *Neuropsychiatric genetics: the official publication of the International Society of Psychiatric Genetics*. 2011;156b (1):79-88.

[69] Shih JC, Chen K, Ridd MJ. Role of MAO A and B in neurotransmitter metabolism and behavior. *Pol J Pharmacol*. 1999;51 (1):25-9.

[70] Domschke K, Tidow N, Kuithan H, Schwarte K, Klauke B, Ambrée O, et al. Monoamine oxidase A gene DNA hypomethylation – a risk factor for panic disorder? *International Journal of Neuropsychopharmacology*. 2012;15 (9):1217-28.

[71] Ziegler C, Richter J, Mahr M, Gajewska A, Schiele MA, Gehrmann A, et al. MAOA gene hypomethylation in panic disorder-reversibility of an epigenetic risk pattern by psychotherapy. *Transl Psychiatry.* 2016;6:e773.

[72] Domschke K, Tidow N, Schrempf M, Schwarte K, Klauke B, Reif A, et al. Epigenetic signature of panic disorder: a role of glutamate decarboxylase 1 (GAD1) DNA hypomethylation? *Progress in neuro-psychopharmacology & biological psychiatry*. 2013;46:189-96.

In: Panic Disorder
Editor: Yong-Ku Kim

ISBN: 978-1-53613-001-0

Chapter 3

IMAGING GENETICS IN PANIC DISORDER

Kang Soo Lee and Sang Hyuk Lee [*]

Department of Psychiatry, School of Medicine, CHA University, CHA Bundang Medical Center, Seongnam, Korea

ABSTRACT

Molecular genetic association studies yielded positive findings of genes encoding cholecystokinin, monoamine oxidase, catechol-O-methyltransferase, serotonin receptor 1A (5-HT1A), serotonin transporter (5-HTT), adenosine receptor, Rgs2, and those in the neuropeptide Y (NPY) gene system in panic disorder (PD). Imaging genetic studies on anxiety traits reveal a significant impact of 5-HTT, 5-HT1A, brain-derived neurotrophic factor (BDNF), NPY, and Rgs2 gene variation on limbic activation during emotional processing of anxiety-relevant stimuli. A functional 5-HT1A polymorphism as well as genetic variation in the noradrenergic and dopaminergic systems distorted emotional processing of anxiety-related stimuli in the limbic-frontal circuit and increased vulnerability to PD. To summarize, imaging genetic studies suggest that genetic factors drive a dysfunctional limbic-frontal interaction during emotional processing in PD.

[*] Corresponding author: E-mail: drshlee27@gmail.com; drshlee@cha.ac.kr.

Panic disorder (PD) is characterized by recurrent attacks of intense fear and anticipatory anxiety about additional attacks. Clinical genetics studies on families and twins have been conducted to elucidate the etiology of PD. In studies on families, PD has been found to be a hereditary disorder with a three-fold increased prevalence in first-degree relatives of patients with the disease [1]. Studies on twins have indicated three times higher concordance rates of PD in monozygotic than in dizygotic twins. The contribution of genetic factors to PD has been calculated to be as high as 48%, with the remaining 52% attributed to environmental factors [2]. However, segregation analyses revealed a complex genetic inheritance pattern with an interaction between environmental factors and multiple predisposing genes, each of which has only a minor influence [3]. Accordingly, molecular genetic linkage studies analyzing co-segregation of particular genetic markers with the disease of interest in pedigrees of affected families have yielded evidence of various potential risk loci for PD on chromosomes 1p, 4q, 7p, 9q, 11p, 15q, 20p, 18, 13, and 22 [4-11]. Furthermore, genetic association studies investigating the allelic frequency of a particular marker in an a-priori candidate gene in a patient sample have reported genes that might be associated with PD. These genes include those encoding cholecystokinin B (CCKB) receptor [12, 13], monoamine oxidase A (MAO-A) [14], catechol- O-methyltransferase (COMT) [15-18], serotonin receptor 1A (5-HT1A) [19, 20], serotonin transporter (5-HTT) [21, 22], adenosine A2A receptor [23, 24], Rgs2 [25, 26], and those in the neuropeptide Y (NPY) gene system [27].

High-throughput genotyping techniques enabled a genome-wide association study (GWAS) for identifying novel candidate genes implicated in anxiety disorders. Compared to those in GWAS on other psychiatric disorders, such as schizophrenia, bipolar disorders, and depression, sample sizes in GWAS on PD published until now are small. The first genome-wide study on PD has been conducted using a Japanese sample population [28]. None of the initially detected associations could be replicated in the subsequent PD association studies [29]. Meta-analysis following a replication analysis and an association analysis of previous candidate genes for PD was published [30]. Unfortunately, no significant results were obtained from genome-wide studies. The most robust and replicated finding from a genome-wide study in PD until now is the association of single-nucleotide polymorphisms (SNPs) in the transmembrane protein 132D gene (*TMEM132D*) [31, 32]. Most of the variants had negative findings, with only two genes, *COMT* and *TMEM132D*, surviving stringent correction for multiple testing.

The amygdala is the central structure of fear conditioning in cognitive and emotional processing. It has been shown that PD is associated with amygdala activity. For instance, significantly increased bilateral amygdala activation was observed in non-medicated patients at rest [33]. Provocation studies with cholecystokinin (CCK-4) showed that healthy probands indicated increased amygdala activity in parallel to increased anxiety levels [34]. Moreover, spontaneous panic attacks in a patient with PD led to increased amygdala activity [35]. It is well documented that the amygdala activation is affected by genes such as those encoding 5-HTT [36] and COMT [37, 38]. Given the pivotal role of the amygdala in the fear circuitry and its involvement in PD, responsiveness of amygdala to anxiety-related stimuli was the first imaging endophenotype investigated in an imaging genetic study. Serotonin transporter gene variation (5-HTTLPR) was significantly involved in amygdala activity in response to angry and fearful faces. This finding suggests a genetic influence on amygdala activation in determining human emotional behavior [39]. It is now well established that certain personality traits or temperaments strongly correlate with PD. Imaging genetic studies on anxiety traits, including phobia proneness, harm avoidance, trait anxiety, behavioral inhibition, introversion, and negative bias, reveal a significant impact of 5-HTT, 5-HT1A, brain-derived neurotrophin (BDNF), NPY, and Rgs2 gene variation on limbic activation during emotional processing of anxiety-relevant stimuli. Multiple candidate genes have been correlated with brain structure and function, but the most robust effects to date come from the serotonin 5-HTTLPR in relation to amygdala functioning in response to negative emotional faces. A meta-analysis investigating 5-HTTLPR and amygdala activity demonstrated a medium effect size [36]. In the current review, we will summarize existing findings sorted by molecular pathways.

Serotonin

Eight variants (rs6295, rs6296, rs6313, rs6318, 5HTTLPR (rs4795541), rs1800532, rs1386494, rs4570625) in five serotonergic genes (*HTR1A*, *HTR1B*, *HTR2A*, *HTR2C*, *SLC6A4*) have been proposed as possible susceptibility factors in PD pathogenesis.

5-HTT presents with a 43-bp insertion/deletion polymorphism in its promoter region, which is referred to as 5-HTT linked polymorphic region (5-HTTLPR). This region most commonly comprises a short (s) and a long (l) variant. The s-allele is associated with 50% reduced transcriptional activity *in vitro* [40]. However, human *in vivo* or post-mortem studies failed to reproduce the same results [41-43] probably because the polymorphism exerts its effect during early neurological development [44]. 5-HTTLPR polymorphisms have been shown to affect connections between the amygdala and the perigenual anterior cingulate cortex (ACC) [45]. Nevertheless, there have been concerns about the reproducibility of genetic association studies [46], and thus, further research is necessary to confirm the experimental results. However, in support of the role of serotonin in fear learning, serotonin-depleted subjects have shown lower activation in the amygdala and orbitofrontal cortex (OFC) during fear acquisition [47]. Together, these reports raise the possibility of the serotonin system playing an important role in fear learning, such that lower serotonin response impairs activation of the insula and amygdala, which are associated with emotional learning.

The 5-HT_{1A} receptor is encoded by *HTR1A*, which is associated with several human polymorphisms. The most investigated SNPs are rs6295, rs1799921, rs1800044, and rs1799920. Patients with PD homozygous for the 5-HT1A-1019G risk allele showed a significantly decreased activation of the ventromedial prefrontal cortex (vmPFC), OFC, and anterior cingulum in response to fearful faces versus that in response to neutral faces. Increased amygdala activity was only detected dependent on the serotonin transporter 5-HTTLPR s-allele in response to happy faces [48]. Increased activation of the prefrontal cortex and amygdala was noted in response to emotional facial stimuli in patients with PD who had -1019C/G

5-HT1A or the short risk allele of 5-HTTLPR [48]. These findings indicated that serotonergic polymorphisms might increase the risk for PD by contributing to distorted emotional processing of anxiety-related stimuli.

The 5HTTLPR polymorphism was related to brain connectivity pattern in ACC-amygdala. Furthermore, these patterns of PD in patients with agoraphobia were associated with response to exposure-based cognitive behavior therapy [49]. The s-allele 5-HTTLPR genotype has been linked to a greater response during fear conditioning in the amygdala, insula, thalamus, and occipital cortex [50]. Similarly, subjects with the s-allele 5-HTTLPR genotype and history of stressful life events have shown greater reactivity in the insula in response to fear conditioning [50, 51]. Some evidence suggests a correlation between 5-HTTPLR genotypes with differences in activation of several important regions associated with fear learning, including the amygdala, insula, dorsal ACC (dACC), and vmPFC. In addition, it was suggested that the 5-HTR1A polymorphism may be associated with the cingulum white matter connectivity in PD [52]. Fractional anisotropy (FA) values in the cingulate gyrus process of the left cingulum were found to be increased in the 5-HTR1A CC genotype compared to those in the GG/CG genotype in PD. Significant positive correlations were shown between interoceptive fear and FA values of the cingulate gyrus in the 5-HTR1A rs6295 GG/CG genotype group [52]. The cingulum is a pivotal white matter tract that supports prefrontal, parietal, and temporal lobe interaction, including the amygdala [53]. Currently, only small neuroimaging studies have investigated genotype associations with differences in the fear learning circuitry in patients with PD/A. Inhibitory ACC-amygdala coupling during fear conditioning was seen specifically in CBT responders with the 5-HTTPLR L/L genotype [49]. In contrast, 5HTR1A risk genotype was associated with reduced effects of CBT on differential activation in the ACC and insula during conditioning [54].

PD with the long VNTR allele for the MAO gene, which is a more active allele, displayed reduced reactivity in the vmPFC, but not increased amygdala reactivity during fear conditioning. This finding supports the notion that functional areas modulating emotional learning, but not those initiating emotional reactions, are compromised [55]. Neuroimaging studies have established a role of the amygdala in early extinction and suggested that vmPFC plays an important role in the retention of the extinction memory [56, 57]. These studies also suggested that serotonin signaling genes modulate learning processes involved in anxiety acquisition and maintenance in patients with PD [56, 57].

DOPAMINE

The dopamine (DA) system may contain several promising candidate genes involved in PD. Studies on fear conditioning, extinction, and CBT have investigated the correlation between PD and the polymorphisms of the catechol-O-methyltransferase (COMT), DA transporter (DAT1), and DA receptor D2 (DRD2) and D4 (DRD4) genes.

COMT is involved in the inactivation of catecholamine neurotransmitters, such as dopamine, epinephrine, and norepinephrine. The COMT has been studied for its role in psychiatric phenotypes, including PD [58]. Previous studies suggested a role of the functional val158met COMT polymorphism in the amygdala and prefrontal activation in response to emotional faces in PD. COMT polymorphism might increase the vulnerability to PD by modulating dopaminergic tones in the amygdala and PFC [58]. Patients with PD displayed higher activation in the amygdala and the OFC in response to fearful faces when carrying at least one COMT 158val risk allele [59].

Kim et al. found an increased white matter connectivity in the right posterior thalamic radiation, right posterior and superior corona radiata, right superior longitudinal fasciculus (SLF), and right sagittal stratum in COMT rs4680 AA/AG genotype compared to that in GG genotype in subjects with PD [60]. It is well known that the dysfunction of SLF might affect the neuro-modulatory effect of the amygdala on the visual cortex [61]. Therefore, patients with PD who carry COMT rs4680 AA/AG genotype have increased white matter connectivity in the amygdala-related structure. These results indicated that genetic variation in the dopaminergic system might distort emotional processing of anxiety-related stimuli in PD.

Using measures of fractional anisotropy, white matter connectivity was related to the Val58Met COMT polymorphism in PD. They reported increased white matter connectivity in Met carriers as compared to Val homozygotes in the posterior thalamic radiation, posterior and superior corona radiate, superior longitudinal fasciculus, and sagittal striatum in the right hemisphere [60]. This may reflect increased fiber density and myelination as well as directional coherence, all of which may contribute to rapid neural transmission. These data suggest that the COMT val158met variant might increase the vulnerability to PD by modulating the dopaminergic or noradrenergic tonus in the amygdala, and thereby altering neuronal processing of anxiety-relevant stimuli. In a different study, subjects with the 9R allele of *DAT1*, a dopamine transporter gene predominantly expressed in the striatum, had significantly higher extinction rates, as well as stronger activation following prediction errors in the ventral striatum [62]. In summary, there is suggestive, but not conclusive, evidence that volumetric alterations and structural connectivity relate to polymorphisms in *COMT*, thereby linking structure to function in imaging genetics studies on PD.

Glutamate

N-methyl-D-aspartate (NMDA) receptors, which have been shown to be involved in long-term potentiation, which is associated with memory and learning, are a class of ionotropic glutamate receptors. NMDA receptor channels are heteromers composed of the key receptor subunit NMDAR1 (GRIN1) and 1 or more of the 4 NMDAR2 subunits—NMDAR2A (GRIN2A), NMDAR2B (GRIN2B), NMDAR2C (GRIN2C), and NMDAR2D (GRIN2D). Subjects with a variant of an NMDA receptor gene (*GRIN2A*) have shown lower amygdala response during fear learning [63].

NEUROPEPTIDE

Seven variants (rs5186, rs1799923, rs18000857, rs1805002, rs1800843, rs110402, and rs324981) in six neuropeptidergic candidate genes (*AGTR1*, *CCK*, *CCKAR*, *CCKBR*, *CRHR1*, and *NPSR1*) have been studied in relation to PD. In studies on samples of the European ancestry, *NPSR1* rs324891 T allele was nominally associated with PD under the allelic model, but it did not survive correction for multiple testing. Conversely, no significant association was observed in studies with samples of the Asian ancestry.

Neuropeptide S (NPS) is a recently discovered neuropeptide, which has been implicated in arousal, anxiety, and fear learning. The human NPS receptor gene, *NPSR1*, harbors a functional A/T SNP, leading to an amino-acid exchange from asparagine to isoleucine. The T-allele is associated with increased NPSR cell surface expression and 10-fold enhanced efficacy of NPS binding to NPSR [64]. In 205 patients with PD and agoraphobia, Domschke et al. showed that T-allele carriers reported significantly stronger increase in perceived symptom intensity elicited by a panic-relevant stimulus again in the absence of the corresponding genotype effect on physiological responding heart rate [65]. The neuropeptide S receptor NPSR1 rs324981 T allele is associated with decreased activity in the dorsolateral PFC, lateral orbitofrontal, and ACC during processing of fearful faces in patients with PD. Hence, converging evidence suggests that the NPSR1 SNP T allele may be associated with exaggerated subjective experience and interpretation of fear reactions or stimuli, in the sense of catastrophizing over-interpretations, which is thought to be crucial for the development and maintenance of PD.

BDNF

The Val66Met SNP of the BDNF gene has been associated with impaired fear extinction in animals and humans [66]. However, neuroimaging studies on Val66Met carriers revealed activation changes only in the amygdala and ACC not during fear extinction, but during fear acquisition [67]. These studies have not been replicated, and results from genetic association studies are often inconsistent.

CORTISOL

The hypothalamic-pituitary-adrenal axis with its primary effector cortisol has a central role in response to stress and its related diseases, such as PD. Corticotropin-releasing hormone (CRH) is a major regulator of the hypothalamic-pituitary-adrenal axis. Weber et al. demonstrated that *CRHR1* risk allele was correlated with aberrant differential conditioning predominantly in the bilateral prefrontal cortex and safety signal processing in the amygdala. In addition, the *CRHR1* risk allele led to reduced flight behavior during fear-provoking situations, but increased anxious apprehension and anxiety sensitivity [68].

OTHERS

A morphometric study investigated the impact of genetic mutations on the gray matter volume with respect to PD. A significant decrease in gray matter volume of the limbic and frontal regions was observed in the PD subgroup with *PINK1* mutations compared to that in age- and sex-matched healthy controls [69]. Thus, *PINK1* mutations, originally associated with Parkinson's disease, might contribute to the etiological risk of PD via distinct gray matter degeneration leading to increased emotional vulnerability.

TMEM132D is a transmembrane protein that is highly expressed in the cortical regions of the human brain, and it has been proposed that this protein could be involved in neural interconnection and signaling [70].

Recent expression analysis of TMEM132D revealed a neuron-specific expression in the cortical regions and its co-localization with actin filaments [71]. This finding suggests that TMEM132D may be involved in neuronal sprouting and connectivity between brain regions that are important for anxiety-related behavior. First evidence supporting this hypothesis comes from resting state networks in healthy participants. Sämann et al. detected a reduction in global connectivity, as well as a specific reduction in cingulate cortex-prefrontal cortex regional connectivity in the carriers of risk allele of rs7309727 [72]. Another risk genotype rs11060369 AA was associated with enhanced TMEM132D mRNA expression in the brain, which was also higher in mice showing extreme anxiety-related behavior. Interestingly, in healthy normal carriers of the rs11060369 AA genotype, enhanced amygdala gray matter volumetric estimates and an anxiety-related personality trait were observed [73].

Patients with PD exhibit hypersensitivity to inhaled carbon dioxide (CO_2). Variation in *ACCN2*, the human ortholog of the ASIC1a (acid sensing ion channel-1a) gene, appears to be associated with PD and with the amygdala phenotypes related to anxiety [74]. The researchers compared variants of *ACCN2* in 414 individuals with PD and 846 healthy controls to examine potential genetic associations with amygdala volume in 1048 subjects and amygdala function in a subset of subjects [74]. The effect was stronger in patients whose panic attacks had prominent respiratory symptoms, including shortness of breath and feelings of suffocation. Furthermore, the panic-associated variants in *ASIC1a* were associated with both the size of the amygdala and a greater amygdala response to emotional threat, even in people without PD. Taken together, these results suggest that *ASIC1a* is a risk factor for PD, as well as is associated with the structure and function of the amygdala and its reaction to threat.

Table 1. Effects on genetic variation on amygdala and related structure in studies with panic disorder

Reference	Gene polymorphism	Sample	Main result
Domschke et al. (2006)	5-HT1A -1019C/G 5-HTTLPR	N = 20 panic disorder	Gene: GG > C carrier happy > neutral faces Brain: Increased amygdala activation
Lueken et al. (2015)	5-HTTLPR	N = 41 panic disorder w/ agoraphobia	Gene: L/L > S carrier in CBT responder Brain: Inhibitory ACC-amygdala activation
Yu et al. (2013)	5-HTR1A	N = 32 panic disorder	Gene: CC > GG/CG Brain: Increased FA in cingulum
Domschke et al. (2008)	COMT val158met	N = 20 panic disorder	Gene: val carrier > met/met (fearful vs. no face) Brain: Increased amygdala activation
Kim et al. (2013)	COMT val158met	N = 26 panic disorder	Gene: AA/AG > GG Brain: Increased FA in thalamic radiation, superior corona radiata, SLF, sagittal stratum
Smoller et al. (2014)	ACCN2	N = 414 panic disorder N = 846 healthy control	Gene: rs1087995 Brain: increased amygdala volume and reactivity
Weber et al. (2015)	CRHR1	N = 292 panic disorder	Gene: rs17689918 Brain: differential conditioning in PFC, amygdala

CONCLUSION

A functional 5-HT1A polymorphism as well as genetic variation in the noradrenergic and dopaminergic systems distorted emotional processing of anxiety-related stimuli in the limbic-frontal circuit, and thereby increased the vulnerability to PD. Additionally, individual differences in NMDA and BDNF may affect fear-learning circuits in the amygdala. In conclusion, studies on serotonergic genes, such as *COMT*, *ACCN2*, and *CRHR1*, and their impact on neuronal activity in relevant brain circuits allow better understanding of the psychopathology of PD. Furthermore, imaging genetic studies suggest that genetic factors drive a dysfunctional cortico-limbic interaction mainly during emotional processing in PD.

REFERENCES

[1] Maier W, Lichtermann D, Minges J, Oehrlein A, Franke P. A controlled family study in panic disorder. *J. Psychiatr. Res.* 1993; 27 (Suppl. 1), 79–87.

[2] Hettema JM, Neale MC, Kendler KS. A review and meta-analysis of the genetic epidemiology of anxiety disorders. *Am. J. Psychiatry* 2001;158, 1568–1578.

[3] Vieland VJ, Goodman DW, Chapman T, Fyer AJ. New segregation analysis of panic disorder. *Am. J. Med. Genet.* 1996; 67, 147–153.

[4] Crowe RR, Noyes Jr R, Wilson AF, Elston RC, Ward LJ. A linkage study of panic disorder. *Arch. Gen. Psychiatry* 1987; 44, 933–937.

[5] Fyer AJ, Hamilton SP, Durner M, Haghighi F, Heiman GA, Costa R, et al. A third-pass genome scan in panic disorder: evidence for multiple susceptibility loci. *Biol. Psychiatry* 2006; 60, 388–401.

[6] Gelernter J, Bonvicini K, Page G, Woods SW, Goddard AW, Kruger S, et al. Linkage genome scan for loci predisposing to panic disorder or agoraphobia. *Am. J. Med. Genet.* 2001; 105, 548–557.

[7] Hamilton SP, Fyer AJ, Durner M, Heiman GA, Baisre de Leon A, Hodge SE, et al. Further genetic evidence for a panic disorder syndrome mapping to chromosome 13q. *Proc. Natl. Acad. Sci. US.* 2003; 100, 2550–2555.

[8] Kaabi B, Gelernter J, Woods SW, Goddard A, Page GP, Elston RC. Genome scan for loci predisposing to anxiety disorders using a novel multivariate approach: strong evidence for a chromosome 4 risk locus. *Am. J. Hum. Genet.* 2006; 78, 543–553.

[9] Knowles JA, Fyer AJ, Vieland VJ, Weissman MM, Hodge SE, Heiman GA, et al. Results of a genome-wide genetic screen for panic disorder. *Am. J. Med. Genet.* 1998; 81, 139–147.

[10] MacKinnon DF, Xu J, McMahon FJ, Simpson SG, Stine OC, McInnis MG, DePaulo JR. Bipolar disorder and panic disorder in families: an analysis of chromosome 18 data. *Am. J. Psychiatry* 1998; 155, 829–831.

[11] Thorgeirsson TE, Oskarsson H, Desnica N, Kostic JP, Stefansson JG, Kolbeinsson H, et al. Anxiety with panic disorder linked to chromosome 9q in Iceland. *Am. J. Hum. Genet.* 2003; 72, 1221–1230.

[12] Hosing VG, Schirmacher A, Kuhlenbaumer G, Freitag C, Sand P, Schlesiger C, et al. Cholecystokinin- and cholecystokinin-B-receptor gene polymorphisms in panic disorder. *J. Neural Transm.* 2004; Suppl. 147–156.

[13] Kennedy JL, Bradwejn J, Koszycki D, King N, Crowe R, Vincent J, Fourie O. Investigation of cholecystokinin system genes in panic disorder. *Mol. Psychiatry* 1999; 4, 284–285.

[14] Deckert J, Catalano M, Syagailo YV, Bosi M, Okladnova O, Di BD, et al. Excess of high activity monoamine oxidase A gene promoter alleles in female patients with panic disorder. *Hum. Mol. Genet.* 1999; 8, 621–624.

[15] Hamilton SP, Slager SL, Heiman GA, Deng Z, Haghighi F, Klein DF, et al. Evidence for a susceptibility locus for panic disorder near the catechol-O-methyltransferase gene on chromosome 22. *Biol. Psychiatry* 2002; 51, 591–601.

[16] Domschke K, Freitag CM, Kuhlenbäumer G, Schirmacher A, Sand P, Nyhuis P, et al. Association of the functional V158M catechol-O-methyltransferase polymorphism with panic disorder in women. *Int. J. Neuropsychopharmacol.* 2004; 7, 183–188.

[17] Rothe C, Koszycki D, Bradwejn J, King N, Deluca V, Tharmalingam S, et al. Association of the Val158Met catechol-Omethyltransferase genetic polymorphism with panic disorder. *Neuropsychopharmacology* 2006; 31, 2237–2242.

[18] Domschke K, Deckert J, O'donovan MC, Glatt SJ. Meta-analysis of COMT val158met in panic disorder: ethnic heterogeneity and gender specificity. *Am. J. Med. Genet. B. Neuropsychiatr. Genet*. 2007; 144, 667–673.

[19] Huang YY, Battistuzzi C, Oquendo MA, Harkavy-Friedman J, Greenhill L, Zalsman G, et al. Human 5-HT1A receptor C(-1019)G polymorphism and psychopathology. *Int. J. Neuropsychopharmacol*. 2004; 7, 441–451.

[20] Rothe C, Gutknecht L, Freitag C, Tauber R, Mossner R, Franke P, et al. Association of a functional 1019CNG 5- HT1A receptor gene polymorphism with panic disorder with agoraphobia. *Int. J. Neuropsychopharmacol*. 2004; 7, 189–192.

[21] Maron E, Tasa G, Toru I, Lang A, Vasar V, Shlik J. Association between serotonin-related genetic polymorphisms and CCK-4-induced panic attacks with or without 5-hydroxytryptophan pretreatment in healthy volunteers. *World J. Biol. Psychiatry* 2004; 5, 149–154.

[22] Maron E, Lang A, Tasa G, Liivlaid L, Toru I, Must A, et al. Associations between serotonin-related gene polymorphisms and panic disorder. *Int. J. Neuropsychopharmacol*. 2005; 8, 261–266.

[23] Deckert J, Nothen MM, Franke P, Delmo C, Fritze J, Knapp M, et al. Systematic mutation screening and association study of the A1 and A2a adenosine receptor genes in panic disorder suggest a contribution of the A2a gene to the development of disease. *Mol. Psychiatry* 1998; 3, 81–85.

[24] Hamilton SP, Slager SL, Baisre de Leon A, Heiman GA, Klein DF, Hodge SE, et al. Evidence for genetic linkage between a polymorphism in the adenosine 2A receptor and panic disorder. *Neuropsychopharmacology* 2004; 29, 558–565.

[25] Leygraf A, Hohoff C, Freitag C, Willis-Owen SA, Krakowitzky P, Fritze J, et al. Rgs 2 gene polymorphisms as modulators of anxiety in humans? *J. Neural Transm*. 2006; 113, 1921–1925.

[26] Smoller JW, Paulus MP, Fagerness JA, Purcell S, Yamaki LH, Hirshfeld-Becker D, et al. Influence of RGS2 on anxiety-related temperament, personality, and brain function. *Arch. Gen. Psychiatry* 2008; 65, 298–308.

[27] Domschke K, Hohoff C, Jacob C, Maier W, Fritze J, Bandelow B, et al. Chromosome 4q31–34 panic disorder risk locus: association of neuropeptide Y Y5 receptor variants. *Am. J. Med. Genet. B. Neuropsychiatr. Genet. 2008*; 5, 510–516.

[28] Otowa T, Yoshida E, Sugaya N, Yasuda S, Nishimura Y, Inoue K, et al. Genome-wide association study of panic disorder in the Japanese population. *J Hum Genet*. 2009;54:122–6.

[29] Otowa T, Tanii H, Sugaya N, Yoshida E, Inoue K, Yasuda S, et al. Replication of a genome-wide association study of panic disorder in a Japanese population. *J Hum Genet*. 2010;55:91–6.

[30] Otowa T, Kawamura Y, Nishida N, Sugaya N, Koike A, Yoshida E, et al. Meta-analysis of genome-wide association studies for panic disorder in the Japanese population. *Transl Psychiatry*. 2012;2:e186.

[31] Erhardt A, Czibere L, Roeske D, Lucae S, Unschuld PG, Ripke S, et al. TMEM132D, a new candidate for anxiety phenotypes: evidence from human and mouse studies. *Mol Psychiatry*. 2011;16:647–63.

[32] Erhardt A, AkulaN, Schumacher J, Czamara D, Karbalai N, Müller-Myhsok B, et al. Replication and meta-analysis of TMEM132D gene variants in panic disorder. *Transl Psychiatry*. 2012;4:2.

[33] Sakai Y, Kumano H, Nishikawa M, Sakano Y, Kaiya H, Imabayashi E, et al. Cerebral glucose metabolism associated with a fear network in panic disorder, *Neuroreport* 2005; 16: 927-931.

[34] Javanmard M, Shlik J, Kennedy SH, Vaccarino FJ, Houle S, Bradwejn J. Neuroanatomic correlates of CCK-4-induced panic attacks in healthy humans: a comparison of two time points. *Biol. Psychiatry* 1999; 45, 872–882.

[35] Pfleiderer B, Zinkirciran S, Arolt V, Heindel W, Deckert J, Domschke K. fMRI amygdala activation during a spontaneous panic attack in a patient with panic disorder, *The World Journal of Biological Psychiatry* 2007; 8: 269-272.

[36] Munafò MR, Brown SM, Hariri AR. Serotonin transporter (5-HTTLPR) genotype and amygdala activation: a meta-analysis, *Biological psychiatry* 2008; 63: 852-857.

[37] Smolka MN, Schumann G, Wrase J, Grüsser SM, Flor H, Mann K, et al. Catechol-O-methyltransferase val158met genotype affects processing of emotional stimuli in the amygdala and prefrontal cortex, *The Journal of neuroscience* 2005; 25: 836-842.

[38] Domschke K, Baune BT, Havlik L, Stuhrmann A, Suslow T, Kugel H, et al. Catechol-O-methyltransferase gene variation: impact on amygdala response to aversive stimuli, *Neuroimage* 2012; 60: 2222-2229.

[39] Hariri AR, Mattay VS, Tessitore A, Kolachana B, Fera F, Goldman D, et al. Serotonin transporter genetic variation and the response of the human amygdala. *Science* 2002; 297: 400–403.

[40] Heils A, Teufel A, Petri S, Seemann M, Bengel D, Balling U et al. Functional promoter and polyadenylation site mapping of the human serotonin (5-HT) transporter gene. *J Neural Transm Gen Sect* 1995; 102: 247–254.

[41] Parsey R, Hastings R, Oquendo M, Hu X, Goldman D, Huang Y et al. Effect of a triallelic functional polymorphism of the serotonin-transporter-linked promoter region on expression of serotonin transporter in the human brain. *Am J Psychiatry* 2006; 163: 48–51.

[42] Reimold M, Smolka M, Schumann G, Zimmer A, Wrase J, Mann K et al. Midbrain serotonin transporter binding potential measured with [C-11]DASB is affected by serotonin transporter genotype. *J Neural Transm* 2007; 114: 635–639.

[43] Van Dyck C, Malison R, Staley J, Jacobsen L, Seibyl J, Laruelle M et al. Central serotonin transporter availability measured with [I-123]beta-CIT SPECT in relation to serotonin transporter genotype. *Am J Psychiatry* 2004; 161: 525–531.

[44] Nordquist N, Oreland L. Serotonin, genetic variability, behaviour, and psychiatric disorders—a review. *Ups J Med Sci* 2010; 115: 2–10.

[45] Pezawas L, Meyer-Lindenberg A, Drabant EM, Verchinski BA, Munoz KE, Kolachana BS et al. 5-HTTLPR polymorphism impacts

human cingulateamygdala interactions: a genetic susceptibility mechanism for depression. *Nat Neurosci* 2005; 8: 828–834.

[46] Munafò MR, Freimer NB, Ng W, Ophoff R, Veijola J, Miettunen J et al. 5-HTTLPR genotype and anxiety-related personality traits: a meta-analysis and new data. *Am J Med Genet B Neuropsychiatr Genet* 2009; 150b: 271–281.

[47] Hindi Attar C, Finckh B, Buchel C. The influence of serotonin on fear learning. *PLoS One* 2012; 7: e42397.

[48] Domschke K, Braun M, Ohrmann P, Suslow T, Kugel H, Bauer J, et al. Association of the functional -1019C/G 5-HT1A polymorphism with prefrontal cortex and amygdala activation measured with 3 T fMRI in panic disorder. *Int. J. Neuropsychopharmacol.* 2006; 9, 349–355.

[49] Lueken U, Straube B, Wittchen HU, Konrad C, Strohle A, Wittmann A et al. Therapygenetics: anterior cingulate cortex-amygdala coupling is associated with 5-HTTLPR and treatment response in panic disorder with agoraphobia. *J Neural Transm* 2015; 122: 135–144.

[50] Klucken T, Alexander N, Schweckendiek J, Merz CJ, Kagerer S, Osinsky R et al. Individual differences in neural correlates of fear conditioning as a function of 5-HTTLPR and stressful life events. *Soc Cogn Affect Neurosci* 2013; 8: 318–325.

[51] Hermann A, Kupper Y, Schmitz A, Walter B, Vaitl D, Hennig J et al. Functional gene polymorphisms in the serotonin system and traumatic life events modulate the neural basis of fear acquisition and extinction. *PLoS One* 2012; 7: e44352.

[52] Yu ST, Kim MK, Kim B, Yoo E, Lee JY, Lee KS, et al. The Effects of 5-HTR1A Polymorphism on Cingulum Connectivity in Patients with Panic Disorder, *Psychiatry investigation* 2013; 10: 399-406.

[53] Jones DK, Christiansen K, Chapman R, Aggleton J. Distinct subdivisions of the cingulum bundle revealed by diffusion MRI fibre tracking: implications for neuropsychological investigations, *Neuropsychologia* 2013; 51: 67-78.

[54] Straube B, Reif A, Richter J, Lueken U, Weber H, Arolt V et al. The functional − 1019C/G HTR1A polymorphism and mechanisms of fear. *Transl Psychiatry* 2014; 4: e490.

[55] Reif A, Weber H, Domschke K et al. MAOA and mechanisms of panic disorder revisited: from bench to molecular psychotherapy. *Mol Psychiatry* 2013.

[56] Phelps EA, Delgado MR, Nearing KI, LeDoux JE. Extinction learning in humans: role of the amygdala and vmPFC. *Neuron* 2004; 43: 897–905.

[57] Milad MR, Quinn BT, Pitman RK, Orr SP, Fischl B, Rauch SL. Thickness of ventromedial prefrontal cortex in humans is correlated with extinction memory. *Proc Natl Acad Sci US* 2005; 102: 10706–10711.

[58] Craddock N, Owen MJ, O'Donovan MC. The catechol-O-methyl transferase (COMT) gene as a candidate for psychiatric phenotypes: evidence and lessons, *Molecular psychiatry* 2006; 11: 446-458.

[59] Domschke K, Ohrmann P, Braun M, Suslow T, Bauer J, Hohoff C, et al. Influence of the catechol-O-methyltransferase val158met genotype on amygdala and orbitofrontal cortex emotional processing in panic disorder. *Psychiatry Res*. 2008; 163, 13–20.

[60] Kim B, Yoo E, Lee JY, Lee KS, Choe AY, Lee JE, et al. The effects of the catechol-O-methyltransferase val158met polymorphism on white matter connectivity in patients with panic disorder, *Journal of affective disorders* 2013; 147: 64-71.

[61] Phillips ML, Drevets WC, Rauch SL, Lane R. Neurobiology of emotion perception II: Implications for major psychiatric disorders, *Biological psychiatry* 2003; 54: 515-528.

[62] Raczka KA, Mechias ML, Gartmann N, Reif A, Deckert J, Pessiglione M et al. Empirical support for an involvement of the mesostriatal dopamine system in human fear extinction. *Transl Psychiatry* 2011; 1: e12.

[63] Cacciaglia R, Nees F, Pohlack ST, Ruttorf M, Winkelmann T, Witt SH et al. A risk variant for alcoholism in the NMDA receptor affects

amygdala activity during fear conditioning in humans. *Biol Psychol* 2013; 94: 74–81.

[64] Bernier V, Stocco R, Bogusky M, Joyce J, Parachoniak C, Grenier K et al. Structure–function relationships in the neuropeptide S receptor—molecular consequences of the asthma-associated mutation N107I. *J Biol Chem* 2006; 281: 24704–24712.

[65] Domschke K, Reif A, Weber H, Richter J, Hohoff C, Ohrmann P, Neuropeptide S receptor gene converging evidence for a role in panic disorder. *Mol Psychiatry* 2011; 16(9):938–948.

[66] Soliman F, Glatt CE, Bath KG, Levita L, Jones RM, Pattwell SS et al. A genetic variant BDNF polymorphism alters extinction learning in both mouse and human. *Science* 2011; 327: 863–866.

[67] Lonsdorf TB, Golkar A, Lindstrom KM, Haaker J, Ohman A, Schalling M et al. BDNF val66met affects neural activation pattern during fear conditioning and 24 h delayed fear recall. *Soc Cogn Affect Neurosci* 2014; 10: 664–671.

[68] Weber H, Richter J, Straube B, Lueken U, Domschke K, Schartner C, et al. Allelic variation in CRHR1 predisposes to panic disorder: evidence for biased fear processing, *Molecular psychiatry* 2015.

[69] Reetz, K., Lencer, R., Steinlechner, S., Gaser, C., Hagenah, J., Buchel, C., et al. Limbic and frontal cortical degeneration is associated with psychiatric symptoms in PINK1 mutation carriers. *Biol. Psychiatry* 2008; 64: 241–247.

[70] Nomoto H, Yonezawa T, Itoh K, Ono K, Yamamoto K, Oohashi T, et al. Molecular cloning of a novel transmembrane protein MOLT expressed by mature oligodendrocytes. *J Biochem*. 2003;134:231–8.

[71] Walser SM, Dedic N, Touma C, Floss T, WurstW, Holsboer F, et al. TMEM132D-a putative cell adhesion molecule involved in panic disorder. *Pharmacopsychiatry*. 2011;44.

[72] Erhardt A, Hoehn D, Czisch M, Kiem S, Holsboer F, et al. Functional connectivity density mapping to explore TMEM 132D, a new candidate for anxiety phenotypes. *Molecular Psychiatry* 2011; 16: 647-663.

[73] Haaker J, Lonsdorf TB, Raczka KA, Mechias ML, Gartmann N and Kalisch R. Higher anxiety and larger amygdala volumes in carriers of a TMEM132D risk variant for panic disorder. *Transl Psychiatry* 2014; 4, e357; doi:10.1038/tp.2014.1.

[74] Smoller JW, Gallagher PJ, Duncan LE, McGrath LM, Haddad SA, Holmes AJ, et al. The human ortholog of acid-sensing ion channel gene ASIC1a is associated with panic disorder and amygdala structure and function, *Biological psychiatry* 2014; 76: 902-910.

In: Panic Disorder
Editor: Yong-Ku Kim
ISBN: 978-1-53613-001-0

Chapter 4

THE ROLE OF THE SYMPATHETIC NERVOUS SYSTEM, NEUROINFLAMMATION AND ALTERATIONS OF THE BRAIN IN PANIC DISORDER

Eunsoo Won, MD, PhD and Yong-Ku Kim*, MD, PhD
Department of Psychiatry,
Korea University College of Medicine,
Seoul, Republic of Korea

ABSTRACT

Panic disorder is characterized by recurrent unexpected panic attacks, with a panic attack being described as an abrupt surge of intense fear or discomfort that reaches a peak within minutes, during which time specific symptoms occur. Such symptoms include palpitations, sweating, shaking, sensations of shortness of breath, feelings of choking, chest pain or discomfort, nausea, dizziness, chills or heat sensations, paresthesias, derealization or depersonalization, fear of losing control, and fear of

* Corresponding author: yongku@korea.ac.kr, yongku0304@gmail.com.

dying. Persistent concern or worrying of additional attacks or significant maladaptive change in behavior related to the attacks should follow at least one of the attacks [1]. Although the exact etiology of panic disorder is still unknown, the sympathetic nervous system and its influence on the immune system seem to play a central role in the development and progression of the disorder. Enhanced inflammation represented as an increase in pro-inflammatory cytokines has been reported in patients diagnosed with panic disorder [2]. Furthermore, increased systemic inflammation can lead to neuroinflammation, which can ultimately lead to alterations in brain structure and function [3], with recent findings supporting alterations in limbic and prefrontal cortical structures in panic disorder [4]. In this chapter, we will revise the influence of the sympathetic nervous system on inflammatory responses involving pro-inflammatory cytokines, and neuroinflammation which may ultimately lead to alterations in the structure and function of specific brain regions that are involved in the etiology of panic disorder.

The Sympathetic Nervous System and Catecholamines in Panic Disorder

Panic disorder has been widely hypothesized to be associated with dysfunction of the autonomic nervous system [5]. Increases in sympathetic tone and decreases in parasympathetic tone have been described in panic disorder [6, 7]. The variety of symptoms presented in panic attacks are considered to be physiological responses of sympathetic nervous system hyperactivity. The sympathetic nervous system's primary process is to stimulate the body's fight-or-flight response, which is normally a physiological reaction that occurs in response to a perceived harmful event, attack, or threat to survival [8]. The reaction is initiated by the amygdala, which triggers a neural response in the hypothalamus. The hypothalamus then secretes corticotropin-releasing hormone (CRH) and arginine vasopressin, which stimulates noradrenergic centers in the brainstem [9]. The locus coeruleus of the brainstem then increases sympathetic activity and reduces parasympathetic activity [10]. The sympathetic system controls catecholamine biosynthesis and secretion from the adrenal medulla which mainly releases epinephrine and norepinephrine into the blood when stimulated by the sympathetic nervous system [11]. Therefore, catecholamine levels increase when the sympathetic nervous system is activated. Catecholamines facilitate immediate physical reactions which include acceleration of heart and lung action, paling or flushing, inhibition of the upper-intestines, lacrimal and salivation glands, dilation of pupils, loss of hearing and peripheral vision, and shaking, which are all symptoms that are present in a panic attack [1]. The parasympathetic nervous system mainly uses acetylcholine as its neurotransmitter, therefore acetylcholine levels decrease when parasympathetic nervous system activity is reduced [12].

Although the dysfunction in the catecholamine system has long been thought to be involved in the pathogenesis of panic disorder, the exact mechanism is still unknown [13]. Genetic studies have suggested functional polymorphisms of the norepinephrine transporter gene to affect synaptic reuptake of noradrenaline in panic disorder [14]. Studies on peripheral receptors are not consistent in panic disorder, with a few studies implying changes in the proportion of high to low affinity adrenoceptors as a result of excessive noradrenaline release during panic attacks [15]. Studies of peripheral catecholamine and metabolites have suggested peripheral alterations in noradrenaline activity in panic disorder, with nocturnal urinary noradrenaline excretion and mean 24 hour urinary 3-methoxy-4-hydroxyphenyglycol, a metabolite of norepinephrine, being elevated in patients with panic attacks [16, 17]. Challenge studies with yohimbine, a α2-adrenergic antagonist which increases noradrenergic concentrations, reported panic disorder patients showing increased rates of panic attacks (18). In carbon dioxide challenge studies, patients with panic disorder showed an increase in panic attacks and subjective anxiety compared to healthy controls (19). Treatment studies have reported various antidepressants that act on norepinephrine levels to alleviate symptoms of panic disorder [20].

Systemic Inflammation and Neuroinflammation in Panic Disorder

Catecholmaines modulate the release of pro-inflammatory cytokines through α- and β-adrenoceptors on immune cells [21], increasing levels of pro-inflammatory cytokines such as tumor necrosis factor (TNF) and interleukin (IL)-6 [22, 23]. Acetylcholine dose-dependently inhibits the release of pro-inflammatory cytokines such as TNF, IL-1, IL-6, and IL-18 [24], having an immunoinhibitory role in the brain [25]. As catecholamine levels seem to be increased due to sympathetic nervous system activity in panic disorder, previous studies have been conducted on the association between systemic inflammation and panic disorder [2, 26]. A broad spectrum of increased peripheral levels of pro-inflammatory cytokines, such as TNF, IL-1 and IL-6, were reported to be elevated in patients with panic disorder [2].

Systemic inflammation can access the brain as pro-inflammatory cytokines can cross the blood–brain barrier (BBB) through circumventricular organs and cytokine specific saturable BBB transporters [27, 28]. Pro-inflammatory cytokine signals can also be conveyed to the brain by cytokine receptor activation [29]. Microglia produce pro-inflammatory cytokines, nitric oxide, and reactive oxygen species, being the primary inflammatory cell type of the brain [30]. It can also produce chemokines that attract monocytes into the brain when activated by increased peripheral inflammation [31], with monocytes then being able to produce pro-inflammatory cytokines [32]. Such increases in pro-inflammatory cytokines can influence the brain by directly exerting neurotoxic effects on specific brain regions.

Neurotoxic Cytokine Effects on the Brain

Certain brain areas have been reported to be directly influenced by increased activation of brain cytokine networks. The brain-derived neurotrophic factor signaling pathway has been shown to be down regulated by increases in pro-inflammatory cytokines, which decreases neurotrophic support and neurogenesis [33-35]. Pro-inflammatory cytokines can decrease cell proliferation through the nuclear factor-kappa B signaling pathway, with the nuclear factor-kappa B being the primary transcription factor of the inflammatory response initiation and conveying peripheral inflammatory signals to the central nervous system [36, 37]. Pro-inflammatory cytokines can increase glutamate that induce excitotoxicity and impaired neurogenesis through N-methyl-D-aspartate receptor activation [38, 39]. Pro-inflammatory cytokines can also induce astrocytes and microglia to release reactive oxygen and nitrogen species that cause oxidative damage on neurons [40, 41].

Limbic and prefrontal structures have been reported to particularly be influenced by increased cytokine levels [70], which are areas that have repeatedly been associated with panic disorder. Healthy controls exposed to laboratory-based stressors were associated with increases in IL-6 and TNF-α, with increases in TNF-α being associated with enhanced dorsal anterior cingulate cortex and anterior insula activity [42]. Healthy individuals injected with bacterial lipopolysaccharide showed increases in TNF-α, IL-1 and IL-6, along with increased state anxiety. Also, these individuals showed enhanced activation of the orbitofrontal cortex in response to emotional visual stimuli when lipopolysaccharide was injected [43]. Healthy controls who received low-dose endotoxin that increases pro-inflammatory cytokine levels, showed decreased ventral striatum activity to anticipated reward, with the ventral striatum being associated with limbic system activity suppression [44, 45]. Healthy participants who received typhoid vaccination and presented increased circulating IL-6, showed mood deterioration correlated increases in subgenual anterior cingulate cortex activity. Also, reduced connectivity of the subgenual anterior cingulate cortex to the amygdala, medial prefrontal cortex, nucleus accumbens, and superior temporal sulcus were also observed, with IL-6 levels seeming to modulate the connectivity of the subgenual anterior cingulate cortex to these regions [46]. Healthy individuals exposed to acute laboratory-based social stressors showed associations between greater increases in IL-6 levels and amygdala activity, and coupling between the amygdala and dorsomedial prefrontal cortex [47].

Structural and Functional Changes of the Brain in Panic Disorder

Since the etiology of panic disorder had been suggested to be associated with impaired coordination of anxiety-related brain circuits that lead to enhanced amygdala activity with subsequent autonomic and behavioral activation [48], numerous imaging studies have been conducted. Recent findings support structural and functional alterations in limbic and pre-frontal structures in panic disorder, including the amygdala and anterior cingulate [4]. Studies on brain structural alterations in panic disorder have reported reduced volumes in the amygdala [49-53], temporal lobe [53-56], parahippocampal gyrus [57], anterior cingulate cortex [49, 58-60] and frontal and orbitofrontal cortices [49, 54, 56, 59, 61, 62], basal ganglia [51, 56] and insula [49]. However, opposite results have also been reported in patients with panic disorder, such as increased volumes in the temporal lobe [60], insula [59, 60] and brainstem [59, 60, 63]. Studies measuring white matter connectivity in panic disorder have reported increased fractional anisotropy values of the anterior and posterior cingulate regions [64]. Meta-analyses of voxel-based morphometry studies in panic disorder have reported grey matter deficits in the caudate [65, 66] and parahippocampal gyrus [65]. Studies measuring resting state function in panic disorder have reported reduced activation in temporal [67, 68], frontal [69-73] and parietal areas [67, 73]. On the other hand, increased activation of the brain stem, midbrain, thalamus, and cerebellum have also been reported [74] along with no difference in function between patients and healthy controls [75, 76]. Although inconsistent results such as increased or decreased volume and function have been reported in previous imaging studies of panic disorder, alterations in limbic and prefrontal structures can be considered to be involved in the pathophysiology of panic disorder.

CONCLUSION

In response to acute stress, such as a perceived harmful event or threat, the amygdala triggers a neural response in the hypothalamus which stimulates noradrenergic centers in the brainstem that increases sympathetic activity and reduces parasympathetic activity. As a result, epinephrine and norepinephrine levels are increased and acetylcholine levels are decreased, which may in turn increase pro-inflammatory cytokine levels. Increased peripheral inflammation can lead to neuroinflammation with increased levels of pro-inflammatory cytokines in the brain, which can directly exert neurotoxic effects on specific brain regions. This may cause alterations in the structure or function of anxiety-related brain circuits, including limbic and pre-frontal structures, priming the brain to be vulnerable to panic disorder. Further research on the use of inflammatory markers and brain imaging in the early diagnosis of panic disorder are needed in order to better identify and manage this disorder.

REFERENCES

[1] APA. *Diagnostic and Statistical Manual of Mental Disorders* 5 ed. Arlington: American Psychiatric Publishing; 2013.

[2] Hoge EA, Brandstetter K, Moshier S, Pollack MH, Wong KK, Simon NM. Broad spectrum of cytokine abnormalities in panic disorder and posttraumatic stress disorder. *Depress Anxiety*. 2009;26(5):447-55.

[3] Kim YK, Na KS, Myint AM, Leonard BE. The role of pro-inflammatory cytokines in neuroinflammation, neurogenesis and the neuroendocrine system in major depression. Prog *Neuropsychopharmacol Biol Psychiatry*. 2016;64:277-84.

[4] Dresler T, Guhn A, Tupak SV, Ehlis AC, Herrmann MJ, Fallgatter AJ, et al. Revise the revised? New dimensions of the neuroanatomical hypothesis of panic disorder. *Journal of neural transmission*. 2013;120(1):3-29.

[5] Stein MB, Asmundson GJ. Autonomic function in panic disorder: cardiorespiratory and plasma catecholamine responsivity to multiple challenges of the autonomic nervous system. *Biological psychiatry*. 1994;36(8):548-58.

[6] Blechert J, Michael T, Grossman P, Lajtman M, Wilhelm FH. Autonomic and respiratory characteristics of posttraumatic stress disorder and panic disorder. *Psychosomatic medicine*. 2007;69(9):935-43.

[7] Cohen H, Benjamin J, Geva AB, Matar MA, Kaplan Z, Kotler M. Autonomic dysregulation in panic disorder and in post-traumatic stress disorder: application of power spectrum analysis of heart rate variability at rest and in response to recollection of trauma or panic attacks. *Psychiatry research*. 2000;96(1):1-13.

[8] Jansen AS, Nguyen XV, Karpitskiy V, Mettenleiter TC, Loewy AD. Central command neurons of the sympathetic nervous system: basis of the fight-or-flight response. *Science*. 1995;270(5236):644-6.

[9] Jones BE, Yang TZ. The efferent projections from the reticular formation and the locus coeruleus studied by anterograde and retrograde axonal transport in the rat. *The Journal of comparative neurology*. 1985;242(1):56-92.

[10] Lewis DI, Coote JH. Excitation and inhibition of rat sympathetic preganglionic neurones by catecholamines. *Brain research*. 1990;530(2):229-34.

[11] Aunis D. Exocytosis in chromaffin cells of the adrenal medulla. *International review of cytology*. 1998;181:213-320.

[12] Wank SA. Cholecystokinin receptors. *The American journal of physiology*. 1995;269(5 Pt 1):G628-46.

[13] Kalk NJ, Nutt DJ, Lingford-Hughes AR. The role of central noradrenergic dysregulation in anxiety disorders: evidence from clinical studies. *Journal of psychopharmacology*. 2011;25(1):3-16.

[14] Sand PG, Mori T, Godau C, Stober G, Flachenecker P, Franke P, et al. Norepinephrine transporter gene (NET) variants in patients with panic disorder. *Neuroscience letters*. 2002;333(1):41-4.

[15] Cameron OG, Smith CB, Lee MA, Hollingsworth PJ, Hill EM, Curtis GC. Adrenergic status in anxiety disorders: platelet alpha 2-adrenergic receptor binding, blood pressure, pulse, and plasma catecholamines in panic and generalized anxiety disorder patients and in normal subjects. *Biological psychiatry*. 1990;28(1):3-20.

[16] Bandelow B, Sengos G, Wedekind D, Huether G, Pilz J, Broocks A, et al. Urinary excretion of cortisol, norepinephrine, testosterone, and melatonin in panic disorder. *Pharmacopsychiatry*. 1997;30(4):113-7.

[17] Garvey MJ, Tollefson GD, Orsulak PJ. Elevations of urinary MHPG in depressed patients with panic attacks. *Psychiatry research.* 1987;20(3):183-7.

[18] Charney DS, Woods SW, Goodman WK, Heninger GR. Neurobiological mechanisms of panic anxiety: biochemical and behavioral correlates of yohimbine-induced panic attacks. *The American journal of psychiatry*. 1987;144(8):1030-6.

[19] Charney DS, Woods SW, Heninger GR. Noradrenergic function in generalized anxiety disorder: effects of yohimbine in healthy subjects and patients with generalized anxiety disorder. *Psychiatry research*. 1989;27(2):173-82.

[20] Baldwin DS, Anderson IM, Nutt DJ, Bandelow B, Bond A, Davidson JR, et al. Evidence-based guidelines for the pharmacological treatment of anxiety disorders: recommendations from the British Association for Psychopharmacology. J*ournal of psychopharmacology*. 2005;19(6):567-96.

[21] Hasko G, Szabo C. Regulation of cytokine and chemokine production by transmitters and co-transmitters of the autonomic nervous system. *Biochemical pharmacology*. 1998;56(9):1079-87.

[22] Spengler RN, Chensue SW, Giacherio DA, Blenk N, Kunkel SL. Endogenous norepinephrine regulates tumor necrosis factor-alpha production from macrophages *in vitro*. *Journal of immunology*. 1994;152(6):3024-31.

[23] Chrousos GP. The stress response and immune function: clinical implications. The 1999 Novera H. Spector Lecture. *Annals of the New York Academy of Sciences*. 2000;917:38-67.

[24] Borovikova LV, Ivanova S, Zhang M, Yang H, Botchkina GI, Watkins LR, et al. Vagus nerve stimulation attenuates the systemic inflammatory response to endotoxin. *Nature.* 2000;405(6785):458-62.

[25] Pavlov VA, Parrish WR, Rosas-Ballina M, Ochani M, Puerta M, Ochani K, et al. Brain acetylcholinesterase activity controls systemic cytokine levels through the cholinergic anti-inflammatory pathway. *Brain, behavior, and immunity.* 2009;23(1):41-5.

[26] Vogelzangs N, Beekman AT, de Jonge P, Penninx BW. Anxiety disorders and inflammation in a large adult cohort. *Translational psychiatry.* 2013;3:e249.

[27] Blatteis CM, Bealer SL, Hunter WS, Llanos QJ, Ahokas RA, Mashburn TA, Jr. Suppression of fever after lesions of the anteroventral third ventricle in guinea pigs. *Brain research bulletin.* 1983;11(5):519-26.

[28] Quan N, Banks WA. Brain-immune communication pathways. *Brain, behavior, and immunity.* 2007;21(6):727-35.

[29] Watkins LR, Goehler LE, Relton JK, Tartaglia N, Silbert L, Martin D, et al. Blockade of interleukin-1 induced hyperthermia by subdiaphragmatic vagotomy: evidence for vagal mediation of immune-brain communication. *Neuroscience letters.* 1995;183(1-2):27-31.

[30] Harry GJ, Kraft AD. Neuroinflammation and microglia: considerations and approaches for neurotoxicity assessment. *Expert Opin Drug Metab Toxicol.* 2008;4(10):1265-77.

[31] D'Mello C, Le T, Swain MG. Cerebral microglia recruit monocytes into the brain in response to tumor necrosis factoralpha signaling during peripheral organ inflammation. *J Neurosci.* 2009;29(7):2089-102.

[32] Peracoli MT, Kurokawa CS, Calvi SA, Mendes RP, Pereira PC, Marques SA, et al. Production of pro- and anti-inflammatory cytokines by monocytes from patients with paracoccidioidomycosis. *Microbes Infect.* 2003;5(5):413-8.

[33] Barrientos RM, Sprunger DB, Campeau S, Higgins EA, Watkins LR, Rudy JW, et al. Brain-derived neurotrophic factor mRNA downregulation produced by social isolation is blocked by intrahippocampal interleukin-1 receptor antagonist. *Neuroscience.* 2003;121(4):847-53.

[34] Ben Menachem-Zidon O, Goshen I, Kreisel T, Ben Menahem Y, Reinhartz E, Ben Hur T, et al. Intrahippocampal transplantation of transgenic neural precursor cells overexpressing interleukin-1 receptor antagonist blocks chronic isolation-induced impairment in memory and neurogenesis. *Neuropsychopharmacology: official publication of the American College of Neuropsychopharmacology.* 2008;33(9):2251-62.

[35] Wu CW, Chen YC, Yu L, Chen HI, Jen CJ, Huang AM, et al. Treadmill exercise counteracts the suppressive effects of peripheral lipopolysaccharide on hippocampal neurogenesis and learning and memory. *J Neurochem.* 2007;103(6):2471-81.

[36] Irwin MR, Wang M, Ribeiro D, Cho HJ, Olmstead R, Breen EC, et al. Sleep loss activates cellular inflammatory signaling. *Biological psychiatry.* 2008;64(6):538-40.

[37] Koo JW, Duman RS. IL-1beta is an essential mediator of the antineurogenic and anhedonic effects of stress. *Proceedings of the National Academy of Sciences of the United States of America.* 2008;105(2):751-6.

[38] Ida T, Hara M, Nakamura Y, Kozaki S, Tsunoda S, Ihara H. Cytokine-induced enhancement of calcium-dependent glutamate release from astrocytes mediated by nitric oxide. *Neuroscience letters.* 2008;432(3):232-6.

[39] Haydon PG, Carmignoto G. Astrocyte control of synaptic transmission and neurovascular coupling. *Physiological reviews.* 2006;86(3):1009-31.

[40] Gavillet M, Allaman I, Magistretti PJ. Modulation of astrocytic metabolic phenotype by proinflammatory cytokines. *Glia.* 2008;56(9):975-89.

[41] Thornton P, Pinteaux E, Gibson RM, Allan SM, Rothwell NJ. Interleukin-1-induced neurotoxicity is mediated by glia and requires caspase activation and free radical release. *J Neurochem.* 2006;98(1):258-66.
[42] Slavich GM, Way BM, Eisenberger NI, Taylor SE. Neural sensitivity to social rejection is associated with inflammatory responses to social stress. *Proceedings of the National Academy of Sciences of the United States of America.* 2010;107(33):14817-22.
[43] Kullmann JS, Grigoleit JS, Lichte P, Kobbe P, Rosenberger C, Banner C, et al. Neural response to emotional stimuli during experimental human endotoxemia. *Human brain mapping.* 2013;34(9):2217-27.
[44] Eisenberger NI, Berkman ET, Inagaki TK, Rameson LT, Mashal NM, Irwin MR. Inflammation-induced anhedonia: endotoxin reduces ventral striatum responses to reward. *Biological psychiatry.* 2010;68(8):748-54.
[45] Williams GV, Rolls ET, Leonard CM, Stern C. Neuronal responses in the ventral striatum of the behaving macaque. *Behavioural brain research.* 1993;55(2):243-52.
[46] Harrison NA, Brydon L, Walker C, Gray MA, Steptoe A, Critchley HD. Inflammation causes mood changes through alterations in subgenual cingulate activity and mesolimbic connectivity. *Biological psychiatry.* 2009;66(5):407-14.
[47] Muscatell KA, Dedovic K, Slavich GM, Jarcho MR, Breen EC, Bower JE, et al. Greater amygdala activity and dorsomedial prefrontal-amygdala coupling are associated with enhanced inflammatory responses to stress. *Brain, behavior, and immunity.* 2015;43:46-53.
[48] Gorman JM, Kent JM, Sullivan GM, Coplan JD. Neuroanatomical hypothesis of panic disorder, revised. *The American journal of psychiatry.* 2000;157(4):493-505.
[49] Asami T, Yamasue H, Hayano F, Nakamura M, Uehara K, Otsuka T, et al. Sexually dimorphic gray matter volume reduction in patients with panic disorder. *Psychiatry research.* 2009;173(2):128-34.

[50] Hayano F, Nakamura M, Asami T, Uehara K, Yoshida T, Roppongi T, et al. Smaller amygdala is associated with anxiety in patients with panic disorder. *Psychiatry and clinical neurosciences*. 2009;63(3):266-76.

[51] Lai CH, Hsu YY, Wu YT. First episode drug-naive major depressive disorder with panic disorder: gray matter deficits in limbic and default network structures. *European neuropsychopharmacology: the journal of the European College of Neuropsychopharmacology*. 2010;20(10):676-82.

[52] Massana G, Serra-Grabulosa JM, Salgado-Pineda P, Gasto C, Junque C, Massana J, et al. Amygdalar atrophy in panic disorder patients detected by volumetric magnetic resonance imaging. *NeuroImage*. 2003;19(1):80-90.

[53] Uchida RR, Del-Ben CM, Santos AC, Araujo D, Crippa JA, Guimaraes FS, et al. Decreased left temporal lobe volume of panic patients measured by magnetic resonance imaging. *Brazilian journal of medical and biological research*. Revista brasileira de pesquisas medicas e biologicas. 2003;36(7):925-9.

[54] Sobanski T, Wagner G, Peikert G, Gruhn U, Schluttig K, Sauer H, et al. Temporal and right frontal lobe alterations in panic disorder: a quantitative volumetric and voxel-based morphometric MRI study. *Psychological medicine*. 2010;40(11):1879-86.

[55] Vythilingam M, Anderson ER, Goddard A, Woods SW, Staib LH, Charney DS, et al. Temporal lobe volume in panic disorder--a quantitative magnetic resonance imaging study. *Psychiatry research*. 2000;99(2):75-82.

[56] Yoo HK, Kim MJ, Kim SJ, Sung YH, Sim ME, Lee YS, et al. Putaminal gray matter volume decrease in panic disorder: an optimized voxel-based morphometry study. *The European journal of neuroscience*. 2005;22(8):2089-94.

[57] Massana G, Serra-Grabulosa JM, Salgado-Pineda P, Gasto C, Junque C, Massana J, et al. Parahippocampal gray matter density in panic disorder: a voxel-based morphometric study. *The American journal of psychiatry*. 2003;160(3):566-8.

[58] Asami T, Hayano F, Nakamura M, Yamasue H, Uehara K, Otsuka T, et al. Anterior cingulate cortex volume reduction in patients with panic disorder. *Psychiatry and clinical neurosciences*. 2008;62(3):322-30.

[59] Protopopescu X, Pan H, Tuescher O, Cloitre M, Goldstein M, Engelien A, et al. Increased brainstem volume in panic disorder: a voxel-based morphometric study. *Neuroreport*. 2006;17(4):361-3.

[60] Uchida RR, Del-Ben CM, Busatto GF, Duran FL, Guimaraes FS, Crippa JA, et al. Regional gray matter abnormalities in panic disorder: a voxel-based morphometry study. *Psychiatry research*. 2008;163(1):21-9.

[61] Roppongi T, Nakamura M, Asami T, Hayano F, Otsuka T, Uehara K, et al. Posterior orbitofrontal sulcogyral pattern associated with orbitofrontal cortex volume reduction and anxiety trait in panic disorder. *Psychiatry and clinical neurosciences*. 2010;64(3):318-26.

[62] Lai CH, Hsu YY. A subtle grey-matter increase in first-episode, drug-naive major depressive disorder with panic disorder after 6 weeks' duloxetine therapy. *The international journal of neuropsychopharmacology*. 2011;14(2):225-35.

[63] Fujiwara A, Yoshida T, Otsuka T, Hayano F, Asami T, Narita H, et al. Midbrain volume increase in patients with panic disorder. *Psychiatry and clinical neurosciences*. 2011;65(4):365-73.

[64] Han DH, Renshaw PF, Dager SR, Chung A, Hwang J, Daniels MA, et al. Altered cingulate white matter connectivity in panic disorder patients. *J Psychiatr Res*. 2008;42(5):399-407.

[65] Lai CH. Gray matter deficits in panic disorder: a pilot study of meta-analysis. *J Clin Psychopharmacol*. 2011;31(3):287-93.

[66] Radua J, van den Heuvel OA, Surguladze S, Mataix-Cols D. Meta-analytical comparison of voxel-based morphometry studies in obsessive-compulsive disorder vs other anxiety disorders. *Arch Gen Psychiatry*. 2010;67(7):701-11.

[67] Bisaga A, Katz JL, Antonini A, Wright CE, Margouleff C, Gorman JM, et al. Cerebral glucose metabolism in women with panic disorder. *The American journal of psychiatry*. 1998;155(9):1178-83.

[68] Lee YS, Hwang J, Kim SJ, Sung YH, Kim J, Sim ME, et al. Decreased blood flow of temporal regions of the brain in subjects with panic disorder. *J Psychiatr Res.* 2006;40(6):528-34.

[69] De Cristofaro MT, Sessarego A, Pupi A, Biondi F, Faravelli C. Brain perfusion abnormalities in drug-naive, lactate-sensitive panic patients: a SPECT study. *Biological psychiatry*. 1993;33(7):505-12.

[70] Eren I, Tukel R, Polat A, Karaman R, Unal S. [Evaluation of regional cerebral blood flow changes in panic disorder with Tc99m-HMPAO SPECT]. *Turk Psikiyatri Derg*. 2002;13(2):89-97.

[71] Eren I, Tukel R, Polat A, Karaman R, Unal S. Evaluation of regional cerebral blood flow changes in panic disorder with Tc99m-HMPAO SPECT. *Psychiatry research*. 2003;123(2):135-43.

[72] Nordahl TE, Stein MB, Benkelfat C, Semple WE, Andreason P, Zametkin A, et al. Regional cerebral metabolic asymmetries replicated in an independent group of patients with panic disorders. *Biological psychiatry*. 1998;44(10):998-1006.

[73] Nordahl TE, Semple WE, Gross M, Mellman TA, Stein MB, Goyer P, et al. Cerebral glucose metabolic differences in patients with panic disorder. *Neuropsychopharmacology: official publication of the American College of Neuropsychopharmacology*. 1990;3(4):261-72.

[74] Sakai Y, Kumano H, Nishikawa M, Sakano Y, Kaiya H, Imabayashi E, et al. Cerebral glucose metabolism associated with a fear network in panic disorder. *Neuroreport*. 2005;16(9):927-31.

[75] Lucey JV, Costa DC, Adshead G, Deahl M, Busatto G, Gacinovic S, et al. Brain blood flow in anxiety disorders. OCD, panic disorder with agoraphobia, and post-traumatic stress disorder on 99mTcHMPAO single photon emission tomography (SPET). *Br J Psychiatry*. 1997;171:346-50.

[76] Lucey JV, Costa DC, Busatto G, Pilowsky LS, Marks IM, Ell PJ, et al. Caudate regional cerebral blood flow in obsessive-compulsive disorder, panic disorder and healthy controls on single photon emission computerised tomography. *Psychiatry research*. 1997;74(1):25-33.

In: Panic Disorder
Editor: Yong-Ku Kim

ISBN: 978-1-53613-001-0

Chapter 5

THE ASSESSMENT AND TREATMENT OF SUICIDE IN PANIC DISORDER

Sun-young Kim and Se-Won Lim*
Department of Psychiatry, Sungkyunkwan University School of Medicine, Kangbuk Samsung Hospital, Republic of Korea

ABSTRACT

Suicide is one of the most common causes of mortality. At present, the known risk factors of suicide are mood disorders, such as, depression, substance use disorders, schizophrenia, and socioeconomic factors, such as, divorce, separation by death, and unemployment [1]. Many researchers have tried to identify a biological marker that can predict suicide. Several studies have reported low serum cholesterol level is associated with suicidality [2], but reported results are inconsistent [3, 4].

In the absence of an available biological marker of suicide, a past suicide attempt is perhaps the best predictor of increased risk of suicide, even in the 21st century [5]. However, in view of the substantial numbers of mortalities resulting from first attempts at suicide [6, 7], the idea of using a past suicide attempt as a predictor of suicidal behavior is near useless in clinical practice.

* Corresponding author. sewon33.lim@samsung.com.

Suicide is believed to have three stages (suicide ideation, suicide plan, and suicide attempt), though suicide ideation and planning could be categorized as suicidal thinking, and suicide attempt as suicidal behavior. Suicidality, a word widely used in the field of psychiatry, refers to suicidal thinking and behavior in combination. To prevent suicide in the real world, it is essential to assess the risk of suicide before suicide behavior has commenced and to start treatment intervention during the suicidal thinking phase.

It is well known that depressive disorders are strongly related with suicidality. However, it remains unclear whether anxiety disorders without other psychiatric comorbidities, such as, mood disorders or substance use disorder are related with suicidality [8]. The majority of research studies on the possible relationships between anxiety disorders and suicidality have usually focused on panic disorder. Although Weissman et al. suggested that panic disorder (PD) is associated with suicidality in their analysis of Epidemiologic Catchment Area (ECA) data [9], Hornig and McNally [10] failed to confirm this association using the same data after controlling for comorbidities using a different statistical method. In this chapter, the authors describe assessment methods for identifying the risk of suicide in PD and suggest interventions for preventing suicide in affected patients.

1. Suicide and Panic Disorder

Previous studies have shown suicide attempt rates among patients with PD vary considerably, from as low as 0.7% [11] or 2% [12] to as high as 42% [13]. Such inconsistencies may be due to cohort demographic differences or methodology, such as, whether the effects of comorbid disorders were controlled. Hornig et al. [10] found that of 50 subjects who qualified for a lifetime diagnosis of PD and attempted suicide in an epidemiologic catchment area (ECA), 40% also met criteria for schizophrenia, 46% criteria for alcohol dependence/abuse, 32% criteria for major depression, and 21% criteria for bipolar disorder. A substantial number of PD patients develop coexisting conditions associated with an increased risk of suicide [14, 15]. However, it has been demonstrated that the presence of PD may increase suicide risk even in individuals with PD without comorbid disorders [9, 16]. In a large community survey, Weissman et al. [9] reported significant associations between panic attacks or PD and a lifetime prevalence of suicidal ideation and suicide attempts. After controlling separately for the effects of major depression, alcohol, drug abuse, and agoraphobia, associations between panic attacks or PD and suicidal ideation or suicide attempts remained significant. These results suggest that PD is independently associated with suicidality.

2. Are Specific Symptoms Associated with Suicidality in Panic Disorder?

PD is characterized by recurrent panic attacks that consist of sudden episodes of intense fear or discomfort. These attacks are associated with several cognitive and somatic symptoms [17], but little is known about the associations between specific DSM panic symptoms in PD and suicidality. Moreover, reports on relationships between specific panic symptoms and suicidality conflict. For example, Schmidt. et al. [18] suggested high scores for certain configurations of panic symptoms may be significantly predict suicide risk. In a sample of patients with PD, it was found that suicide risk was predicted by high levels of (1) overall anxiety symptoms; (2) anticipatory anxiety; (3) avoidance of bodily sensations; (4) attentional vigilance toward bodily perturbations; and (5) phrenophobia. In another study, Yaseen et al. [19] revealed a positive association between suicide risk and fear of dying among patients with panic attacks. These studies raise important questions about potential relationships between specific panic symptoms and suicidality in patients with PD. Recently, Lim et al. [20] reported that specific symptoms (e.g., "palpitation" and "fear of losing control or going crazy") of PD were associated with a higher risk of suicidality in their cross-sectional study of a Korean population. Because various sociocultural factors contribute to suicidality, a prospective study of a patient cohort with a diverse sociocultural background would help understand the link between specific symptoms of PD and suicidality.

3. Relationships between Agoraphobia and Other Comorbid Illnesses

Agoraphobia (AG) is defined as anxiety about being in places or situations from which escape might be difficult or embarrassing or in which help might not be available when escape is needed. AG frequently occurs jointly with PD, but may occur independently (AG without PD). Thibodeau et al. concluded AG without PD was not associated with lifetime suicide attempts in the National Epidemiologic survey on Alcohol and Related Condition (NESARC), but this possibility contradicted the findings of the National Comorbidity Survey Replication (NCS-R). This discrepancy may have been caused by methodologic differences, for example, few individuals with AG without PD and with a history of suicide attempt were included in NESARC, and this might be related with insufficient statistical power [21]. Previous studies have shown patients with PD that report suicidal ideation or attempts have more pronounced agoraphobia [9, 22]. However, Starcevic et al. reported that individuals with PD and AG with suicidal ideation were significantly more likely to have a personality disorder and more than one comorbid psychiatric disorder [23].

The relationship between PD and suicide is substantially impacted by the presence of other co-occurring disorders. Evidence suggests depressive disorder and bipolar disorder [18, 24], GAD and social anxiety disorder [22, 25] alcohol and substance abuse [26, 27, 9], somatoform disorder [28, 29, 30], eating disorder [27], schizophrenia [10, 31], and personality disorder [23, 32] are associated with suicide in patients with PD.

Although the mechanisms underlying associations between psychiatric comorbidities and suicide are not well understood, several studies have shown that comorbidities may mediate the relationship between PD and suicide [18, 33]. For example, PD can precede the development of depression [34], lead to alcohol/substance use as a form of self-medication [35], and exacerbate general medical conditions [36], which are known risk factors of suicide. Therefore, clinicians should be aware that when PD is comorbid with agoraphobia and another psychiatric illness, the risk of suicide might be increased. In addition, if the symptoms of panic disorder are severe, clinicians are more likely to focus on the apparently manifesting panic disorder and overlook the need to search for coexistent psychiatric diseases. It is recommended that a structured clinical interview, such as, MINI (MINI neuropsychiatric interview) [37], be used to detect possible comorbidities.

4. Assessment of Suicidality in Panic Disorder

Although several psychometric scales are available to measure suicidality, no specific scales have been designed specifically to assess suicidality in panic disorder. Considering that suicidality includes both suicidal thinking and behavior, the suicidality module in MINI has some strength in terms of ease for usage and comprehensiveness [37]. The suicidality section of MINI is composed of 6 questions that address the essential components of suicidality. Total scores for the MINI suicidality module range from 0 to 33. The authors of MINI categorized the risk of suicide as follows: no current risk of suicide as 0 points, low risk 1 to 5 points, moderate risk 6 to 9 points, and high risk 10 or more points. Recently several researchers dichotomized total scores as the absence (total score < 6; no or low risk of suicide) or the presence (total score ≥ 6; moderate to high risk of suicide) of suicidality [38, 39, 20]. However, it should be remembered that clinical scales are only ancillary tools that support the judgements of clinicians. Therefore, whenever suicidality in PD is assessed, all relevant factors, such as, severity of symptoms, the presence of comorbid psychiatric illnesses and of specific symptoms likely to be associated with suicidality, and general medical status as well as suicidality scales should be carefully considered.

5. Treatment of Suicidality in Panic Disorder

Currently, no evidence is available as to which drugs are more effective at treating PD with suicidality. Generally, when panic symptoms are severe, anxiety itself and comorbid conditions, secondary to symptoms of PD, are known to increase risk of suicide. Therefore, the use of serotonergic antidepressants, which considerable evidence indicates reduce the symptoms of PD, may be a reasonable choice in cases of PD with suicidality. However, as some patients taking selective serotonin reupake inhibitors (SSRIs) may experience adverse events, such as, violent behavior, mania, or aggression, which can all lead to suicide, careful observation is essential when prescribing SSRIs to PD patients with suicidality, especially during the early phase of treatment. In addition, in PD patients with comorbid bipolar disorder, the use of SSRIs might induce mania or result in a mixed or rapid cycling state, which is known to be associated with higher risk of suicide. Thus, primary mood stabilizers (valproate, lithium, carbamazepine) [40, 41] and second generation antipsychotics (olanzapine and quetiapine), which have been shown to have some efficacy in PD with bipolar disorder, may be a safer choice [42, 43].

Psychological interventions are critical for the successful treatment of PD patients with suicidality. It has been reported that 67% of suicide attempters with PD believed suicide was an attempt to regain control. [44]. In other words, suicide attempts by PD patients might be desperate attempts to control the catastrophic experience of panic disorder.

For some patients, suicide can be a way of escape from suffering rooted in affective distress related to PD. Feldener et al. reported that patients with PD have greater levels of emotional suppression, which exacerbates both anxious response during bodily perturbation and the perception of intolerable experience [45]. Moreover, some PD patients with depressive disorder are more likely to consider suicide as a means of escape from a life that is “too much to bear” caused by not only emotion suppression but also rumination and maladaptive beliefs, such as, pessimistic thoughts related to depression [46, 47]. Previous studies have shown that emotional acceptance instructions may decrease intense fear, catastrophic thinking, and behavioral avoidance, which are helpful for treating anxiety and mood disorders. [48]. Therefore, clinicians should aware emotional acceptance and mindfulness based therapy can be helpful for PD patients with suicidality and that comorbid depressive disorders should be actively treated.

Avoidant behaviors caused by symptoms of PD can weaken protective factors and increase risk factors of suicide. Cox et al. reported that individuals with PD perceived avoidance-oriented coping as the most effective way of dealing with anxiety [49]. However, avoidance may thwart resiliency factors that prevent suicide, such as, social relationships, and exacerbate risk factors like loneliness [50, 51].

Recently, a positive feedback model for suicide in PD was proposed [52]. This model was based on the premise that limbic-autonomic arousal and catastrophic cognition of panic attack are mutually activating, and that this positive feedback amplifies catastrophic cognitions, induces suicidal ideation, and finally, the combination of suicidal ideation and heightened limbic-autonomic arousal drives the transition to action in the form of a suicide attempt. Considering that catastrophic cognition, which is central to this model, exacerbates maladaptive coping strategies of escape-avoidance, cognitive therapy might be of considerable benefit in PD patients with suicidality

Conclusion

In this chapter, PD is considered as an independent risk factor of suicidality even after controlling for other psychiatric disorders. Recently, some studies suggest that specific symptoms of PD might be related with increased risk of suicidality. The relationship between PD and suicide is substantially impacted by the presence of co-occurring disorders, and evidence suggests AG, mood disorder, other anxiety disorders, alcohol/substance abuse, somatoform disorder, eating disorder, schizophrenia, and personality disorder are associated with suicide in patients with PD.

In terms of assessing suicidality in PD, the suicidality module in MINI has some strengths in terms of its ease of usage and ability to comprehensively measure suicidality. In addition, all relating factors, such as, symptom severity, the presence of comorbid psychiatric illnesses or specific symptoms more likely to be associated with suicidality, and general medical status should be carefully considered.

The use of the serotonergic antidepressants can be a reasonable choice even in PD patients with suicidality. However, in the presence of comorbid bipolar disorder, the use of SSRIs should be approached cautiously. Clinicians should be aware emotional acceptance and mindfulness based therapy can be helpful for PD with suicidality and that comorbid depressive disorders should be actively treated. Cognitive therapy might be very helpful for correcting catastrophic cognitions that produce suicidal ideation in PD patients with suicidality.

REFERENCES

[1] Sadock, BJ; Sadock, VA; Ruiz, P. *Comprehensive textbook of psychiatry* 9th edition. Lippincott Williams & Wilkins, 2009, 2723-24.

[2] Kim, YK; Lee, HJ; Kim, JY; Yoon, DK; Choi, SH; Lee, MS. Low serum cholesterol is correlated to suicidality in a Korean sample. *Acta Psychiatrica Scandinavica*., 2002, 105(2), 141-8.

[3] Deisenhammer, EA; Kramer-Reinstadler, K; Liensberger, D; Kemmler, G; Hinterhuber, H; Fleischhacker, WW. No evidence for an association between serum cholesterol and the course of depression and suicidality. *Psychiatry Research*, 2004,121(3), 253-61.

[4] De Leon, J; Mallory, P; Maw, L; Susce, MT; Perez-Rodriguez, MM; Baca-Garcia, E. Lack of replication of the association of low serum

cholesterol and attempted suicide in another country raises more questions. *Annals of clinical psychiatry.*, 2011, 23(3), 163-70.

[5] Harris, EC; Barraclough, B. Suicide as an outcome for mental disorders. A meta-analysis. *The British Journal of Psychiatry.*, 1997, 170(3), 205-28.

[6] Suominen, K; Isometsa, E; Suokas, J; Haukka, J; Achte, K; Lonnqvist, J. Completed suicide after a suicide attempt: a 37-year follow-up study. *American Journal of Psychiatry.*, 2004, 161(3), 562-3.

[7] Cavanagh, JT; Carson, AJ; Sharpe, M; Lawrie, SM. Psychological autopsy studies of suicide: a systematic review. *Psychological medicine.*, 2003, 33(3), 395-405.

[8] Khan, A; Leventhal, RM; Khan, S; Brown, WA. Suicide risk in patients with anxiety disorders: a meta-analysis of the FDA database. *Journal of Affective Disorders.*, 2002, 68(2), 183-90.

[9] Weissman, MM; Klerman, GL; Markowitz, JS; Ouellette, R. Suicidal ideation and suicide attempts in panic disorder and attacks. *New England Journal of Medicine.*, 1989, 321(18), 1209-14.

[10] Hornig, CD; McNally, RJ. Panic disorder and suicide attempt. A reanalysis of data from the Epidemiologic Catchment Area study. *The British Journal of Psychiatry.*, 1995, 167(1), 76-9.

[11] Beck, A; Steer, RA; Sanderson, WC; Skeie, TM. Panic disorder and suicidal ideation and behavior: discrepant findings in psychiatric outpatients. *American Journal of Psychiatry.*, 1992, 149(10), 1412-3.

[12] Friedman, S; Jones, JC; Chernen, L; Barlow, DH. Suicidal ideation and suicide attempts among patients with panic disorder: a survey of two outpatient clinics. *American Journal of Psychiatry.*, 1992, 149(5), 680-5.

[13] Lepine, JP; Chignon, JM; Teherani, M. Suicide attempts in patients with panic disorder. *Archives of General Psychiatry.*, 1993, 50(2), 144-9.

[14] Henriksson, M; Isometsa, ET; Kuoppasalmi, KI; Heikkinen, ME; Marttunen, MJ; Lonnqvist, JK. Panic disorder in completed suicide. *Journal of Clinical Psychiatry.*, 1996, 57(7), 275-81.

[15] Rudd, MD; Dahm, PF; Rajab, MH. Diagnostic comorbidity in persons with suicidal ideation and behavior. *American Journal of Psychiatry.*, 1993, 150(6), 928-34.
[16] Johnson, J; Weissman, MM; Klerman, GL. Panic disorder, comorbidity, and suicide attempts. *Archives of General Psychiatry.*, 1990, 47(9), 805-8.
[17] American Psychiatric Association: Diagnostic and statistical manual of mental disorders: DSM-5. ed 4, revised. *American Psychiatric Publishing.*, 2013.
[18] Schmidt, NB; Woolaway-Bickel, K; Bates, M. Evaluating panic-specific factors in the relationship between suicide and panic disorder. *Behaviour research and therapy.*, 2001, 39(6), 635-49.
[19] Yaseen, ZS; Chartrand, H; Mojtabai, R; Bolton, J; Galynker, II. Fear of dying in panic attacks predicts suicide attempt in comorbid depressive illness: prospective evidence from the national epidemiological survey on alcohol and related conditions. *Depression and anxiety.*, 2013, 30(10), 930-9.
[20] Lim, SW; Ko, EM; Shin, DW; Shin, YC; Oh, KS. Clinical symptoms associated with suicidality in patients with panic disorder. *Psychopathology.*, 2015, 48(3), 137-44.
[21] Thibodeau, MA; Welch, PG; Sareen, J; Asmundson, GJ. Anxiety disorders are independently associated with suicide ideation and attempts: propensity score matching in two epidemiological samples. *Depression and anxiety.*, 2013, 30(10), 947-54.
[22] Norton, GR. Suicidal ideation and suicide attempts in panic disorder and social phobia. *American Journal of Psychiatry.*, 1994, 15(1), 882-7.
[23] Starcevic, V; Bogojevic, G; Marinkovic, J; Kelin, K. Axis I and axis II comorbidity in panic/agoraphobic patients with and without suicidal ideation. *Psychiatry Research.*, 1999, 88(2), 153-61.
[24] Kilbane, EJ; Gokbayrak, NS; Galynker, I; Cohen, L; Tross, S. A review of panic and suicide in bipolar disorder: does comorbidity increase risk?. *Journal of affective disorders.*, 2009, 115(1), 1-10.

[25] Massion, AO; Warshaw, MG; Keller, MB. Quality of life and psychiatric morbidity in panic disorder and generalized anxiety disorder. *American Journal of Psychiatry.*, 1993, 4, 600–7.

[26] Norton, GR; Rockman, GE; Luy, B; Marion, T. Suicide, chemical abuse, and panic attacks: a preliminary report. *Behaviour Research and Therapy.*, 1993, 31(1), 37–40.

[27] Warshaw, MG; Massion, AO; Peterson, LG; Pratt, LA; Keller, MB. Suicidal behavior in patients with panic disorder: retrospective and prospective data. *Journal of Affective Disorders.*, 1995, 34, 235–47.

[28] Merikangas, KR; Angst, J; Eaton, W; Canino, GRSM. Comorbidity and boundaries of affective disorders with anxiety disorders and substance misuse: results of an international task force. *The British Journal of Psychiatry.*, 1996, 168(suppl30), 58–67.

[29] Wittchen, HU; Nelson, CB; Lachner, G. Prevalence of mental disorders and psychosocial impairments in adolescents and young adults. *Psychological medicine.*, 1988, 28(1), 109–26.

[30] Faravelli, C. The Sesto Fiorentino Study. point and one year prevalences of psychiatric disorders in an Italian community sample using clinical interviewers. *Psychotherapy and psychosomatics.*, 2004, 73(4), 226–34.

[31] Goodwin, R; Lyons, JS; McNally, RJ. Panic attacks in schizophrenia. *Schizophrenia research.*, 2002, 58(2), 213-20.

[32] Ozkan, M; Altindag, A. Comorbid personality disorders in subjects with panic disorder: do personality disorders increase clinical severity? *Comprehensive Psychiatry.*, 2005, 46(1), 20-6.

[33] Sareen, J; Cox, BJ; Afifi, TO; de Graaf, R; Asmundson, GJ; ten Have, M; Stein, MB. Anxiety disorders and risk for suicidal ideation and suicide attempts: a population-based longitudinal study of adults. *Archives of general psychiatry.*, 2005, 62(11), 1249-57.

[34] Cole, DA; Peeke, LG; Martin, JM; Truglio, R; Seroczynski, AD. A longitudinal look at the relation between depression and anxiety in children and adolescents. *Journal of consulting and clinical psychology.*, 1998, 66(3), 451.

[35] Bolton, J; Cox, B; Clara, I; Sareen, J. Use of alcohol and drugs to self-medicate anxiety disorders in a nationally representative sample. *The Journal of nervous and mental disease*., 2006, 194(11), 818–25.

[36] Roest, AM; Martens, EJ; de Jonge, P; Denollet, J. Anxiety and risk of incident coronary heart disease: a meta-analysis. *American College of Cardiology*., 2010, 56(1), 38–46.

[37] Sheehan, DV; Lecrubier, Y; Sheehan, KH; Amorim, P; Janavs, J; Weiller, E; Hergueta, T; Baker, R; Dunbar, GC. The Mini-International Neuropsychiatric Interview (M.I.N.I.): the development and validation of a structured diagnostic psychiatric interview for DSM-IV and ICD-10. *Journal of clinical psychiatry*., 1998, 59 (Suppl 20), 22-33.

[38] Pompili, M; Rihmer, Z; Akiskal, H; Amore, M; Gonda, X; Innamorati, M; Lester, D; Perugi, G; Serafini, G; Telesforo, L; Tatarelli, R; Girardi, P. Temperaments mediate suicide risk and psychopathology among patients with bipolar disorders. *Comprehensive psychiatry*., 2012, 53(3), 280-5.

[39] Chen, L; Liu, YH; Zheng, QW; Xiang, YT; Duan, YP; Yang, FD; Wang, G; Fang, YR; Lu, Z; Yang, HC; Hu, J; Chen, ZY; Huang, Y; Sun, J; Wang, XP; Li, HC; Zhang, JB; Chen, DF; Si, TM. Suicide risk in major affective disorder: Results from a national survey in China. *Journal of affective disorders*., 2014, 155, 174-9.

[40] Keck, PE Jr; McElroy, SL; Friedman, LM. Valproate and carbamazepine in the treatment of panic and posttraumatic stress disorders, withdrawal states, and behavioral dyscontrol syndromes. *Journal of Clinical Psychopharmacology*., 1992, 12(Suppl1), 36S–41S.

[41] Ghaemi, SN; Hsu, DJ; Soldani, F; Goodwin, FK. Antidepressants in bipolar disorder: the case for caution. *Bipolar disorders*., 2003,5(6), 421-33.

[42] Hirschfeld, RM; Weisler, RH; Raines, SR; Macfadden, W. Quetiapine in the treatment of anxiety in patients with bipolar I or II depression: a secondary analysis from a randomized, double-blind,

placebo-controlled study. *Journal of Clinical Psychiatry.*, 2006, 67(3), 355–63.

[43] Oruc, L; Cavuljuga, S. Olanzapine in treatment of patients with bipolar I disorder and panic comorbidity: a case study. *Bosnian Journal of Basic Medical Science.*, 2003, 3(4), 67–9.

[44] Borden, JW. Panic disorder and suicidality: prevalence and risk factors. *Journal of anxiety disorders.*, 1994, 8(3), 217-25.

[45] Feldner, MT; Zvolensky, MJ; Leen-Feldner, EW. A critical review of the empirical literature on coping and panic disorder. *Clinical Psychology Review.*, 2004, 24(2), 123-48.

[46] Jobes, DA; Mann, RE. Reasons for living versus reasons for dying: examining the internal debate of suicide. *Suicide and Life-Threatening Behavior.*, 1999, 29(2), 97–104.

[47] Foster, T. Suicide note themes and suicide prevention. *The international Journal of Psychiatry in Medicine.*, 2003, 33(4), 323–31.

[48] Campbell-Sills, L; Barlow, DH; Brown, TA; Hofmann, SG. Effects of suppression and acceptance on emotional responses of individuals with anxiety and mood disorders. *Behaviour research and therapy.*, 2006, 44(9), 1251-63.

[49] Cox, BJ; Endler, NS; Swinson, RP; Norton, GR. Situations and specific coping strategies associated with clinical and nonclinical panic attacks. *Behaviour Research and Therapy,* 1992, 30(1), 67-9.

[50] Joiner, TE Jr; Brown, JS; Wingate, LR. The psychology and neurobiology of suicidal behavior. *Annual Review of Psychology.*, 2005, 56, 287–314.

[51] Stravynski, A; Boyer, R. Loneliness in relation to suicide ideation and parasuicide: a population-wide study. *Suicide and Life-Threatening Behavior.*, 2001, 31(1), 32–40.

[52] Katz, C; Yaseen, ZS; Mojtabai, R; Cohen, LJ; Galynker, II. Panic as an independent risk factor for suicide attempt in depressive illness: findings from the National Epidemiological Survey on Alcohol and Related Conditions (NESARC). *The Journal of clinical psychiatry,*. 2011, 72(12), 1628-35.

In: Panic Disorder
Editor: Yong-Ku Kim
ISBN: 978-1-53613-001-0

Chapter 6

RISK FACTORS AND PREVENTIONS IN PANIC DISORDER

Cheolmin Shin[1], Kwang-Yeon Choi[2] and Yong-Ku Kim[1,*]
[1]Department of Psychiatry,
Korea University College of Medicine, Republic of Korea
[2]Department of Psychiatry,
Chungnam National University Hospital, Republic of Korea

ABSTRACT

Panic disorder (PD) is one of the most common anxiety disorders, with lifetime prevalence rates in general population of 2.1%-4.7% [1, 2]. PD usually progressed chronically, resulting in economic burden and a loss of quality of life [3, 4]. Therefore, proper prevention and treatment of PD is important. In particular, there is an increasing interest in developing methods to prevent anxiety disorders, which require a clear comprehension of the risk factors for predicting the disorder [5, 6]. To date, risk factor of PD are not well determined. In studies of risk factors, PD is often studied as an anxiety disorder.

---

* Corresponding author. yongku@korea.ac.kr, yongku0304@gmail.com.

Nevertheless, from many clinical and epidemiological studies, this chapter attempts to sum up all risk factors regarding the development of PD as well as its progress. As such, cross-sectional designs and longitudinal studies on risk factors of PD are reviewed. Genetic risk factors are excluded here since they are dealt with in a separate chapter.

Risk Factors for Panic Disorder

Demographic Factors

As for gender, it was found that there is a significant association between females and the development of PD [7-9]. When it comes to age regarding PD, Gräsbeck et al. found that ages of 30-44 increase the risk of the disorder [8], while Grant et al. who observed 35,000 people in their large-scale epidemiologic survey, reported ages of 20-54 had higher chances of a 1-year incidence rate than ages of 55 or more [7]. Wittchen and Essau presented different hazard rates of PD according to gender. In this study, the highest hazard rates of PD were ranged from 25 to 34 years for women and 30 to 44 for men [9]. Previous research has found no relation between educational level and occurrence of PD [7]. Although there are few comparative studies of ethnicity and PD, a study reported that ethnicities such as Caucasian, Black or Hispanic had no effect on development of PD [7]. Finally, Grant et al. reported that lower socioeconomic status led to a higher chance of PD [7], while other previous researches concluded socioeconomic status had nothing to do with PD [10].

Psychosocial Factors

Stressful Life Event

Stressful live events are known to be associated with PD and panic attack. Previous research supported the relationship between stressful life events and the onset of adult PD or panic attack. Better understanding the role of stressful live events in PD can help the clinician predict factors that can exacerbate the patient's illness. Uhde et al. reported that 80% of patients with PD had experienced at least one major life stress event within six months of the initial panic attack, and explained that the gene-environment interaction between the stress factor of life events and genes give rise to panic attacks [11]. According to a study that examined the differences in how the patient versus control groups cope with life events, while patients with PD and other anxiety disorders did not differ from the comparison subjects in the number of negative life events experienced within 6 months, they tended to experience those events as having more negative impact [12]. Life events related to the onset of panic attacks and PD include interpersonal conflict, crises experienced in important relationships, such as breakup or loss, and health threats, such as physical illness.

Moreover, stressful live events worked as a risk factor for worsening disease course in PD [13]. Moitra et al. observed the changes in anxiety symptoms of 418 subjects in a psychiatric clinic, during 12 weeks before and after a stressful live events. The results showed that PD or panic attack symptoms worsened over the course of 12 weeks, but not on the day that the stressful live events occurred or the week of stressful live events. However, due to the residual effect of events related to family, friends, and the workplace, the panic symptoms of participants then became severely worse across 12 weeks.

Scocco et al. found that patients with PD occasionally experience interpersonal life events, such as sadness, interpersonal deficits, role transition, and loss of a relative or significant other prior to the onset [14]. Likewise, Milrod et al. reported that 47% of patients with PD suffered interpersonal loss 6 weeks prior to development of PD [15]. Jacobs et al. examining the prevalence of PD during the 6 months after individuals experience loss of a significant other, found that the rate of PD was higher for those who have experienced loss compared to the control group, with more serious effects on females than males [16]. A systematic review of research examining the prevalence and incidence of mood and anxiety disorders after loss of a spouse showed that the risk of PD increased, comorbid to a considerable degree with major depressive disorder (MDD) [17].

Early Stressful Life Event

Unlike the research focusing on the life events in adulthood and development of PD, most research evaluating the effect of life events in childhood on PD focuses on a specific life event rather than accumulated life events. Specific life event in childhood is considered especially interesting because the death of parents or the experience of the separation or loss from divorce has a special influence which can later affect psychopathology. Only one study reported that individuals whose onset of PD took place in adulthood had more life events during childhood and adolescence than the control group [18].

Several studies report that the effect of separation from mother or father, parental divorce, or loss and separation, such as death of the parents or siblings, is related to the later onset of PD [19-21]. However, studies report conflicting results regarding the characteristics of separation or loss. Faravelli et al. suggested that maternal separation and parental divorce after the age of 4 can influence PD, but that such experience before the age of 4 has no such association [21]. Kendler et al. found a relationship between PD and death of parents in childhood, and between mother's death and PD, but reported no relationship between separation from the father and PD [20]. In addition, no study reports any difference between the patient and control groups regarding the death or divorce of parents. Laraia et al. reported in a retrospective study no differences between PD patient and control groups in the death or divorce of parents [22]. Peter et al. also found no relation between separation anxiety and childhood separation experience, and stated that childhood separation is confounded with adult separation event [23]. Therefore, even though loss or separation events are more frequently observed in patients with PD, 30% or more of patients with PD report no childhood traumatic experience [19]. However, as childhood trauma influences a wide spectrum of anxiety disorders [24], and is related to increase in the concurrence of MDD and suicide attempts, clinical attention to it is needed [21].

Early traumatic events such as childhood physical and sexual abuse, have been reported to increase the risk of PD in adulthood. There is observational evidence that the experience of child abuse plays an important role in the pathogenesis of PD. Many studies of clinical samples have reported research on the childhood traumatic events and the onset of anxiety disorders, including PD [25-27]. According to research by Young et al. 35% of patients with PD or MDD have experienced abuse, and the risk of PD increased as the severity of abuse increased. However, some studies reported negative findings. Friedman et al. failed to find a difference in anxiety disorders across the experience of abuse [28]. Moreover, one study reports that, while the experience of sexual abuse in childhood does increase the incidence of PD at the time, it does not increase the rate of lifetime PD [29]. Lastly, a twin study reported that sexual abuse in childhood increased not only the prevalence lifetime PD, but also the risk of lifetime diagnosis of MDD, conduct disorder, alcohol use disorder [30].

Clinical Factors

Comorbid Psychiatric Illnesses

PD is often associated with other anxiety disorders and depression [7, 31-33]. The National Comorbidity Survey Replication (NCS-R) in its study on nationally representative samples observed one or more comorbid conditions in 71.9% of those who experienced panic attacks without PD and agoraphobia and in 83.1% who suffered PD without agoraphobia [2]. In other study, odds ratio (OR) (2.5-25.8) of PD accompanied by agoraphobia tended to be higher than that (2.0-54) of PD without agoraphobia [34]. In a cohort study to investigate risk factors for PD in pregnancy, incidence of PD without depressive comorbidity was predicted by a history of previous episodes of anxiety disorders while the development of PD with depression was predicted by a history of previous depressive episodes [35].

Other psychiatric illnesses including alcohol use disorder, personality disorder and sleep disorder are often linked to PD. In the sample of the NCS-R, alcohol use disorder was associated with panic attack and PD [2]. In other nationally representative sample, binge drinking was associated with development of PD in women [36]. Early studies have reported associations between PD and dependent personality trait [37]. However, anecdotal studies have reported several personality associations with PD [7, 38]. In a community-based cohort study, sleep disturbances increased the risk of developing PD by 1.62 fold after 4 years [39].

Comorbid Physical Illnesses

In terms of physical illness, several studies have been reported pulmonary diseases are a risk factor for PD. Smoller et al. reported that the conditions for the precipitating symptom of breathing difficulty could develop PD [40]. Also, chronic obstructive pulmonary disorder was reported as a risk factor for PD [41]. Patients with anxiety disorders, including PD, have a higher risk of physical illnesses such as angina, mitral valve prolapse, idiopathic cardiomyopathy, labile hypertension, migraine headaches, peptic ulcer disease, diabetes mellitus, or thyroid disease [42]. In a critical review, Fleet et al. examined the prevalence of PD in patients with coronary artery disease (CAD), PD developed after the diagnosis of CAD from overreaction to cardiovascular symptoms [43]. These results are supported by the fact that the prevalence of PD increased for patients with chronic heart failure [44]. No significant link has been found between miscarriage and PD [45] On the other hand, Rudaz et al. discovered an important association between the number of physical disorders experienced and future development of PD in the list of 14 symptoms and illnesses [32]. They also reported that physical symptoms measured on Whiteley Index and body sensations assessed on Body Sensations Questionnaire had no relation with PD. Finally, Bulbena et al. found that joint hypermobility syndrome was significantly associated with the development of PD [46].

Smoking

Smoking is considered a problem in the field of mental health, as it is well established that smoking among psychiatric patients, including patients with anxiety disorders, is more common than the general population [47]. Smoking and nicotine dependence have been studied to relate with anxiety disorders. Therefore, there has been much research that smoking and nicotine dependence may be a risk factor for PD.

In the early study of the chart review of psychiatric outpatients, smoking was found in 47% and 57% of patients diagnosed with PD and agoraphobia with panic attack. This comorbidity is more than individuals with specific phobia (47%), generalized anxiety disorder (GAD) (29%) Phobia (27%) and obsessive-compulsive disorder (9%) [48]. Other studies in the US clinical settings found that women with PD had a higher rate of smoking at the onset of illness than those in the control group [49]. Smoking is also known to co-occur in epidemiologic studies. Zvolensky et al. reported that patients diagnosed with PD had much more daily smoking rate (19-56%) than those without mental health problem. smoke daily [50].

Several prospective studies suggested that smoking is one of risk factors that could lead to the increase in the development of PD. First, in an early study, Breslau et al. proved in their epidemiologic investigation that daily smoking increased the risk of experiencing panic attack and PD even after controlled for major depression and gender [51]. Johnson et al. examined 688 adolescents aged 16 or younger who smoked 20 or more cigarettes per day in their community-based research and found the subjects face much greater risk of contracting PD and agoraphobia when they reached 22 [52, 55]. In a 4-year follow-up prospective community study, panic attacks and PD had a relationship with prior smoking [53]. Interestingly, smoking and development of PD were unidirectional in all of the three studies (Prior PD didn't raise the risk of smoking).

In cross-sectional study which assessed concurrent associations between current smoking and various panic-related indicators, smokers with PD had a much more severe anxiety symptom, and were more socially impaired than non-smokers with PD [54]. In another cross-sectional study, the onset (OR = 2.6) of the PD was associated with smoking during the previous year, and nicotine-dependent smokers had a greater risk of PD than non-smokers or non-nicotine dependent smokers [55].

Caffeine Intake

Experimental and epidemiological data have suggested that caffeine may exert an anxiogenic effect against panic attack and PD. The investigation of caffeine intake found self-reported levels of anxiety and depression to be correlated with the amount of caffeine intake in patients with PD. In addition, this self-report questionnaire showed that patients with PD have increased sensitivity to the effect of a single cup of coffee. Many patients reported to have discontinued coffee intake due to the side effect of PD, and to have clear sensitivity to caffeine.

PD may influence perceived effects of caffeine. Early studies observed that patients of PD exhibited greater sensitivity to anxiety caused by large doses of caffeine (more than 400mg in general) [56, 57]. Such high sensitivity to anxiety led by much caffeine was also observed among first degree relatives of PD patients [58]. When PD patients with caffeine-driven panic attack were examined using the Symptom Checklist-90-Revised, they presented more non-specific general psychopathologies than PD patients who didn't go through a caffeine-induced panic attack [59].

In twin study, all groups defined as caffeine intake, heavy caffeine user, toxicity, and dependence according to degree of caffeine intake were moderately associated with PD, but the risk for PD was not causal [60].

Psychological Factors

Anxiety Sensitivity

Anxiety sensitivity is a premorbid cognitive vulnerability, a fear that symptoms of anxiety cause harmful consequences [61, 62]. Anxiety sensitivity is known to trigger fear conditioning toward aversive stimuli, that is anxiety reaction and, thus, it is considered a risk factor of anxiety disorder and PD [61-63]. Anxiety sensitivity index (ASI) is a widely accepted tool to measure anxiety sensitivity [63]. It's a questionnaire consisting of 16 questions on anxiety-related senses, which can be categorized into three factors of physical concerns, mental incapacitation concerns and social concerns, according to factor analysis [64]. Previous research reported that anxiety disorder patients, especially PD patients, presented higher ASI. While both PD and GAD patients go through anxiety symptoms, those suffering PD present a specific psychopathology that they are excessively afraid of anxiety symptoms themselves, indicating the increase of anxiety sensitivity [65].

Longitudinal studies also confirm the link between anxiety sensitivity and PD. For example, Schmidt et al. handed out an ASI questionnaire to a cadet cohort ahead of stressful military drills and found 6% of them answered that they experienced panic attack [66]. Higher ASI scores was a predictor of panic attack even after being controlled for trait anxiety and previous panic history. A longitudinal study, which followed up 505 healthy university students 10 years after concluded that, while ASI was a predictor of panic symptoms and panic attacks, it could predict development of PD [67]. Finally, a 1-year follow-up study on 136 PD patients suggested anxiety sensitivity could predict clinical course of PD by ASI's forecasting episode time of PD [68].

One of the reasons anxiety sensitivity is highlighted as a risk factor of PD is that it's a factor which could be corrected clinically. anxiety sensitivity is a trait-like factor, but was normalized via cognitive behavioral therapy (CBT) [69]. Furthermore, medicine treatment using Benzodiazepine resulted in a significant decline of ASI [70, 71]. However, Fava et al. reported anxiety sensitivity alleviated by benzodiazepine could block anxiety symptoms, thereby stopping cognitive reorganization that anxiety symptoms are not harmful [72]. Meanwhile, improvement in anxiety sensitivity through CBT was the most reliable predictor of successful reduction of benzodiazepine [73].

Prevention for Panic Disorder

The primary prevention of PD is to prevent PD from developing in high-risk subjects. However, because PD is a relatively rare condition and the risk factors are not clearly determined, primary prevention cannot be actively provided. Therefore, it is important to provide secondary prevention to patients who already have PD. It includes to treat current disability and to prevent recurrence of the disorder. The most important thing of secondary prevention will be the providing optimal treatment to patients of PD.

It will also be important to correct adjustable risk factors that affect the course. As shown in this text, CBT for anxiety sensitivity, reducing smoking or caffeine intake and treatment of comorbid condition could affect the course of PD, and may be important to prevent aggravation and recurrence of symptoms of PD.

Conclusion

This review showed various risk factors contributing to development of PD. In most factors shown above, more prospective design studies are needed to clarify causality. Nonetheless, this knowledge will help to understand patients in clinical settings and will be useful for the development of intervention for the prevention of PD in the future.

References

[1] Batelaan NM, De Graaf R, Van Balkom AJ, Vollebergh WA, Beekman AT. [Epidemiology of panic]. *Tijdschr Psychiatr.* 2006;48(3):195-205.

[2] Kessler RC, Chiu WT, Jin R, Ruscio AM, Shear K, Walters EE. The epidemiology of panic attacks, panic disorder, and agoraphobia in the

National Comorbidity Survey Replication. *Arch Gen Psychiatry.* 2006;63(4):415-24.

[3] Baxter AJ, Vos T, Scott KM, Ferrari AJ, Whiteford HA. The global burden of anxiety disorders in 2010. *Psychol Med.* 2014;44(11):2363-74.

[4] Carta MG, Moro MF, Aguglia E, Balestrieri M, Caraci F, Dell'Osso L, et al. The attributable burden of panic disorder in the impairment of quality of life in a national survey in Italy. *Int J Soc Psychiatry.* 2015;61(7):693-9.

[5] Feldner MT, Zvolensky MJ, Babson K, Leen-Feldner EW, Schmidt NB. An integrated approach to panic prevention targeting the empirically supported risk factors of smoking and anxiety sensitivity: theoretical basis and evidence from a pilot project evaluating feasibility and short-term efficacy. *J Anxiety Disord.* 2008;22(7):1227-43.

[6] Schmidt NB, Zvolensky MJ. Risk factor research and prevention for anxiety disorders: introduction to the special series on risk and prevention of anxiety pathology. *Behav Modif.* 2007;31(1):3-7.

[7] Grant BF, Goldstein RB, Chou SP, Huang B, Stinson FS, Dawson DA, et al. Sociodemographic and psychopathologic predictors of first incidence of DSM-IV substance use, mood and anxiety disorders: results from the Wave 2 National Epidemiologic Survey on Alcohol and Related Conditions. *Mol Psychiatry.* 2009;14(11):1051-66.

[8] Grasbeck A, Hagnell O, Otterbeck L, Rorsman B. Anxiety in the Lundby Study: re-evaluation according to DSM-III-R, incidence and risk. *Neuropsychobiology.* 1993;27(1):1-8.

[9] Wittchen HU, Essau CA. Epidemiology of panic disorder: progress and unresolved issues. *J Psychiatr Res.* 1993;27 Suppl 1:47-68.

[10] Katerndahl DA, Realini JP. Lifetime prevalence of panic states. *Am J Psychiatry.* 1993;150(2):246-9.

[11] Uhde TW, Boulenger JP, Roy-Byrne PP, Geraci MF, Vittone BJ, Post RM. Longitudinal course of panic disorder: clinical and biological considerations. *Prog Neuropsychopharmacol Biol Psychiatry.* 1985;9(1):39-51.

[12] Rapee RM, Litwin EM, Barlow DH. Impact of life events on subjects with panic disorder and on comparison subjects. *Am J Psychiatry.* 1990;147(5):640-4.

[13] Moitra E, Dyck I, Beard C, Bjornsson AS, Sibrava NJ, Weisberg RB, et al. Impact of stressful life events on the course of panic disorder in adults. *J Affect Disord.* 2011;134(1-3):373-6.

[14] Scocco P, Barbieri I, Frank E. Interpersonal problem areas and onset of panic disorder. *Psychopathology.* 2007;40(1):8-13.

[15] Milrod B, Leon AC, Shear MK. Can interpersonal loss precipitate panic disorder? *Am J Psychiatry.* 2004;161(4):758-9.

[16] Jacobs S, Hansen F, Kasl S, Ostfeld A, Berkman L, Kim K. Anxiety disorders during acute bereavement: risk and risk factors. *J Clin Psychiatry.* 1990;51(7):269-74.

[17] Onrust SA, Cuijpers P. Mood and anxiety disorders in widowhood: a systematic review. *Aging Ment Health.* 2006;10(4):327-34.

[18] Horesh N, Amir M, Kedem P, Goldberger Y, Kotler M. Life events in childhood, adolescence and adulthood and the relationship to panic disorder. *Acta Psychiatr Scand.* 1997;96(5):373-8.

[19] Bandelow B, Spath C, Tichauer GA, Broocks A, Hajak G, Ruther E. Early traumatic life events, parental attitudes, family history, and birth risk factors in patients with panic disorder. *Compr Psychiatry.* 2002;43(4):269-78.

[20] Kendler KS, Neale MC, Kessler RC, Heath AC, Eaves LJ. Childhood parental loss and adult psychopathology in women. A twin study perspective. *Arch Gen Psychiatry.* 1992;49(2):109-16.

[21] Faravelli C, Webb T, Ambonetti A, Fonnesu F, Sessarego A. Prevalence of traumatic early life events in 31 agoraphobic patients with panic attacks. *Am J Psychiatry.* 1985;142(12):1493-4.

[22] Laraia MT, Stuart GW, Frye LH, Lydiard RB, Ballenger JC. Childhood environment of women having panic disorder with agoraphobia. *Journal of Anxiety Disorders.* 1994;8(1):1-17.

[23] Peter H, Bruckner E, Hand I, Rufer M. Childhood separation anxiety and separation events in women with agoraphobia with or without panic disorder. *Can J Psychiatry.* 2005;50(14):941-4.

[24] Torgersen S. Childhood and family characteristics in panic and generalized anxiety disorders. *Am J Psychiatry*. 1986;143(5):630-2.
[25] Sheikh JI, Swales PJ, Kravitz J, Bail G, Taylor CB. Childhood abuse history in older women with panic disorder. *Am J Geriatr Psychiatry*. 1994;2(1):75-7.
[26] Stein MB, Walker JR, Anderson G, Hazen AL, Ross CA, Eldridge G, et al. Childhood physical and sexual abuse in patients with anxiety disorders and in a community sample. *Am J Psychiatry*. 1996;153(2):275-7.
[27] Tekin A, Meric C, Sagbilge E, Kenar J, Yayla S, Ozer OA, et al. The relationship between childhood sexual/physical abuse and sexual dysfunction in patients with social anxiety disorder. *Nord J Psychiatry*. 2016;70(2):88-92.
[28] Friedman S, Smith L, Fogel D, Paradis C, Viswanathan R, Ackerman R, et al. The incidence and influence of early traumatic life events in patients with panic disorder: a comparison with other psychiatric outpatients. *J Anxiety Disord*. 2002;16(3):259-72.
[29] Saunders BE, Villeponteaux LA, Lipovsky JA, Kilpatrick DG, Veronen LJ. Child sexual assault as a risk factor for mental disorders among women: A community survey. *Journal of Interpersonal Violence*. 1992;7(2):189-204.
[30] Dinwiddie S, Heath AC, Dunne MP, Bucholz KK, Madden PA, Slutske WS, et al. Early sexual abuse and lifetime psychopathology: a co-twin-control study. *Psychol Med*. 2000;30(1):41-52.
[31] Kinley DJ, Walker JR, Enns MW, Sareen J. Panic attacks as a risk for later psychopathology: results from a nationally representative survey. *Depress Anxiety*. 2011;28(5):412-9.
[32] Rudaz M, Craske MG, Becker ES, Ledermann T, Margraf J. Health anxiety and fear of fear in panic disorder and agoraphobia vs. social phobia: a prospective longitudinal study. *Depress Anxiety*. 2010;27(4):404-11.
[33] Pietrzak RH, Kinley J, Afifi TO, Enns MW, Fawcett J, Sareen J. Subsyndromal depression in the United States: prevalence, course,

and risk for incident psychiatric outcomes. *Psychol Med.* 2013;43(7):1401-14.

[34] Faravelli C, Paionni A. *Panic Disorder: Clinical Course, Morbidity and Comorbidity. Anxiety Disorders*: John Wiley & Sons, Ltd; 2001. p. 51-79.

[35] Marchesi C, Ampollini P, Paraggio C, Giaracuni G, Ossola P, De Panfilis C, et al. Risk factors for panic disorder in pregnancy: a cohort study. *J Affect Disord.* 2014;156:134-8.

[36] Chou KL, Liang K, Mackenzie CS. Binge drinking and Axis I psychiatric disorders in community-dwelling middle-aged and older adults: results from the National Epidemiologic Survey on Alcohol and Related Conditions (NESARC). *J Clin Psychiatry.* 2011;72(5):640-7.

[37] Nystrom S, Lindegard B. Predisposition for mental syndromes: A study comparing predisposition for depression, neurasthenia and anxiety state. *Acta Psychiatr Scand.* 1975;51(2):69-76.

[38] Johnson JG, Cohen P, Kasen S, Brook JS. Personality disorders evident by early adulthood and risk for anxiety disorders during middle adulthood. *J Anxiety Disord.* 2006;20(4):408-26.

[39] Batterham PJ, Glozier N, Christensen H. Sleep disturbance, personality and the onset of depression and anxiety: prospective cohort study. *Aust N Z J Psychiatry.* 2012;46(11):1089-98.

[40] Smoller JW, Simon NM, Pollack MH, Kradin R, Stern T. Anxiety in patients with pulmonary disease: comorbidity and treatment. *Semin Clin Neuropsychiatry.* 1999;4(2):84-97.

[41] Wingate BJ, Hansen-Flaschen J. Anxiety and depression in advanced lung disease. *Clin Chest Med.* 1997;18(3):495-505.

[42] Harter MC, Conway KP, Merikangas KR. Associations between anxiety disorders and physical illness. *Eur Arch Psychiatry Clin Neurosci.* 2003;253(6):313-20.

[43] Fleet R, Lavoie K, Beitman BD. Is panic disorder associated with coronary artery disease? A critical review of the literature. *J Psychosom Res.* 2000;48(4-5):347-56.

[44] Muller-Tasch T, Frankenstein L, Holzapfel N, Schellberg D, Lowe B, Nelles M, et al. Panic disorder in patients with chronic heart failure. *J Psychosom Res*. 2008;64(3):299-303.

[45] Geller PA, Klier CM, Neugebauer R. Anxiety disorders following miscarriage. *J Clin Psychiatry*. 2001;62(6):432-8.

[46] Bulbena A, Gago J, Pailhez G, Sperry L, Fullana MA, Vilarroya O. Joint hypermobility syndrome is a risk factor trait for anxiety disorders: a 15-year follow-up cohort study. *Gen Hosp Psychiatry*. 2011;33(4):363-70.

[47] Hughes JR, Hatsukami DK, Mitchell JE, Dahlgren LA. Prevalence of Smoking among Psychiatric Outpatients. *Am J Psychiat*. 1986;143(8):993-7.

[48] Himle J, Thyer BA, Fischer DJ. Prevalence of smoking among anxious outpatients. *Phobia Practice and Research Journal*. 1988;1(1):25-31.

[49] Pohl R, Yeragani VK, Balon R, Lycaki H, McBride R. Smoking in patients with panic disorder. *Psychiatry Res*. 1992;43(3):253-62.

[50] Zvolensky MJ, Feldner MT, Leen-Feldner EW, McLeish AC. Smoking and panic attacks, panic disorder, and agoraphobia: a review of the empirical literature. *Clin Psychol Rev*. 2005;25(6): 761-89.

[51] Breslau N, Klein DF. Smoking and panic attacks: an epidemiologic investigation. *Arch Gen Psychiatry*. 1999;56(12):1141-7.

[52] Johnson JG, Cohen P, Pine DS, Klein DF, Kasen S, Brook JS. Association between cigarette smoking and anxiety disorders during adolescence and early adulthood. *JAMA*. 2000;284(18):2348-51.

[53] Isensee B, Wittchen HU, Stein MB, Hofler M, Lieb R. Smoking increases the risk of panic: findings from a prospective community study. *Arch Gen Psychiatry*. 2003;60(7):692-700.

[54] Zvolensky MJ, Schmidt NB, McCreary BT. The impact of smoking on panic disorder: an initial investigation of a pathoplastic relationship. *J Anxiety Disord*. 2003;17(4):447-60.

[55] Breslau N, Novak SP, Kessler RC. Psychiatric disorders and stages of smoking. *Biol Psychiatry*. 2004;55(1):69-76.

[56] Boulenger JP, Uhde TW, Wolff EA, 3rd, Post RM. Increased sensitivity to caffeine in patients with panic disorders. Preliminary evidence. *Arch Gen Psychiatry*. 1984;41(11):1067-71.

[57] Charney DS, Heninger GR, Jatlow PI. Increased anxiogenic effects of caffeine in panic disorders. *Arch Gen Psychiatry*. 1985;42(3):233-43.

[58] Nardi AE, Valenca AM, Nascimento I, Freire RC, Veras AB, de-Melo-Neto VL, et al. A caffeine challenge test in panic disorder patients, their healthy first-degree relatives, and healthy controls. *Depress Anxiety*. 2008;25(10):847-53.

[59] Masdrakis VG, Papakostas YG, Vaidakis N, Papageorgiou C, Pehlivanidis A. Caffeine challenge in patients with panic disorder: baseline differences between those who panic and those who do not. *Depress Anxiety*. 2008;25(9):E72-9.

[60] Kendler KS, Myers J, C OG. Caffeine intake, toxicity and dependence and lifetime risk for psychiatric and substance use disorders: an epidemiologic and co-twin control analysis. *Psychol Med*. 2006;36(12):1717-25.

[61] Reiss S. Expectancy model of fear, anxiety, and panic. *Clinical Psychology Review*. 1991;11(2):141-53.

[62] McNally RJ. Anxiety sensitivity and panic disorder. *Biol Psychiatry*. 2002;52(10):938-46.

[63] Reiss S, Peterson RA, Gursky DM, McNally RJ. Anxiety sensitivity, anxiety frequency and the prediction of fearfulness. *Behav Res Ther*. 1986;24(1):1-8.

[64] Zinbarg RE, Barlow DH, Brown TA. Hierarchical structure and general factor saturation of the Anxiety Sensitivity Index: Evidence and implications. *Psychological assessment*. 1997;9(3):277.

[65] Taylor S, Koch WJ, McNally RJ. How does anxiety sensitivity vary across the anxiety disorders? *Journal of Anxiety Disorders*. 1992;6(3):249-59.

[66] Schmidt NB, Lerew DR, Jackson RJ. The role of anxiety sensitivity in the pathogenesis of panic: prospective evaluation of spontaneous

panic attacks during acute stress. *J Abnorm Psychol.* 1997; 106(3):355-64.

[67] Plehn K, Peterson RA. Anxiety sensitivity as a predictor of the development of panic symptoms, panic attacks, and panic disorder: a prospective study. *J Anxiety Disord.* 2002;16(4):455-74.

[68] Benitez CI, Shea MT, Raffa S, Rende R, Dyck IR, Ramsawh HJ, et al. Anxiety sensitivity as a predictor of the clinical course of panic disorder: a 1-year follow-up study. *Depress Anxiety.* 2009;26(4):335-42.

[69] McNally RJ, Foa EB. Cognition and agoraphobia: Bias in the interpretation of threat. *Cognitive Therapy and Research.* 1987;11(5):567-81.

[70] Otto MW, Reilly-Harrington NA, Taylor S. The impact of treatment on anxiety sensitivity. *Anxiety sensitivity: Theory, research, and treatment of the fear of anxiety.* 1999:321-36.

[71] Fava GA, Grandi S, Belluardo P, Savron G, Raffi AR, Conti S, et al. Benzodiazepines and anxiety sensitivity in panic disorder. *Prog Neuropsychopharmacol Biol Psychiatry.* 1994;18(7):1163-8.

[72] Fava GA. Anxiety sensitivity. *Am J Psychiatry.* 1996;153(8):1109-10.

[73] Bruce TJ, Spiegel DA, Gregg SF, Nuzzarello A. Predictors of alprazolam discontinuation with and without cognitive behavior therapy in panic disorder. *Am J Psychiatry.* 1995;152(8):1156-60.

In: Panic Disorder
Editor: Yong-Ku Kim

ISBN: 978-1-53613-001-0

Chapter 7

PANIC DISORDER NEUROIMAGING FOCUSED ON MRI

Chien-Han Lai*

Department of Psychiatry,
Ditmanson Medical Foundation Chia-Yi Christian Hospital,
Chia-Yi City, Taiwan
Institute of Biophotonics, National Yang-Ming University,
Taipei, Taiwan

ABSTRACT

Recently, neuroimaging has been an important tool to solve underlying pathophysiology of panic disorder (PD). Within the many kinds of modalities of neuroimaging, magnetic resonance imaging (MRI) is the most convenient and popular method to investigate the brain pathophysiology due to relatively excellent spatial and temporal resolution of MRI acquisition imaging. The researchers can utilize MRI to study structural and functional alterations in neurological and psychiatric illnesses. The PD has been hypothesized as the dysregulation of fear network [1]. The connection between fear network and the autonomic nervous system is considered as an important aspect of

* E-mail: stephenlai99@gmail.com.

pathophysiology for PD. In this chapter, we reviewed the findings discovered by MRI. In addition, the alterations of brain function and structure in PD were also discussed.

1. Fear Network Hypothesis in PD

The PD is characterized with recurrent panic attacks, such as chest tightness, dizziness, paresthesia, abdominal discomforts, palpitations, sweating, fear of losing control, feel like dying and shortness of breathing. It is an important anxiety illness but usually under-recognized [2]. The impairments in somatic feelings and life qualities of patients are also observed [3]. PD also has a high tendency to be comorbid with other psychiatric disorders [4]. The pathophysiology of PD basically originated from Gorman's hypothesis of "fear network" [1]. The fear network included many regions of frontal and limbic areas, such as medial frontal gyrus, anterior cingulate, insula, thalamus, amygdala, brainstem, hypothalamus, hippocampus, periacqueductal gyrus, locus cerulus, parabrachial nucleus and nucleus of solitary tract. The frontal lobe system modulated the overresponse of the limbic system, which would be associated with panic symptoms, such as chest tightness, palpitations, dizziness, abdominal pain, nausea, shortness of breathing, fear of losing control and feel like dying [1].

In addition to original fear network hypothesis, there are some modifications of this original hypothesis of fear network model. Dresler et al. suggested the potential extension of original fear network model to other regions, such as the limbic and cortical regions. The fear circuit determined the subtype of PD and treatment options [5]. This theory is well-known as the fear network circuit theory, which is considered as the etiology of PD. The alterations of fear network model can be proved, such as the decreased volume of distribution in serotonin 5-HT1A receptors of the cingulate and raphe nucleus [6], the reduced 5-HT 1A receptor bindings in amygdala, temporal cortex, orbitofrontal cortex and amygdala [7], and the reduced gray matter in the preaqueductal gray matter and anterior cingulate cortex [8]. Therefore the fear network model has been examined in some imaging modalities, including the MRI and positron emission tomography. From the neuroimaging perspectives, the pathophysiology of PD can be explored more extensively in the brain. In addition, the translational medicine characteristics of functional MRI can be used to clarify the role of brain etiology in the formation of PD symptoms. The biomarker of PD can also be discovered and utilized as the treatment target for the medication, psychotherapy and the innovation study for new potential drug discovery of pharmaceutics. Therefore the application of MRI in the dissection of pathophysiology for PD will be a very intrigue issue, especially for future study.

2. MRI Applications and Introductions

The MRI is an important tool to investigate structure and function of brain [9]. The MRI contrast comes from the hydrogen ion fluctuations derived from the directional magentic field or moment. The images result from the MRI contrast. For the brain function, fluctuations of brain magnetic effects due to the changes in the oxygenation of blood hemoglobin can be used for the production of blood oxygen level dependent (BOLD) signals. The BOLD signals can be the basis to detect the brain function, such as the cognitive function, language andmemory [9, 10]. As the advances occurred in these years, the functional MRI techniques of brain have been evolved to survey the resting-state functional MRI signal changes, which reflected the resting-state brain activities [11-14]. The resting-state functional MRI signals can reveal default brain activities, which originated from the astrocyte-neuron coupling mechanism. The advance of analysis method can derive the network representations. The whole-brain network exhibits "small-world" properties shared with many other complex systems, such as the social system. This network with a high efficiency (with a very low wiring and energy cost) also allows for a high level of adaptation. In addition, degree distribution of brain networks demonstrates highly connected hubs that are crucial for the whole-network functioning [12].

The structural study of brain in MRI can obtain the data of gray matter and white matter from voxel-based and surface-based segmentation, voxel-based morphometry, cortical thickness, cortical regions and deep brain nuclei [15]. The voxe-based morphometry can obtain the gray matter from the segmentation. Then the non-parametric independent 2 sample test was performed for the group comparison to identify the significant structural alteratins of endophenotype for specific kind of illness. The volume, thickness and shape of brain can also be derived from the structural brain analysis [16]. In addition, the diffusion tensor imaging technique of MRI can derive the white matter tract [17]. Diffusion MRI and tractography techniques can be used to probe the architecture of both white and gray matter. These techniques showed their significant influences in the investigation of the macro-, meso-, and microscopic organization of brain connectivity and anatomy. Diffusion MRI-based techniques can therefore obtain the neuroanatomical structures of white matter tract by analyzing the water diffusion property and water molecule free movement (Brownian motion) within the fasciculus [18].

Therefore there are many kinds of modalities for the MRI to investigate the brain morphology and activities. The applications of these modalities in PD pathophysiology will be addressed in the following section.

3. Gray Matter Alteration Study in PD

The gray matter is an important structure for the cognitive function, high cortical function, thought, attention, executive function, coordination between different modalities of cognitive dimensions [19]. The important role is based on the rich distribution of neurons within the gray matter, which is also the important structure of cerebral cortex [20]. From the neuroimaging perspectives, the survey of gray matter can help us understand the cognition-related structures of brain.

There are several past articles using voxel-based morphometry (VBM) to suvery the deficits in brain structures of PD [21-31]. The regions of gray matter volume (GMV) alterations include the amygdala, hippocampus, orbitofrontal cortex, middle temporal lobe, medial orbitofrontal cortex, posterior cingulate gyrus, putamen, parahippocampal gyrus and superior temporal gyrus. Several regions from these articles replicate the regions of fear network model for PD, which can interact within this model to influence the formation of panic responses [1, 32, 33]. In addition to the traditional fear network model, the temporal lobe seems to play a role in the pathophysiology for PD [21-24, 27, 28, 34]. Several VBM studies also demonstrate inconsistent findings in the temporal region [22, 28, 29] of GMV. Another study of anxiety disorders in the temporal lobe showed significant deficits of GMV [35]. These results suggested the possible extension of fear circuitry model of PD might include the temporal lobe.

Frontal regions of gray matter deficits are also reported in PD [22, 25-27, 29, 34, 35]. The reductions of GMV were found in the inferior frontal cortex and the reductions were also associated with panic severity [29]. The frontal lobe might regulate sensory messages using a top-down mechanism. The modulation of signals from the temporal lobe and thalamus will control panic symptoms. In addition, decreased 5 HT-1A receptor bindings were found in the fronto-temporal area [7]. Lower activity of inferior frontal cortex will lose controlling ability for panic attacks if exposing to anxiogenic agents [36].

The insula is also another important structure [8, 22, 28], which receives sensory information filtered by thalamus [1]. Insula might modulate panic responses with frontal and temporal regions through integrating multimodal sensory information [37, 38].

The gray matter alterations of hypothalamus and midbrain periacqueductal gray matter might be associated with the innate and learned response to threat. The different threats, interoceptive threats and painful stimuli will induce the subsequent panic response. The threatening messages are processed by corticolimbic circuit, such as the amygdala, the hippocampus and the prefrontal and insular cortices. Then the messages are passed downstream to the hypothalamic and brainstem circuits. The formation of anticipatory anxiety is modulated by stimulation of 5-HT2C and 5-HT1A receptors [39].

Our study group showed that PD comorbid with depression had significant alterations in GMV of the "fronto-limbic" structures, such as the right anterior cingulate cortex, right medial frontal gyrus, left posterior cingulate cortex, right parahippocampal gyrus, limbic areas, occipital lingual gyrus and bilateral cerebellums [34]. The structural study of subcortical surface morphology in PD comorbid with depression showed smaller volumes of left hippocampus, thalamus, and putamen, which replicated the fear network theory of PD [40]. The comorbidity study shows the integrating effects of fear network theory and fronto-limbic etiology of depression in the GMV and structural studies. Another study demonstrated gray matter reductions in the frontal, temporal and insula areas [41]. The VBM study can show the detailed information of GMV using the non-parametric independent two sample T test to compare the individual dataset of GMV of patient to the control group. Therefore we can obtain the important information of GMV alterations of between-group difference. In the following years, we also compared the GMV of pure PD patients to those of pure depression patients. Then we found that PD patients had less severe alterations in GMV than depression patients. Our data revealed that higher gray matter volume were found in PD patients than MDD group in the right medial frontal cortex and right temporal gyrus. The PD patients had GMV reductions in the right inferior frontal gyrus and right insula when compared to controls [42]. Therefore we can suggest that the GMV alteration pattern of PD should be intermediate between the controls and depression.

From the above literature, the current GMV study in PD confirmed the important role of "fear network model" in the pathophysiology of PD. However, there are still many additional regions with GMV alterations for the so-called "extended fear network model" [5]. For example, the cortical regions (such as the temporal and occipital regions) and limbic regions (such as the putamen, posterior cingulate cortex), are not listed on the original fear network model. The current VBM study of PD suggested that the above several areas can be the components of "extended fear network model" for PD. In addition, the PD patients have less alterations in GMV than depression patients. The relatively non-severe features of GMV alterations in PD seems compatible with the clinical features of PD when compared to depression.

4. White Matter Alteration Study in PD

There are not many articles mentioning the white matter (WM) study in the pathophysiology for PD. The WM is an important structure connecting different gray matter regions via the fasciculus structure. The oligodendrocyte formed the myelin and the enhancing transport signals through the WM tracts. Therefore the connection fluency of WM tract fasciculus is the crucial factor for the message sending between different gray matter regions, which host most high cortical functions and cognitive abilities. WM hyperintensity in frontal region was found in PD patients and the hyperintensity was correlated with severity of PD symptoms [43]. The WM volume reductions in the orbitofrontal cortex seem associated with social, personal and occupational function impairments in PD patients [44]. In addition to the traditional hyperintensity and volume study for the macrostructure, the advanced new method, diffusion tensor imaging (DTI), has been used in the WM microstructure study in PD [45, 46]. If PD is comorbid with depression, there are fractional anisotropy (FA) reductions in all WM tracts [47]. However, PD patients had greater FA values than controls in the left anterior cingulate and right posterior cingulate regions, which were positively correlated with clinical severity [48]. In addition, the alterations in the FA values were associated with catechol-O-methyltransferase specific genotype [49]. Another study showed the connection between 5-HTR1A polymorphism and cingulum connectivity in PD [50]. Our DTI study in PD revealed FA alterations in right inferior fronto-occipital fasculi, left body of corpus callosum and left superior longitudinal fasciculus [51]. The alterations in the frontal WM and corpus callosum of bilateral hemispheres are also associated with anxiety severity in PD [52]. There are still a part of PD patients with suicide attempts due to recurrent panic attacks. Therefore a study about PD with suicide attempt revealed more reductions in the FA values of internal capsule, splenium of the corpus callosum, superior and posterior corona radiata, thalamic radiations, sagittal stratum, and superior longitudinal fasciculus [53]. However, the influences and biases from the co-morbidity of depression for this kind of PD patients should not be ignored. The anxiety sensitivity is also associated with alterations in the FA values of the insula, the splenium of the corpus callosum, the tapetum, the fornix/stria terminalis, the posterior limb of the internal capsule, the retrolenticular part of the internal capsule, the posterior thalamic radiation, the sagittal striatum, and the posterior corona radiata located in temporo-parieto-limbic regions for the interoceptive processing [54]. From the serial study about WM study in Kim's group, it suggested that WM alterations occurred in frontal WM, corpus callosum, limbic-related WM tracts, occipital and temporo-parietal related WM tracts. Combined with the findings in our study, the importance of the frontal, temporal, occipital and limbic regions-related WM tracts are emerging. It also corresponds to the extended fear network model mentioned in the previous section of gray mater alterations in PD. In addition, our recent published article also mentioned the alterations of WM microintegrity should be intermediate between depression and controls. The depression group had lower WM microintegrity than the PD group in the left anterior thalamic radiation, left uncinate fasciculus, left inferior fronto-occipital fasciculus, and bilateral corpus callosum [55]. In summary, the extended fear network model is also replicated in WM microintegrity study. The WM alterations in PD should not be as severe as depression.

5. Resting-State Functional MRI Alteration Study in PD

Resting-state functional MRI (Rs-FMRI) is an recent important method to explore the baseline brain activities. There are many kinds of indicators among Rs-FMRI, including the fractional amplitude of low-frequency oscillations (fALFF) [56], regional homogeneity (ReHo) [57], voxel-morrored homotopic connectivity (VMHC) [58] and functional connectivity (FC).

The low frequency oscillations of human brain can reveal the baseline brain activities [59]. Rs-FMRI studies on fALFF will detect the neuronal fluctuations [59, 60]. fALFF can weaken the biases of physiological noise and provide more accurate measures of impacts of amplitude of low frequency fluctuations within specific band of frequency [56]. ReHo is a measure of similarities of several time series from signals of Rs-FMRI. The ReHo represents the synchronizing abilities of neuronal activations in a specific region and is a complementary tool to understand the complexity of resting brain activities and the regional stability [57]. The VMHC method can measure the synchrony of spontaneous brain activities between geometrically corresponding regions in each hemisphere [61]. There are not many studies mentioning this issue in PD. Our study of fALFF in PD showed that decreased fALFF values in the right middle occipital gyrus and increased fALFF values in the right putamen and right ventral lateral nucleus of thalamus of patients. In addition, the fALFF alterations were associated with panic severity in PD. A occipito-striato-thalamic pattern of fALFF alterations might correspond to the fear network model due to the findings in the putamen and thalamus [62]. Among the Rs-FMRI, the most crucial findings will be focused on the the default mode network (DMN), which is constituted of the ventromedial prefrontal cortex, anterior cingulate, posterior cingulate and lateral parietal cortex [63]. For VMHC, our findings also revealed that PD patients had significant alterations in the VMHC values of posterior cingulate cortex and precuneus, which are crucial structures of posterior sub-network of DMN [64]. Our study in PD revealed decreased ReHo in the left lingual gyrus and increased ReHo in the right cuneus cortex of patient, which might be associated with sensory and inhibitory dysfunction. ReHo values of patients were negatively correlated with PD ratings in the right cuneus [65]. The FC study in PD revealed that alterations of extended fear network model, including the brainstem, somatosensory cortex, insula, thalamus, anterior, and mid-cingulate cortex and medial prefrontal cortex [66, 67]. The FC was altered in the DMN, fear network, cognitive-sensory network [68, 69]. The FC in the fronto-cingulate and fear network can also predict the treatment responses in PD [68; 70]. Aberrant FC alterations in the limbic and salience network in PD have also been mentioned [71]. Our findings of FC network model in PD showed that decreased functional connectivity in the edges between the following nodes of extended fear network for PD, such as the left parahippocampal gyrus, bilateral precentral gyri, bilateral middle cingulate gyri, bilateral supramarginal gyri, bilateral calcarine fissures, and right lingual gyrus. The central hubs were the left parahippocampal gyrus and left precentral gyrus. Our results suggested the importance of limbic areas and connection with the sensory and motor regions. It might shed light on the revision of fear network model for the pathophysiology of PD [72]. Among the Rs-FMRI study in PD, the occipital lobe and parietal lobe occasionally would appear in the alterations of brain. It might be associated with the face recognition, emotion processing, levels of trait anxiety and sensitivity to fearful stimuli of occipital lobe [73, 74]. The anxiety would influence dorsal attention system, which includes the occipital lobe. The system controls top-down procedure for selective attention and sensory modulation [75]. The connectivity between occipital lobe and other regions would be impaired due to excessive anxiety and correlated with fear degree [76, 77]. The abnormal activities in occipital lobes, basal ganglion and thalamus occur while receiving negative emotion stimulus in PD [78]. The occipital lobe is also involved in the neural processing of social cognition, social rejection sensitivity and low confidence fear stress of social interaction [79-81]. The occipital lobe also regulates the vigilance, anxiety, cardiovascular functions [82] and visual processing and orientation-specific function [83]. Therefore the occipital lobe's role in the Rs-FMRI study of PD can been recognized as the additional part for the extensive fear network model for PD. In summary, the Rs-FMRI results might suggest certain dysregulations between the fear, sensory, autonomic and cognitive-related regions in PD patients. Most regions of extended fear network model in PD have also been replicated in the Rs-FMRI study.

6. Medication Treatment MRI Study in PD

The medication-related effects in brain of PD patients are important for the clinicans to understand the theory of medicine treatment in PD. Among the many tools to understand the effects in brain, the functional MRI is a crucial tool for translational medicine research. The typical treatment for PD is the antidepressant. There are some studies to investigate the antidepressant's effects in the psychiatric illnesses and some modulating effects of GMV are noted [84-86]. From the cell and molecular study, the antidepressants showed promised effects in the brain tissue cells. Antidepressants can elevate serotonin level in brain and increase the expression of the brain-derived growth factor in specific regions in brain, which might contribute to the synaptic plasticity and GMV increase [87]. The antidepressants can lead to the proliferation of glial cells and improvement in the long-term survival of progenitor stem cells [88], which might activate neurons via the neuron-glia coupling mechanism [89]. Antidepressants might also induce increases in the astrocytic protein and glial cell number, which might in turn increase the brain volume [90]. In addition, the synaptic remodeling effects of antidepressant could also alter GMV [91]. Antidepressants might also change GMV by prevention of oxidative stress or modulation of glutamate receptor function [92]. Our several studies also found subtle increases in GMV, improvements in WM microintegrity and modulations in ReHo after antidepressant treatment [84, 93-98]. When we examined the antidepressant's effects in brain of PD patients comorbid with depression, the 6-week therapy seemed to induce the subtle GMV increases in the left infero-frontal cortex, right fusiform gyrus, and right cerebellum VIIIa areas [84]. In the perspective of pure PD diagnosis patients, the increased GMV in the left superior frontal gyrus (state-dependent biomarker) after antidepressant treatment. However, there were significant GMV deficits in the right precentral gyrus (trait-dependent biomarker) after remission of PD symptoms [97]. We also found significant improvements in WM microintegrity of some regions of right uncinate fasciculus and left fronto-occipital fasciculus in PD patients after 6-week antidepressant treatment with remission status [98]. The antidepressant therapy can also increase ReHo in the frontal region and decrease ReHo in the temporal region of PD patinets comorbid with depression, which suggest that the antidepressant can enhance the reasonable thinking ability and reduce the primitive and nonreasonable response [96]. From the current literature, the antidepressant seems to modulate the alterations in brain structure and function in the fear network model of PD patients. Therefore the antidepressant is proved to be effective in the treatment in PD, from the viewpoint of MRI perspectives.

CONCLUSION

From the above MRI studies in PD, at least we can confirm the crucial role of fear network model in the pathophysiology of PD, especially for the extended version of fear network theory. The extended fear network, with the new members of occipital and parietal lobes, might be associated with the etiology of PD (Figure 1). The medication treatment can also modulate the structural and functional alterations in the extended fear network model.

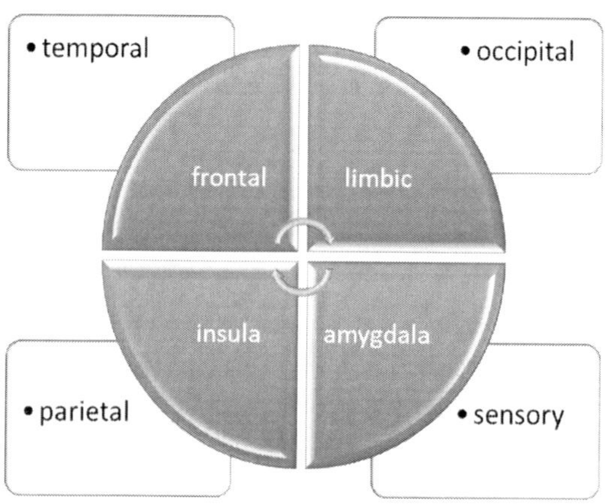

Figure 1. The basic part and extended part of fear network model for PD. The core blue part is composed of the traditional fear network model regions. The outside white part represents the extended fear network model regions.

REFERENCES

[1] Gorman, J. M., Kent, J. M., Sullivan, G. M., & Coplan, J. D. Neuroanatomical hypothesis of panic disorder, revised. *Am J Psychiatry* (2000), 157(4), 493-505.

[2] Wood, W. G. The diagnosis and management of panic disorder. *Psychiatr Med* (1990), 8(3), 197-209.

[3] Culpepper, L. Identifying and treating panic disorder in primary care. *J Clin Psychiatry* (2004), 65 Suppl 5, 19-23.

[4] Weissman, M. M., Wickramaratne, P., Adams, P. B., Lish, J. D., Horwath, E., Charney, D., et al. The relationship between panic disorder and major depression. A new family study. *Arch Gen Psychiatry* (1993), 50(10), 767-80.

[5] Dresler, T., Guhn, A., Tupak, S. V., Ehlis, A. C., Herrmann, M. J., Fallgatter, A. J., et al. Revise the revised? New dimensions of the neuroanatomical hypothesis of panic disorder. *J Neural Transm* (2013), 120(1), 3-29.

[6] Neumeister, A., Bain, E., Nugent, A. C., Carson, R. E., Bonne, O., Luckenbaugh, D. A., et al. Reduced serotonin type 1A receptor binding in panic disorder. *J Neurosci* (2004), 24(3), 589-91.

[7] Nash, J. R., Sargent, P. A., Rabiner, E. A., Hood, S. D., Argyropoulos, S. V., Potokar, J. P., et al. Serotonin 5-HT1A receptor binding in people with panic disorder: positron emission tomography study. *Br J Psychiatry* (2008), 193(3), 229-34.

[8] Graeff, F. G., & Del-Ben, C. M. Neurobiology of panic disorder: from animal models to brain neuroimaging. *Neurosci Biobehav Rev* (2008), 32(7), 1326-35.

[9] Le Bihan, D. Functional MRI of the brain principles, applications and limitations. *J Neuroradiol* (1996), 23(1), 1-5.

[10] Chen, W., Liu, X., Zhu, X. H., & Zhang, N. Functional MRI study of brain function under resting and activated states. *Conf Proc IEEE Eng Med Biol Soc* (2009), 2009, 4061-3.

[11] Andellini, M., Cannata, V., Gazzellini, S., Bernardi, B., & Napolitano, A. Test-retest reliability of graph metrics of resting state

MRI functional brain networks: A review. *J Neurosci Methods* (2015), 253, 183-92.

[12] Guye, M., Bettus, G., Bartolomei, F., & Cozzone, P. J. Graph theoretical analysis of structural and functional connectivity MRI in normal and pathological brain networks. *MAGMA* (2010), 23(5-6), 409-21.

[13] Joo, S. H., Lim, H. K., & Lee, C. U. Three Large-Scale Functional Brain Networks from Resting-State Functional MRI in Subjects with Different Levels of Cognitive Impairment. *Psychiatry Investig* (2016), 13(1), 1-7.

[14] Smyser, C. D., Snyder, A. Z., & Neil, J. J. Functional connectivity MRI in infants: exploration of the functional organization of the developing brain. *Neuroimage* (2011), 56(3), 1437-52.

[15] Helms, G. Segmentation of human brain using structural MRI. *MAGMA* (2016), 29(2), 111-24.

[16] Bigler, E. D. Structural Image Analysis of the Brain in Neuropsychology Using Magnetic Resonance Imaging (MRI) Techniques. *Neuropsychol Rev* (2015), 25(3), 224-49.

[17] Richardson, F. M., & Price, C. J. Structural MRI studies of language function in the undamaged brain. *Brain Struct Funct* (2009), 213(6), 511-23.

[18] Bastiani, M., & Roebroeck, A. Unraveling the multiscale structural organization and connectivity of the human brain: the role of diffusion MRI. *Front Neuroanat* (2015), 9, 77.

[19] Zheng, D., Sun, H., Dong, X., Liu, B., Xu, Y., Chen, S., et al. Executive dysfunction and gray matter atrophy in amnestic mild cognitive impairment. *Neurobiol Aging* (2014), 35(3), 548-55.

[20] Schmidt-Wilcke, T., Poljansky, S., Hierlmeier, S., Hausner, J., & Ibach, B. Memory performance correlates with gray matter density in the ento-/perirhinal cortex and posterior hippocampus in patients with mild cognitive impairment and healthy controls--a voxel based morphometry study. *Neuroimage* (2009), 47(4), 1914-20.

[21] Asami, T., Hayano, F., Nakamura, M., Yamasue, H., Uehara, K., Otsuka, T., et al. Anterior cingulate cortex volume reduction in

patients with panic disorder. *Psychiatry Clin Neurosci* (2008), 62(3), 322-30.

[22] Asami, T., Yamasue, H., Hayano, F., Nakamura, M., Uehara, K., Otsuka, T., et al. Sexually dimorphic gray matter volume reduction in patients with panic disorder. *Psychiatry Res* (2009), 173(2), 128-34.

[23] Hayano, F., Nakamura, M., Asami, T., Uehara, K., Yoshida, T., Roppongi, T., et al. Smaller amygdala is associated with anxiety in patients with panic disorder. *Psychiatry Clin Neurosci* (2009), 63(3), 266-76.

[24] Massana, G., Serra-Grabulosa, J. M., Salgado-Pineda, P., Gasto, C., Junque, C., Massana, J., et al. Parahippocampal gray matter density in panic disorder: a voxel-based morphometric study. *Am J Psychiatry* (2003), 160(3), 566-8.

[25] Protopopescu, X., Pan, H., Tuescher, O., Cloitre, M., Goldstein, M., Engelien, A., et al. Increased brainstem volume in panic disorder: a voxel-based morphometric study. *Neuroreport* (2006), 17(4), 361-3.

[26] Roppongi, T., Nakamura, M., Asami, T., Hayano, F., Otsuka, T., Uehara, K., et al. Posterior orbitofrontal sulcogyral pattern associated with orbitofrontal cortex volume reduction and anxiety trait in panic disorder. *Psychiatry Clin Neurosci* (2010), 64(3), 318-26.

[27] Sobanski, T., Wagner, G., Peikert, G., Gruhn, U., Schluttig, K., Sauer, H., et al. Temporal and right frontal lobe alterations in panic disorder: a quantitative volumetric and voxel-based morphometric MRI study. *Psychol Med* (2010), 40(11), 1879-86.

[28] Uchida, R. R., Del-Ben, C. M., Busatto, G. F., Duran, F. L., Guimaraes, F. S., Crippa, J. A., et al. Regional gray matter abnormalities in panic disorder: a voxel-based morphometry study. *Psychiatry Res* (2008), 163(1), 21-9.

[29] Yoo, H. K., Kim, M. J., Kim, S. J., Sung, Y. H., Sim, M. E., Lee, Y. S., et al. Putaminal gray matter volume decrease in panic disorder: an optimized voxel-based morphometry study. *Eur J Neurosci* (2005), 22(8), 2089-94.

[30] Na, K. S., Ham, B. J., Lee, M. S., Kim, L., Kim, Y. K., Lee, H. J., et al. Decreased gray matter volume of the medial orbitofrontal cortex

in panic disorder with agoraphobia: a preliminary study. *Prog Neuropsychopharmacol Biol Psychiatry* (2013), 45, 195-200.

[31] Atmaca, M., Yildirim, H., Gurok, M. G., & Akyol, M. Orbito-frontal cortex volumes in panic disorder. *Psychiatry Investig* (2012), 9(4), 408-12.

[32] de Carvalho, M. R., Rozenthal, M., & Nardi, A. E. The fear circuitry in panic disorder and its modulation by cognitive-behaviour therapy interventions. *World J Biol Psychiatry* (2010), 11(2 Pt 2), 188-98.

[33] Johnson, L. R., Hou, M., Prager, E. M., & Ledoux, J. E. Regulation of the Fear Network by Mediators of Stress: Norepinephrine Alters the Balance between Cortical and Subcortical Afferent Excitation of the Lateral Amygdala. *Front Behav Neurosci* (2011), 5, 23.

[34] Lai, C. H., Hsu, Y. Y., & Wu, Y. T. First episode drug-naive major depressive disorder with panic disorder: gray matter deficits in limbic and default network structures. *Eur Neuropsychopharmacol* (2010), 20(10), 676-82.

[35] van Tol, M. J., van der Wee, N. J., van den Heuvel, O. A., Nielen, M. M., Demenescu, L. R., Aleman, A., et al. Regional brain volume in depression and anxiety disorders. *Arch Gen Psychiatry* (2010), 67(10), 1002-11.

[36] Boshuisen, M. L., Ter Horst, G. J., Paans, A. M., Reinders, A. A., & den Boer, J. A. rCBF differences between panic disorder patients and control subjects during anticipatory anxiety and rest. *Biol Psychiatry* (2002), 52(2), 126-35.

[37] Nagai, M., Kishi, K., & Kato, S. Insular cortex and neuropsychiatric disorders: a review of recent literature. *Eur Psychiatry* (2007), 22(6), 387-94.

[38] Dresler, T., Hahn, T., Plichta, M. M., Ernst, L. H., Tupak, S. V., Ehlis, A. C., et al. Neural correlates of spontaneous panic attacks. *J Neural Transm* (2011).

[39] Canteras, N. S., & Graeff, F. G. Executive and modulatory neural circuits of defensive reactions: implications for panic disorder. *Neurosci Biobehav Rev* (2014), 46 Pt 3, 352-64.

[40] Lai, C. H. Hippocampal and subcortical alterations of first-episode, medication-naive major depressive disorder with panic disorder patients. *J Neuropsychiatry Clin Neurosci* (2014), 26(2), 142-9.

[41] Lai, C. H., & Wu, Y. T. Fronto-temporo-insula gray matter alterations of first-episode, drug-naive and very late-onset panic disorder patients. *J Affect Disord* (2012), 140(3), 285-91.

[42] Lai, C. H., & Wu, Y. T. The gray matter alterations in major depressive disorder and panic disorder: Putative differences in the pathogenesis. *J Affect Disord* (2015), 186, 1-6.

[43] Bae, S., Kim, J. E., Hwang, J., Lee, Y. S., Lee, H. H., Lee, J., et al. Increased prevalence of white matter hyperintensities in patients with panic disorder. *J Psychopharmacol* (2010), 24(5), 717-23.

[44] Konishi, J., Asami, T., Hayano, F., Yoshimi, A., Hayasaka, S., Fukushima, H., et al. Multiple white matter volume reductions in patients with panic disorder: relationships between orbitofrontal Gyrus volume and symptom severity and social dysfunction. *PLoS One* (2014), 9(3), e92862.

[45] Ayling, E., Aghajani, M., Fouche, J. P., & van der Wee, N. Diffusion tensor imaging in anxiety disorders. *Curr Psychiatry Rep* (2012), 14(3), 197-202.

[46] Del Casale, A., Serata, D., Rapinesi, C., Kotzalidis, G. D., Angeletti, G., Tatarelli, R., et al. Structural neuroimaging in patients with panic disorder: findings and limitations of recent studies. *Psychiatr Danub* (2013), 25(2), 108-14.

[47] Kim, B., Kim, M. K., Yoo, E., Lee, J. Y., Choe, A. Y., Yook, K. H., et al. Comparison of panic disorder with and without comorbid major depression by using brain structural magnetic resonance imaging. *Prog Neuropsychopharmacol Biol Psychiatry* (2013), 43, 188-96.

[48] Han, D. H., Renshaw, P. F., Dager, S. R., Chung, A., Hwang, J., Daniels, M. A., et al. Altered cingulate white matter connectivity in panic disorder patients. *J Psychiatr Res* (2008), 42(5), 399-407.

[49] Kim, B., Yoo, E., Lee, J. Y., Lee, K. S., Choe, A. Y., Lee, J. E., et al. The effects of the catechol-O-methyltransferase val158met

polymorphism on white matter connectivity in patients with panic disorder. *J Affect Disord* (2013), 147(1-3), 64-71.

[50] Yu, S. T., Kim, M. K., Kim, B., Yoo, E., Lee, J. Y., Lee, K. S., et al. The Effects of 5-HTR1A Polymorphism on Cingulum Connectivity in Patients with Panic Disorder. *Psychiatry Investig* (2013), 10(4), 399-406.

[51] Lai, C. H., & Wu, Y. T. Fronto-occipital fasciculus, corpus callosum and superior longitudinal fasciculus tract alterations of first-episode, medication-naive and late-onset panic disorder patients. *J Affect Disord* (2013), 146(3), 378-82.

[52] Kim, B., Kim, J. H., Kim, M. K., Lee, K. S., Kim, Y., Choi, T. K., et al. Frontal white matter alterations in short-term medicated panic disorder patients without comorbid conditions: a diffusion tensor imaging study. *PLoS One* (2014), 9(4), e95279.

[53] Kim, B., Oh, J., Kim, M. K., Lee, S., Tae, W. S., Kim, C. M., et al. White matter alterations are associated with suicide attempt in patients with panic disorder. *J Affect Disord* (2015), 175, 139-46.

[54] Kim, M. K., Kim, B., Kiu Choi, T., & Lee, S. H. White matter correlates of anxiety sensitivity in panic disorder. *J Affect Disord* (2017), 207, 148-56.

[55] Lai, C. H., & Wu, Y. T. The White Matter Microintegrity Alterations of Neocortical and Limbic Association Fibers in Major Depressive Disorder and Panic Disorder: The Comparison. *Medicine (Baltimore)* (2016), 95(9), e2982.

[56] Zou, Q. H., Zhu, C. Z., Yang, Y., Zuo, X. N., Long, X. Y., Cao, Q. J., et al. An improved approach to detection of amplitude of low-frequency fluctuation (ALFF) for resting-state fMRI: fractional ALFF. *J Neurosci Methods* (2008), 172(1), 137-41.

[57] Zang, Y., Jiang, T., Lu, Y., He, Y., & Tian, L. Regional homogeneity approach to fMRI data analysis. *Neuroimage* (2004), 22(1), 394-400.

[58] Zuo, X. N., Kelly, C., Di Martino, A., Mennes, M., Margulies, D. S., Bangaru, S., et al. Growing together and growing apart: regional and sex differences in the lifespan developmental trajectories of functional homotopy. *J Neurosci* (2010), 30(45), 15034-43.

[59] Biswal, B., Yetkin, F. Z., Haughton, V. M., & Hyde, J. S. Functional connectivity in the motor cortex of resting human brain using echo-planar MRI. *Magn Reson Med* (1995), 34(4), 537-41.

[60] Fox, M. D., & Raichle, M. E. Spontaneous fluctuations in brain activity observed with functional magnetic resonance imaging. *Nat Rev Neurosci* (2007), 8(9), 700-11.

[61] Salvador, R., Suckling, J., Coleman, M. R., Pickard, J. D., Menon, D., & Bullmore, E. Neurophysiological architecture of functional magnetic resonance images of human brain. *Cereb Cortex* (2005), 15(9), 1332-42.

[62] Lai, C. H., & Wu, Y. T. Patterns of fractional amplitude of low-frequency oscillations in occipito-striato-thalamic regions of first-episode drug-naive panic disorder. *J Affect Disord* (2012), 142(1-3), 180-5.

[63] Sheline, Y. I., Barch, D. M., Price, J. L., Rundle, M. M., Vaishnavi, S. N., Snyder, A. Z., et al. The default mode network and self-referential processes in depression. *Proc Natl Acad Sci U S A* (2009), 106(6), 1942-7.

[64] Lai, C. H., & Wu, Y. T. The alterations in inter-hemispheric functional coordination of patients with panic disorder: the findings in the posterior sub-network of default mode network. *J Affect Disord* (2014), 166, 279-84.

[65] Lai, C. H., & Wu, Y. T. Decreased regional homogeneity in lingual gyrus, increased regional homogeneity in cuneus and correlations with panic symptom severity of first-episode, medication-naive and late-onset panic disorder patients. *Psychiatry Res* (2013), 211(2), 127-31.

[66] Feldker, K., Heitmann, C. Y., Neumeister, P., Bruchmann, M., Vibrans, L., Zwitserlood, P., et al. Brain responses to disorder-related visual threat in panic disorder. *Hum Brain Mapp* (2016), 37(12), 4439-53.

[67] Cui, H., Zhang, J., Liu, Y., Li, Q., Li, H., Zhang, L., et al. Differential alterations of resting-state functional connectivity in

generalized anxiety disorder and panic disorder. *Hum Brain Mapp* (2016), 37(4), 1459-73.

[68] Kircher, T., Arolt, V., Jansen, A., Pyka, M., Reinhardt, I., Kellermann, T., et al. Effect of cognitive-behavioral therapy on neural correlates of fear conditioning in panic disorder. *Biol Psychiatry* (2013), 73(1), 93-101.

[69] Sylvester, C. M., Corbetta, M., Raichle, M. E., Rodebaugh, T. L., Schlaggar, B. L., Sheline, Y. I., et al. Functional network dysfunction in anxiety and anxiety disorders. *Trends Neurosci* (2012), 35(9), 527-35.

[70] Lueken, U., Straube, B., Konrad, C., Wittchen, H. U., Strohle, A., Wittmann, A., et al. Neural substrates of treatment response to cognitive-behavioral therapy in panic disorder with agoraphobia. *Am J Psychiatry* (2013), 170(11), 1345-55.

[71] Pannekoek, J. N., Veer, I. M., van Tol, M. J., van der Werff, S. J., Demenescu, L. R., Aleman, A., et al. Aberrant limbic and salience network resting-state functional connectivity in panic disorder without comorbidity. *J Affect Disord* (2013), 145(1), 29-35.

[72] Lai, C. H., & Wu, Y. T. The Explorative Analysis to Revise Fear Network Model for Panic Disorder: Functional Connectome Statistics. *Medicine (Baltimore)* (2016), 95(18), e3597.

[73] Japee, S., Crocker, L., Carver, F., Pessoa, L., & Ungerleider, L. G. Individual differences in valence modulation of face-selective M170 response. *Emotion* (2009), 9(1), 59-69.

[74] Bayle, D. J., & Taylor, M. J. Attention inhibition of early cortical activation to fearful faces. *Brain Res* (2010), 1313, 113-23.

[75] Liao, W., Chen, H., Feng, Y., Mantini, D., Gentili, C., Pan, Z., et al. Selective aberrant functional connectivity of resting state networks in social anxiety disorder. *Neuroimage* (2010), 52(4), 1549-58.

[76] Liao, W., Xu, Q., Mantini, D., Ding, J., Machado-de-Sousa, J. P., Hallak, J. E., et al. Altered gray matter morphometry and resting-state functional and structural connectivity in social anxiety disorder. *Brain Res* (2011), 1388, 167-77.

[77] Mather, M., Mitchell, K. J., Raye, C. L., Novak, D. L., Greene, E. J., & Johnson, M. K. Emotional arousal can impair feature binding in working memory. *J Cogn Neurosci* (2006), 18(4), 614-25.

[78] Ohrmann, P., Pedersen, A., Braun, M., Bauer, J., Kugel, H., Kersting, A., et al. Effect of gender on processing threat-related stimuli in patients with panic disorder: sex does matter. *Depress Anxiety* (2010), 27(11), 1034-43.

[79] Premkumar, P., Ettinger, U., Inchley-Mort, S., Sumich, A., Williams, S. C., Kuipers, E., et al. Neural processing of social rejection: The role of schizotypal personality traits. *Hum Brain Mapp* (2011).

[80] Killgore, W. D., & Yurgelun-Todd, D. A. Social anxiety predicts amygdala activation in adolescents viewing fearful faces. *Neuroreport* (2005), 16(15), 1671-5.

[81] Pathology and management of dizziness. *Lancet* (1984), 2(8417-8418), 1439.

[82] Nehlig, A., Armspach, J. P., & Namer, I. J. SPECT assessment of brain activation induced by caffeine: no effect on areas involved in dependence. *Dialogues Clin Neurosci* (2010), 12(2), 255-63.

[83] Schiltz, C., Bodart, J. M., Dubois, S., Dejardin, S., Michel, C., Roucoux, A., et al. Neuronal mechanisms of perceptual learning: changes in human brain activity with training in orientation discrimination. *Neuroimage* (1999), 9(1), 46-62.

[84] Lai, C. H., & Hsu, Y. Y. A subtle grey-matter increase in first-episode, drug-naive major depressive disorder with panic disorder after 6 weeks' duloxetine therapy. *Int J Neuropsychopharmacol* (2011), 14(2), 225-35.

[85] Li, C. T., Lin, C. P., Chou, K. H., Chen, I. Y., Hsieh, J. C., Wu, C. L., et al. Structural and cognitive deficits in remitting and non-remitting recurrent depression: a voxel-based morphometric study. *Neuroimage* (2010), 50(1), 347-56.

[86] Sijens, P. E., Mostert, J. P., Irwan, R., Potze, J. H., Oudkerk, M., & De Keyser, J. Impact of fluoxetine on the human brain in multiple sclerosis as quantified by proton magnetic resonance spectroscopy and diffusion tensor imaging. *Psychiatry Res* (2008), 164(3), 274-82.

[87] Brunoni, A. R., Lopes, M., & Fregni, F. A systematic review and meta-analysis of clinical studies on major depression and BDNF levels: implications for the role of neuroplasticity in depression. *Int J Neuropsychopharmacol* (2008), 11(8), 1169-80.

[88] Kodama, M., Fujioka, T., & Duman, R. S. Chronic olanzapine or fluoxetine administration increases cell proliferation in hippocampus and prefrontal cortex of adult rat. *Biol Psychiatry* (2004), 56(8), 570-80.

[89] Magistretti, P. J. Cellular bases of functional brain imaging: insights from neuron-glia metabolic coupling. *Brain Res* (2000), 886(1-2), 108-12.

[90] Manev, H., Uz, T., & Manev, R. Glia as a putative target for antidepressant treatments. *J Affect Disord* (2003), 75(1), 59-64.

[91] Guest, P. C., Knowles, M. R., Molon-Noblot, S., Salim, K., Smith, D., Murray, F., et al. Mechanisms of action of the antidepressants fluoxetine and the substance P antagonist L-000760735 are associated with altered neurofilaments and synaptic remodeling. *Brain Res* (2004), 1002(1-2), 1-10.

[92] Witkin, J. M., Marek, G. J., Johnson, B. G., & Schoepp, D. D. Metabotropic glutamate receptors in the control of mood disorders. *CNS Neurol Disord Drug Targets* (2007), 6(2), 87-100.

[93] Lai, C. H., & Wu, Y. T. Duloxetine's modest short-term influences in subcortical structures of first episode drug-naive patients with major depressive disorder and panic disorder. *Psychiatry Res* (2011), 194(2), 157-62.

[94] Lai, C. H. Escitalopram increased gray matter and white matter in a first-episode drug-naive panic disorder patient within 6 weeks. *J Neuropsychiatry Clin Neurosci* (2012), 24(2), E23-4.

[95] Lai, C. H., & Wu, Y. T. Frontal regional homogeneity increased and temporal regional homogeneity decreased after remission of first-episode drug-naive major depressive disorder with panic disorder patients under duloxetine therapy for 6 weeks. *J Affect Disord* (2012), 136(3), 453-8.

[96] Lai, C. H., & Wu, Y. T. Changes in regional homogeneity of parieto-temporal regions in panic disorder patients who achieved remission with antidepressant treatment. *J Affect Disord* (2013), 151(2), 709-14.

[97] Lai, C. H., & Wu, Y. T. Changes in gray matter volume of remitted first-episode, drug-naive, panic disorder patients after 6-week antidepressant therapy. *J Psychiatr Res* (2013), 47(1), 122-7.

[98] Lai, C. H., Wu, Y. T., Yu, P. L., & Yuan, W. Improvements in white matter micro-structural integrity of right uncinate fasciculus and left fronto-occipital fasciculus of remitted first-episode medication-naive panic disorder patients. *J Affect Disord* (2013), 150(2), 330-6.

In: Panic Disorder
Editor: Yong-Ku Kim
ISBN: 978-1-53613-001-0

Chapter 8

ALTERATIONS OF THE HYPOTHALAMIC-PITUITARY-ADRENAL AXIS IN PANIC DISORDER

Gloria-Beatrice Wintermann, PhD [*]
Department of Psychotherapy and Psychosomatic Medicine,
Medizinische Fakultät Carl Gustav Carus,
Technische Universität Dresden, Dresden, Germany

ABSTRACT

Stressors play a pivotal role in the first onset of Panic Disorder (PD). Furthermore, symptoms occurring during a panic attack resemble those during the stress response in healthy individuals. Following, PD can be regarded as stress-related disorder. Findings concerning the involvement in one of the major stress regulating systems, the Hypothalamic-Pituitary-adrenal (HPA)- axis, did not bring about unequivocal results with evidence for both hyper- and hypo-reactivity as well as no differences under basal and stimulated conditions. Existing findings could not show consistent endocrine dysfunctions whereas findings hint toward only a

[*] Corresponding author. E-mail: gloria.wintermann@uniklinikum-dresden.de.

subtle alteration of HPA axis activity. In the present chapter we review the main findings in this research area and give an outlook for future studies which should take into account influencing variables of cortisol secretion. Future research should better unravel the sensitivity and functioning of glucocorticoid (GC) receptors in different target tissues besides the assessment of GC concentration alone. Further insight into the functioning of the HPA axis is required for a more profound understanding of the etiopathogenesis of PD.

1. The HPA Axis and Its Role in PD

Patients with PD show symptoms characteristic of reactions under stress in healthy subjects (e.g., shortness of breath, sweating, trembling, dizziness, palpitation) [1]. This leads to the assumption that at least some patients with Panic Disorder (PD) show alterations in one of the major stress regulating systems, the hypothalamic-pituitary-adrenal (HPA) axis. Above, repetitive stress exposure plays a crucial role in the onset of psychological disorders such as PD [2]. Findings have associated the development of PD with dysregulations in the HPA axis and suggested PD as maladaptive response pattern to various stressors [3]. Following, in order to gain insights into the etiopathogenesis of this anxiety disorder investigations of the HPA axis and its exudates are of essential importance. Above, subgroups of patients with a distinctive neuroendocrine response pattern may be related to therapy response or non-response and thus, in the future, help to improve the assignment of specific patient groups to appropriate treatment options [4].

The HPA axis has been widely investigated in patients with affective disorders, particularly major depression, as main hormonal system being involved in the etiopathogenesis and pathophysiology of these disorders [5, 6]. The main regulator of the HPA axis is the Corticotropin-Releasing-Factor (CRF). Hypophysiotropic neurons in the medial parvocellular subdivision of the paraventricular nucleus (PVN) synthesize CRF and vasopressin (AVP). Under stress, CRF is released into the anterior pituitary via hypophysial portal vessels. There, CRF binds to CRF type 1 receptors

(CRFR1) placed on pituitary corticotropes, initiates cyclic adenosine monophosphate (cAMP) cascades and ends up in the release of Adrenocorticotropic Hormone (ACTH, also called corticotropin) into the systemic circulation. CRF has synergistic effects with AVP on the ACTH release. Target for circulating ACTH is the adrenal cortex where it binds to melanocortin type 2 receptors (MC2-R), stimulates steroidogenesis, the secretion of glucocorticoids, mineralcorticoids, androgenic steroids as well as the synthesis and secretion of cortisol from the zona fasciculata [7] (see Figure 1). Further HPA axis activation is regulated by negative feedback inhibition, controlling the magnitude and duration of glucocorticoid release. 80% to 90% of the total cortisol concentration is bound to the protein cortisol-binding-globulin (CBG) or transcortin [8]. Following, the availability of biologically active cortisol is decisively determined by the current concentration of CBG [9].

The physiological effects of cortisol are mediated by glucocorticoid receptors, widely centrally and peripherally distributed cytosolic proteins. The ligand-receptor complex translocates into the nucleus where it binds to specific DNA motifs or glucocorticoid response elements (GRE) and deploys genetic effects by means of interaction with transcription factors [7]. Glucocorticoid receptors (GR, type II) are highly expressed in stress-related neural areas such as hypothalamus, hippocampus, amygdalae, brain stem nuclei, pituitary gland and mediate negative feedback under stress. Mineralocorticoid receptors (MR, type I) occur mainly in the limbic system and regulate the circadian fluctuations as well as basal HPA axis tone. In this process, the number and function of GR is regulated ligand-dependently or ligand-independently. Cortisol has several physiologic effects, influences metabolic, muscle, brain and immune functions. Besides, it enables an adaptive stress response. Inadequately excessive or diminished release can have detrimental effects leading to pathologies and a lack of adaptation under stress [10].

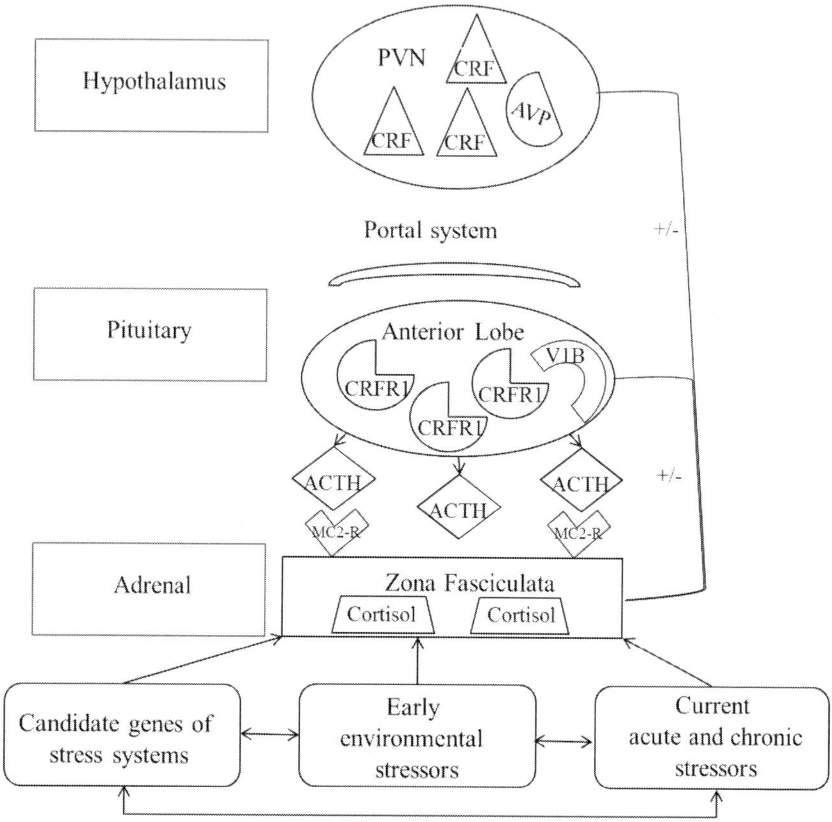

Figure 1. Schema of the Hypothalamic-Pituitary-Adrenal (HPA) axis according to Smith & Vale [7] with the main agents Corticotropin-Releasing-Factor (CRF), Adrenocorticotropic Hormone (ACTH) and the end product cortisol. In patients with mental disorders in general and PD in particular, interacting stress-related genetic and environmental factors determine the variation in HPA axis reactivity [11]. See text for further details. AVP-Vasopressin r; CRFR1-CRF type 1 receptor; MC2-R-Melanocortin type 2 receptor; V1B-Vasopressin V1B receptor,

2. Abnormalities of HPA Axis in PD

Abnormalities in the HPA axis activity and response pattern in patients with PD have been shown under various stress and basal conditions using urinary, salivary and plasma ACTH/ cortisol as outcome variables (for a structured review see [12]; for a literature review see [13]). While salivary cortisol reflects the free, biologically active fraction of cortisol and allows together with serum/ plasma cortisol the representation of acute, stress induced changes of cortisol concentrations, urinary cortisol indicates an integrative measurement of HPA axis activity usually over 24 hours [13, 14].

Paradigms investigating the activity of the HPA axis comprise simply measuring the distinct basal diurnal rhythm [15], stress induction by way of physiological or pharmacological stimulation (e.g., Dexemethasone-Corticotrophine-Releasing-Hormone Test, ergometry, cold pressure test) or psychosocial stress exposure (e.g., Trier Social Stress Test, TSST). Findings either show raised, blunted levels or no differences of the end product cortisol under diverse conditions. The different cortisol secretion profiles have been associated with the severity of PD, psychotherapy outcome and treatment response [4, 16, 17]. Current findings suggest an association between an attenuated cortisol response under psychosocial stress with psychotherapy non-response [4, 18]. Vice versa, higher absolute cortisol levels during exposure therapy facilitated fear extinction whereas unequivocal evidence is still owed [16, 19].

Present results hint towards a rather subtle change of the HPA axis in PD under physiological stimulation (e.g., [20, 21]). Besides, there is preliminary evidence that a hypofunctional HPA axis responsivity rather displays a vulnerability factor or trait characteristic for the etiopathogenesis of PD than a consequence of the psychopathology [22]. This is underlined by an allelic variation of the receptor CRHR1 which increases the risk for pronounced anxiety sensitivity and the occurrence of PD, particularly in females [23].

3. Basal Cortisol in PD

Findings regarding the diurnal secretion pattern in PD are heterogeneous. The majority of studies could find an elevated cortisol level during the evening and night but not during the morning and afternoon [24-29]. Findings regarding the natural rise of cortisol during the first hour after waking from sleep (Cortisol Awakening Response) hint towards no change in HPA axis activity in PD [29, 30]. Differing results can be ascribed to influencing variables such as preceding strains, anticipated demands, meals and smoking. Moreover, inconsistent results were moderated by illness severity and the recruitment strategy of patients. In the study by Abelson and Curtis [25], patients recruited through clinical referral channels had a greater cortisol secretion than patients recruited by advertisements.

Measuring HPA axis response under natural panic attacks gave evidence for elevated salivary cortisol indicated by a decrease 24h later [31]. However, investigating HPA axis during natural panic attacks raises some methodological problems since standardization is limited. The time point when the panic attack occurs varies inter-individually. Likewise, the perceived intensity of the panic attack may differ between patients. However, whether panic attacks lead to an activation of the HPA axis remains equivocal and demands the application of more standardized stress procedures leading to a reliable HPA axis response in both patients and healthy controls [32].

4. Physiological Stimulation

Results of studies applying the Dexamethasone (Dex) and Corticotropin-Releasing-Hormone (CRH) test do not allow a final conclusion regarding an involvement of the HPA axis in the pathophysiology of PD (Dex test: e.g., [33-38]; CRH test: e.g., [24, 39-41]). Divergent findings may be ascribed to differences in the dose and administration of dexamethasone/ CRH, application of different cut-off values and differences in the time of testing. Both the Dex- and the CRH-test only have a small to moderate sensitivity in order to detect dysfunctions of the HPA axis. Besides, a reduced glucocorticoid feedback sensitivity at the pituitary level cannot be proven, therefore the DEX-CRH test was introduced [42, 43].

The Dex-CRH test turned out to be independent from influencing variables such as smoking, weight, test-induced stress, age and psychopharmaceutical drug treatment [20, 44]. Studies hint toward a hyperreactivity (> 110 nmol/l) of the HPA axis compared with healthy controls [20, 21, 42]. This response pattern was present in 69% of the patients and 20% of the healthy controls [21]. However, final conclusions based on these results cannot be drawn since patients received antidepressant drug treatment [20], the study sample was small (n = 13, [21]) and differences in gender distribution between patient and control samples confounded the results [21]. More recent results could show a dissociation between plasma ACTH and cortisol in the DEX-CRH test in patients with PD [45, 46]. The latter result alludes to a hypo-responsiveness of the adrenal cortex to ACTH. Increased reactivity of HPA axis seems to be mainly driven by a comorbid depressive disorder as well as the severity of psychopathology and duration of disorder [45, 46].

Regarding the HPA axis reactivity under stimulation with anxiogenic agents such as lactate, CO_2, caffeine, yohombine, respiratory stimulant, cholecystokinin B, there is evidence that these stimuli indeed trigger panic but do not result in a reliable activation of the HPA axis in patients with PD (e.g., [28, 47, 48]). An exaggerated HPA axis response has been associated with hypersensitivity to novelty and contextual cues, a trait predisposing toward the development of psychopathology [28]. A recently published study has shown an increase in ACTH and cortisol after caffeine administration [49]. However, caffeine-induced panic does not seem to be mediated by HPA axis activation since post-caffeine panickers and non-panickers did not differ with respect to the increases [49].

5. Psychosocial Stimulation

The application of standardized psychosocial stress procedures were motivated by the supposition that a simulated public speaking can activate similar neural areas like panic attacks and elicit a significant HPA axis response [50, 51]. Studies could not show an increase in cortisol values during a simulated public speaking or showing a frightening video [51-53]. Presumably the intensity, the personal relevance, the duration and the extent of social-evaluative threat of the stressor were not sufficient to induce a stress response [54, 55]. Therefore, the application of a more potent stressor was required. The Trier Social Stress Test (TSST, [56]) is most likely to elicit a reliable HPA axis response by means of social-evaluative threat and uncontrollability [15, 57]. The stress protocol comprises a free speech and an arithmetic task in front of a panel of two persons. While 82% of the healthy individuals presented a cortisol response only about 9% of the patients with PD did [30]. There is broad evidence of an attenuated cortisol response in patients with PD being exposed to the TSST (e.g., [22, 30, 58]). The cortisol non-response is in line with findings showing an attenuated plasma and saliva cortisol response during a psychosocial stressor (speech of an emotionally charged topic) in healthy subjects with high trait anxiety [59]. A decreased response pattern might be related to the theory of allostastis and allostatic load [60, 61] proposing an exhaustion of the HPA axis due to repeated stressors such as panic attacks (repeated hits), presumably resulting in a down-regulation of corticosteroid receptors and an maladaptive stress response on the long-run [13, 62]. However, the theory of allostasis and allostatic load is challenged by findings of an absent HPA axis activity during panic attacks and thus needs further evidence in patients with PD [31].

6. Summary and Implications for Future Research

To summarize, there is a plethora of studies investigating the HPA axis reactivity in patients with PD under natural and stimulated conditions. Current findings could not reveal a consistent pattern of abnormal HPA axis response under both basal and stimulated conditions in patients with PD. The results should be critically evaluated with respect to the specifics of the sample (e.g., comorbidities, extent of agoraphobic avoidance, illness severity), the sample size, measurement regime (e.g., sampling times, circadian phase/ time of the day, hypoglycemic state) and stress protocol (e.g., potency of the stressor to elicit HPA axis response). Future research should use prospective designs with standardized measurement of cortisol in both saliva and blood, using sub-group analysis and analysis of mediators as well as moderators (e.g., gender, use of hormonal contraceptives, menstrual cycle, medication, smoking, duration of disorder, specific symptomatology, comorbidities, preceding traumatic events, measurement context, state anxiety) of the HPA axis stress response ([22]; for a systematic review and meta-analysis see [10]). Especially conditions such as intake of oral contraceptives and menstrual cycle which affect the concentration of cortisol-binding proteins should not be disregarded (for a systematic review see [13]). In order to account for the large intra- and inter-individual variations of cortisol levels due to the above mentioned confounding variables and circadian rhythm, future research may consider hair cortisol as non-invasive and retrospective measure of long-term stress exposure in PD [14].

Above, future studies should investigate the effect treatments (e.g., Cognitive-behavioral therapy, antidepressants) have on the HPA axis under stress conditions (for a structured review see: [12]). Specific neuroendocrine response patterns should shed light on individual treatment decisions. Moreover, succeeding studies should unravel which specific part of the HPA axis show aberrant functioning, e.g., in order to specify the sensitivity of the adrenal cortex future research should apply the synacthen stimulation test. Furthermore, factors influencing the adrenal glucocorticoid synthesis and release independently of pituitary ACTH such as immune cells, cytokines, adipocyte-derived factors, neurons, and neuropeptides should be further considered and systematically investigated [63]. In the future, results ought to better differentiate between the central and peripheral functioning of the HPA axis. The sensitivity of glucocorticoid receptors within different target tissues should be outlined [64, 65]. Furthermore, the interaction of the HPA axis with the immune system should be profoundly investigated since an attenuated stress response may increase the risk for a low-grade systemic proinflammatory state and consequently the pathogenesis of autoimmune or other somatic diseases [64, 66, 67]. According to this research branch, the existing findings are still ambiguous and need clarification [67, 68]. In this context, the role of the transcription factor nuclear factor kappa b should be considered more in detail in patients with PD [69].

Finally, another branch of research should intensely focus allelic variations of candidate genes along the HPA axis (e.g., CRHR1) and relate them with behavioral as well as neurofunctional alterations in PD. Thus, a deeper understanding and insight into the pathogenesis of PD would be allowed based on the involvement of a neural fear network and differentiating between the endocrine and neuronal regulation of the HPA axis [7, 23]. Prospective studies ought to unravel the transition of acutely increased cortisol levels to a hypocortisolaemic stress response concurrently considering salutogenetic or protecting variables [14, 70].

REFERENCES

[1] Holsboer F, Spengler D, Heuser I. The role of corticotropin-releasing hormone in the pathogenesis of Cushing's disease, anorexia nervosa, alcoholism, affective disorders and dementia. *Prog Brain Res* 1992;93:385-417.

[2] Moreno-Peral P, Conejo-Ceron S, Motrico E, Rodriguez-Morejon A, Fernandez A, Garcia-Campayo J, et al. Risk factors for the onset of panic and generalised anxiety disorders in the general adult population: a systematic review of cohort studies. *J Affect Disord* 2014;168:337-348.

[3] de Kloet ER, Joels M, Holsboer F. Stress and the brain: from adaptation to disease. *Nat Rev Neurosci* 2005;6(6):463-475.

[4] Wichmann S, Kirschbaum C, Lorenz T, Petrowski K. Effects of the cortisol stress response on the psychotherapy outcome of panic disorder patients. *Psychoneuroendocrinology* 2017;77:9-17.

[5] Pariante CM. Depression, stress and the adrenal axis. *J Neuroendocrinol* 2003;15(8):811-812.

[6] Pariante CM. The glucocorticoid receptor: part of the solution or part of the problem? *J Psychopharmacol* 2006;20(4 Suppl):79-84.

[7] Smith SM, Vale WW. The role of the hypothalamic-pituitary-adrenal axis in neuroendocrine responses to stress. *Dialogues Clin Neurosci* 2006;8(4):383-395.

[8] Lewis JG, Bagley CJ, Elder PA, Bachmann AW, Torpy DJ. Plasma free cortisol fraction reflects levels of functioning corticosteroid-binding globulin. *Clin Chim Acta* 2005;359(1-2):189-194.

[9] Wiegratz I, Kutschera E, Lee JH, Moore C, Mellinger U, Winkler UH, et al. Effect of four different oral contraceptives on various sex hormones and serum-binding globulins. *Contraception* 2003;67(1):25-32.

[10] Zorn JV, Schur RR, Boks MP, Kahn RS, Joels M, Vinkers CH. Cortisol stress reactivity across psychiatric disorders: A systematic review and meta-analysis. *Psychoneuroendocrinology* 2017;77:25-36.

[11] Pagliaccio D, Luby JL, Bogdan R, Agrawal A, Gaffrey MS, Belden AC, et al. Stress-system genes and life stress predict cortisol levels and amygdala and hippocampal volumes in children. *Neuropsychopharmacology* 2014;39(5):1245-1253.

[12] Elnazer HY, Baldwin DS. Investigation of cortisol levels in patients with anxiety disorders: a structured review. *Curr Top Behav Neurosci* 2014;18:191-216.

[13] Jakuszkowiak-Wojten K, Landowski J, Wiglusz MS, Cubala WJ. Cortisol as an indicator of hypothalmic-pitituary-adrenal axis dysregulation in patients with panic disorder: a literature review. *Psychiatr Danub* 2015;27 Suppl 1:S445-451.

[14] Staufenbiel SM, Penninx BW, Spijker AT, Elzinga BM, van Rossum EF. Hair cortisol, stress exposure, and mental health in humans: a systematic review. *Psychoneuroendocrinology* 2013;38(8):1220-1235.

[15] Skoluda N, Strahler J, Schlotz W, Niederberger L, Marques S, Fischer S, et al. Intra-individual psychological and physiological responses to acute laboratory stressors of different intensity. *Psychoneuroendocrinology* 2015;51:227-236.

[16] Fischer S, Cleare AJ. Cortisol as a predictor of psychological therapy response in anxiety disorders-Systematic review and meta-analysis. *J Anxiety Disord* 2017;47:60-68.

[17] Siegmund A, Koster L, Meves AM, Plag J, Stoy M, Strohle A. Stress hormones during flooding therapy and their relationship to therapy outcome in patients with panic disorder and agoraphobia. *J Psychiatr Res* 2011;45(3):339-346.

[18] de Quervain DJ, Bentz D, Michael T, Bolt OC, Wiederhold BK, Margraf J, et al. Glucocorticoids enhance extinction-based psychotherapy. *Proc Natl Acad Sci U S A* 2011;108(16):6621-6625.

[19] Meuret AE, Trueba AF, Abelson JL, Liberzon I, Auchus R, Bhaskara L, et al. High cortisol awakening response and cortisol levels moderate exposure-based psychotherapy success. *Psychoneuroendocrinology* 2015;51:331-340.

[20] Erhardt A, Ising M, Unschuld PG, Kern N, Lucae S, Putz B, et al. Regulation of the hypothalamic-pituitary-adrenocortical system in patients with panic disorder. *Neuropsychopharmacology* 2006;31(11):2515-2522.

[21] Schreiber W, Lauer CJ, Krumrey K, Holsboer F, Krieg JC. Dysregulation of the hypothalamic-pituitary-adrenocortical system in panic disorder. *Neuropsychopharmacology* 1996;15(1):7-15.

[22] Wintermann GB, Kirschbaum C, Petrowski K. Predisposition or side effect of the duration: the reactivity of the HPA-axis under psychosocial stress in panic disorder. *Int J Psychophysiol* 2016;107:9-15.

[23] Weber H, Richter J, Straube B, Lueken U, Domschke K, Schartner C, et al. Allelic variation in CRHR1 predisposes to panic disorder: evidence for biased fear processing. *Mol Psychiatry* 2016;21(6):813-822.

[24] Roy-Byrne PP, Uhde TW, Post RM, Gallucci W, Chrousos GP, Gold PW. The corticotropin-releasing hormone stimulation test in patients with panic disorder. *Am J Psychiatry* 1986;143(7):896-899.

[25] Abelson JL, Curtis GC. Hypothalamic-pituitary-adrenal axis activity in panic disorder. 24-hour secretion of corticotropin and cortisol. *Arch Gen Psychiatry* 1996;53(4):323-331.

[26] Bandelow B, Sengos G, Wedekind D, Huether G, Pilz J, Broocks A, et al. Urinary excretion of cortisol, norepinephrine, testosterone, and melatonin in panic disorder. *Pharmacopsychiatry* 1997;30(4):113-117.

[27] Bandelow B, Wedekind D, Sandvoss V, Broocks A, Hajak G, Pauls J, et al. Diurnal variation of cortisol in panic disorder. *Psychiatry Res* 2000;95(3):245-250.

[28] Abelson JL, Khan S, Liberzon I, Young EA. HPA axis activity in patients with panic disorder: review and synthesis of four studies. *Depress Anxiety* 2007;24(1):66-76.

[29] Jakuszkowiak-Wojten K, Landowski J, Wiglusz MS, Cubala WJ. Cortisol awakening response in drug-naive panic disorder. *Neuropsychiatr Dis Treat* 2016;12:1581-1585.

[30] Petrowski K, Herold U, Joraschky P, Wittchen HU, Kirschbaum C. A striking pattern of cortisol non-responsiveness to psychosocial stress in patients with panic disorder with concurrent normal cortisol awakening responses. *Psychoneuroendocrinology* 2010;35(3):414-421.

[31] Bandelow B, Wedekind D, Pauls J, Broocks A, Hajak G, Ruther E. Salivary cortisol in panic attacks. *Am J Psychiatry* 2000;157(3):454-456.

[32] Cameron OG, Lee MA, Curtis GC, McCann DS. Endocrine and physiological changes during "spontaneous" panic attacks. *Psychoneuroendocrinology* 1987;12(5):321-331.

[33] Curtis GC, Cameron OG, Nesse RM. The dexamethasone suppression test in panic disorder and agoraphobia. *Am J Psychiatry* 1982;139(8):1043-1046.

[34] Lieberman JA, Brenner R, Lesser M, Coccaro E, Borenstein M, Kane JM. Dexamethasone suppression tests in patients with panic disorder. *Am J Psychiatry* 1983;140(7):917-919.

[35] Grunhaus L, Tiongco D, Haskett RF, Greden JF. The dexamethasone suppression test in inpatients with panic disorder or agoraphobia with panic attacks. *Biol Psychiatry* 1987;22(4):517-521.

[36] Coryell W, Noyes R. HPA axis disturbance and treatment outcome in panic disorder. *Biol Psychiatry* 1988;24(7):762-766.

[37] Kopp MS, Arato M, Magyar I, Buza K. Basal adrenocortical activity and DST in electrodermally differentiated subgroups of panic patients. *Int J Psychophysiol* 1989;7(1):77-83.

[38] Coryell W, Noyes R, Jr., Reich J. The prognostic significance of HPA-axis disturbance in panic disorder: a three-year follow-up. *Biol Psychiatry* 1991;29(2):96-102.

[39] Holsboer F, von Bardeleben U, Buller R, Heuser I, Steiger A. Stimulation response to corticotropin-releasing hormone (CRH) in patients with depression, alcoholism and panic disorder. *Horm Metab Res Suppl* 1987;16:80-88.

[40] Brambilla F, Bellodi L, Perna G, Battaglia M, Sciuto G, Diaferia G, et al. Psychoimmunoendocrine aspects of panic disorder. *Neuropsychobiology* 1992;26(1-2):12-22.

[41] Curtis GC, Abelson JL, Gold PW. Adrenocorticotropic hormone and cortisol responses to corticotropin-releasing hormone: changes in panic disorder and effects of alprazolam treatment. *Biol Psychiatry* 1997;41(1):76-85.

[42] Heuser I, Yassouridis A, Holsboer F. The combined dexamethasone/CRH test: a refined laboratory test for psychiatric disorders. *J Psychiatr Res* 1994;28(4):341-356.

[43] Watson S, Gallagher P, Smith MS, Ferrier IN, Young AH. The dex/CRH test--is it better than the DST? *Psychoneuroendocrinology* 2006;31(7):889-894.

[44] Kunzel HE, Binder EB, Nickel T, Ising M, Fuchs B, Majer M, et al. Pharmacological and nonpharmacological factors influencing hypothalamic-pituitary-adrenocortical axis reactivity in acutely depressed psychiatric in-patients, measured by the Dex-CRH test. *Neuropsychopharmacology* 2003;28(12):2169-2178.

[45] Petrowski K, Wintermann GB, Kirschbaum C, Bornstein SR. Dissociation between ACTH and cortisol response in DEX-CRH test in patients with panic disorder. *Psychoneuroendocrinology* 2012;37(8):1199-1208.

[46] Petrowski K, Wintermann G-B, Kirschbaum C, Bornstein SR. A Comorbid Major Depression in Patients with Panic Disorder Affects the HPA Axis Response in the DEX-CRH Test. *Journal of Psychophysiology* 2014;28(4):257-264.

[47] Seier FE, Kellner M, Yassouridis A, Heese R, Strian F, Wiedemann K. Autonomic reactivity and hormonal secretion in lactate-induced panic attacks. *Am J Physiol* 1997;272(6 Pt 2):H2630-2638.

[48] van Duinen MA, Schruers KR, Jaegers E, Maes M, Griez EJ. Salivary cortisol in panic: are males more vulnerable? *Neuro Endocrinol Lett* 2004;25(5):386-390.

[49] Masdrakis VG, Markianos M, Oulis P. Lack of specific association between panicogenic properties of caffeine and HPA-axis activation. A placebo-controlled study of caffeine challenge in patients with panic disorder. *Psychiatry Res* 2015;229(1-2):75-81.

[50] Silva M, Hetem LA, Guimaraes FS, Graeff FG. Opposite effects of nefazodone in two human models of anxiety. *Psychopharmacology (Berl)* 2001;156(4):454-460.

[51] Garcia-Leal C, Parente AC, Del-Ben CM, Guimaraes FS, Moreira AC, Elias LL, et al. Anxiety and salivary cortisol in symptomatic and nonsymptomatic panic patients and healthy volunteers performing simulated public speaking. *Psychiatry Res* 2005;133(2-3):239-252.

[52] Hoehn T, Braune S, Scheibe G, Albus M. Physiological, biochemical and subjective parameters in anxiety patients with panic disorder during stress exposure as compared with healthy controls. *Eur Arch Psychiatry Clin Neurosci* 1997;247(5):264-274.

[53] Stones A, Groome D, Perry D, Hucklebridge F, Evans P. The effect of stress on salivary cortisol in panic disorder patients. *J Affect Disord* 1999;52(1-3):197-201.

[54] Dickerson SS, Kemeny ME. Acute stressors and cortisol responses: a theoretical integration and synthesis of laboratory research. *Psychol Bull* 2004;130(3):355-391.

[55] Dickerson SS, Mycek PJ, Zaldivar F. Negative social evaluation, but not mere social presence, elicits cortisol responses to a laboratory stressor task. *Health Psychol* 2008;27(1):116-121.

[56] Kirschbaum C, Pirke KM, Hellhammer DH. The 'Trier Social Stress Test'--a tool for investigating psychobiological stress responses in a laboratory setting. *Neuropsychobiology* 1993;28(1-2):76-81.

[57] Schommer NC, Hellhammer DH, Kirschbaum C. Dissociation between reactivity of the hypothalamus-pituitary-adrenal axis and the sympathetic-adrenal-medullary system to repeated psychosocial stress. *Psychosom Med* 2003;65(3):450-460.

[58] Petrowski K, Wintermann GB, Schaarschmidt M, Bornstein SR, Kirschbaum C. Blunted salivary and plasma cortisol response in patients with panic disorder under psychosocial stress. *Int J Psychophysiol* 2013;88(1):35-39.

[59] Jezova D, Makatsori A, Duncko R, Moncek F, Jakubek M. High trait anxiety in healthy subjects is associated with low neuroendocrine activity during psychosocial stress. *Prog Neuropsychopharmacol Biol Psychiatry* 2004;28(8):1331-1336.

[60] McEwen BS. Stress, adaptation, and disease. Allostasis and allostatic load. *Ann N Y Acad Sci* 1998;840:33-44.

[61] McEwen BS. Protection and damage from acute and chronic stress: allostasis and allostatic overload and relevance to the pathophysiology of psychiatric disorders. *Ann N Y Acad Sci* 2004;1032:1-7.

[62] Fries E, Hesse J, Hellhammer J, Hellhammer DH. A new view on hypocortisolism. *Psychoneuroendocrinology* 2005;30(10):1010-1016.

[63] Bornstein SR, Engeland WC, Ehrhart-Bornstein M, Herman JP. Dissociation of ACTH and glucocorticoids. *Trends Endocrinol Metab* 2008;19(5):175-180.

[64] Rohleder N, Joksimovic L, Wolf JM, Kirschbaum C. Hypocortisolism and increased glucocorticoid sensitivity of pro-Inflammatory cytokine production in Bosnian war refugees with posttraumatic stress disorder. *Biol Psychiatry* 2004;55(7):745-751.

[65] Rohleder N, Wolf JM, Wolf OT. Glucocorticoid sensitivity of cognitive and inflammatory processes in depression and posttraumatic stress disorder. *Neurosci Biobehav Rev* 2010;35(1):104-114.

[66] Smoller JW, Pollack MH, Wassertheil-Smoller S, Jackson RD, Oberman A, Wong ND, et al. Panic attacks and risk of incident cardiovascular events among postmenopausal women in the Women's Health Initiative Observational Study. *Arch Gen Psychiatry* 2007;64(10):1153-1160.

[67] Hoge EA, Brandstetter K, Moshier S, Pollack MH, Wong KK, Simon NM. Broad spectrum of cytokine abnormalities in panic disorder and posttraumatic stress disorder. *Depress Anxiety* 2009;26(5):447-455.

[68] van Duinen MA, Schruers KR, Kenis GR, Wauters A, Delanghe J, Griez EJ, et al. Effects of experimental panic on neuroimmunological functioning. *J Psychosom Res* 2008;64(3):305-310.

[69] Wolf JM, Rohleder N, Bierhaus A, Nawroth PP, Kirschbaum C. Determinants of the NF-kappaB response to acute psychosocial stress in humans. *Brain Behav Immun* 2009;23(6):742-749.

[70] de Kloet ER. About stress hormones and resilience to psychopathology. *J Neuroendocrinol* 2008;20(6):885-892.

In: Panic Disorder
Editor: Yong-Ku Kim
ISBN: 978-1-53613-001-0

Chapter 9

NEUROBIOLOGY AND NEUROANATOMY OF PANIC DISORDER

Michel Bourin[*]
University of Nantes, Neurobiology of Anxiety and Depression ,
Nantes, France

INTRODUCTION

Panic disorder is an extremely common anxiety disorder since its prevalence rate, whole lifetime; in the population is 4.5%. It is associated with a mood disorder in 20% of cases [1). The main characteristic of the disorder is the sudden and unpredictable appearance of panic attacks. Symptoms of panic attack include palpitation, sweating, tremors or muscle twitches, a feeling of "blowing away" or a feeling of suffocation chest pain or discomfort, a feeling of dizziness, Instability, empty head or fainting impression, a derealisation (feelings of unreality) or depersonalization (being detached from oneself), fear of losing control of oneself to go mad, fear of dying. Consequently, comorbidity of panic disorder with medical illness is significant [2].

[*] Corresponding author E-mail: michel.bourin@univ-nantes.fr.

The interest of the neurobiology of panic attacks became apparent when it was discovered that they could be experimentally induced in the laboratory under controlled conditions. The fundamental observation was carried out by Pitts and McClure in 1967 which showed the induction of panic attacks by sodium lactate, based on the observation that anxious patients were intolerant to stress and developed concentrations of lactic acid [3].

Moreover, hyperpnoea is a reaction which is an integral part of the physical effort and the alert reaction. It is an innate mechanism for survival in case of danger. On the other hand, if we breathe rapidly or deeply without having significant muscular activity, breathing is poorly adapted to the state of our organism: it leads to the expulsion of carbon dioxide too quickly. This results in respiratory alkalosis that prevents oxygen from reaching the tissues. This causes changes in the nervous, cardio-vascular, cerebral and muscular levels. The experimental neurochemical provocation of panic attacks in sensitive subjects or healthy volunteers has considerably enriched our knowledge of the pathophysiology and psychopharmacology of panic disorder [4]. Furthermore, the use of substances having selective effects on particular neurotransmission systems has been widely developed. Their anxiolytic or anxiogenic effects can then be attributed to a specific mode of action on a neurotransmission system [5].

Today, our knowledge is the result of experiments in animals and humans that allow us to build coherent hypotheses. For example, a neuroanatomic model of panic disorder with brainstem, limbic and prefrontal cortex that would be involved in panic attacks, anticipatory anxiety and phobic avoidance, other models are more based on an "anatomical network of fear" [6].

In this chapter, we will mainly discuss the anomalies encountered in the various neurotransmission systems and the neuroanatomy of panic disorder.

1. Role of the Noradrenergic System

Redmond and Huang [7] were the first to assume that hyperactivity of the locus coeruleus (LC) is related to anxiety. Their theory was based on the observation that stimulation of the locus coerulus induced fear in monkeys. This behaviour appeared after electrical stimulation of the LC as well as after chemical stimulation with alpha-2 adrenergic receptor antagonists such as yohimbine.

Yohimbine acts by blocking the presynaptic alpha 2 receptor, increasing the amount of noradrenaline which is thus likely to stimulate the locus coeruleus. This hypothesis seemed to be confirmed when it was shown that yohimbine induced more anxiety and panic attacks in panic patients than in normal subjects [8]. These data suggest that the sensitivity of presynaptic alpha 2 receptors is increased in panic attackers. This is difficult to reconcile with the noradrenergic growth theory, however, it is possible that the sensitivity of alpha 2 autoreceptors may be decreased (as a primary mechanism leading to increased noradrenaline bioavailability or the result of down-regulation compensatory secondary to increased noradrenaline concentrations).

The anxiogenic effect of yohimbine, however, did not appear to be correlated with an increase in plasma noradrenaline in one study in 10 healthy volunteers, 10 mg per os diazepam antagonized anxiety induced by 30 mg per os of yohimbine but did not antagonize the increase in concentrations of the main metabolite of noradrenaline MHPG. One might argue that the fact that there has been no change in MHPG during panic attacks in many studies is due to their artificial nature, however, it should be noted that natural panic attacks not induced by pharmacological agent do not increase the blood concentrations of MHPG.

Therapeutic studies in panic disorder seem to be arguments against the role of alpha 2 receptor abnormalities in panic. If norepinephrine hyperactivity is involved in panic states, it would have been hoped that compounds that decrease noradrenergic activity may be active in therapy, which is not the case. In contrast, clonidine agonist alpha 2 receptors appears to be effective in the treatment of respiratory signs of panic disorder, so it could play a crucial role on the anxiety symptoms induced by noradrenergic hyperactivity in these patients. [9] Generally speaking, stimulation of the LC generates fear and anxiety [10]. Yohimbine was studied in the role of avoidance-oriented coping strategies and fear of anxiety-related symptoms as risk and maintenance factors in the development of panic symptoms, particularly within a biological challenge model [11].

2. Role of the Serotoninergic System

Many animal studies show that decreased serotonergic function leads to reduced anxiety while its increase can induce anxiety. Studies in humans demonstrate that serotonin acts on 3 receptor subtypes, 5-HT1a, 5-HT2, and 5-HT3, which are thought to be involved in the regulation of anxiety [12, 13]. In humans m-chloro-phenyl-piperazine (mCPP) which is a 5-HT1 and 5-HT2 receptor agonist induces anxiety. The mCPP injected intravenously at a dose of 0.1 mg / kg induces anxiety and panic attacks in panic patients as in healthy subjects. Using lower oral doses (0.25 mg / kg), it was found that mCPP may increase anxiety and panic attacks in panic patients but not in normal subjects [14].

Thus, the hypothesis was made that panic patients are hypersensitive to the anxiogenic effects of mCPP; this is probably due to an increase in the post-synaptic sensitivity of 5-HT receptors. Hormonal responses to the mCPP seem to corroborate these assumptions. While a low dose of mCPP at 0.25 mg/kg orally induces an increase in cortisol release only in panic disorder patients, higher doses, i.e., 0.1 mg/kg and this time intravenously increases the cortisol level in both patients and control subjects. Oral administration of fenfluramine (long used as an anorectic agent), which is a 5-HT2b agonist, provides additional information on the hypothesis of hypersensitivity to receptors [15]. Fenfluramine induces anxiety and panic attacks and increases the release of cortisol and prolactin in female panic attackers in contrast to normal subjects and patients with major depression.

If the increase in serotonergic function is anxiogenic and some 5-HT receptors are hypersensitive in panic attackers, it is hoped that treatment with 5-HT agonists will lead to worsening in panic attackers. This seems to be the case in the therapeutic studies in panickers with indirect serotonergic agonists such as 5-hydroxy-tryptophan (5-HTP), clomipramine and fluvoxamine which are serotonin reuptake inhibitors Evidence of biphasic responses, i.e., there is an improvement following an exacerbation of the initial symptom [16]. This aggravation could be attributed to increased noradrenergic activity. However, there has been reported a diphasic effect with much purer serotonin reuptake inhibitors such as fluvoxamine and fluoxetine. The anti-panic efficacy of 5-HT agonists was explained by the fact that there could be downregulation of these hypersensitive serotoninergic receptors.

3. The Role of the GABA-Ergic System

Several studies using an antagonist and an agonist have shown in a formal way that the benzodiazepine site may be involved in panic disorder. Nutt et al. [17] showed that intravenous injection of 2 mg of flumazenil was able to induce panic attacks in eight patients (in a group of 10) with panic disorder. All patients experienced severe or severe anxiety, the onset of the disorder was rapid and the effects were considered by patients to be the neighbors of a non induced panic attack. These results cannot be attributed to the concomitant or recent use of alcohol or benzodiazepines at addictive doses.

Another study using a 1 mg/intravenous dose of flumazenil in anxiety patients treated with benzodiazepines illustrates the problem of validating an inducing agent. Patients became anxious after flumazenil administration and two with panic disorder had a panic attack. This goes against the theory of inversion of action of the receptor after administration of benzodiazepines. Indeed, it should be possible to block the effect of flumazenil by benzodiazepines. It is possible that panic disorder is linked to hyposensitivity to benzodiazepine agonists [18].

On the other hand, a significant decrease in GABA, expressed as the ratio of GABA over total creatine was detected in the anterior cingulate cortex/medial prefrontal cortex in PD patients, which tends to be pronounced in patients with a PD family history [19].

4. Role of Cholecystokinine

Researches have led to the hypothesis that the alteration of the CCK-ergic system could contribute to the pathophysiology of panic disorder [20].

The starting point of these studies is an electrophysiological experimentation which showed that benzodiazepine agonists selectively and specifically antagonized the CCK-8-induced excitation of hippocampal pyramidal neurons in rats [21]. These studies proved that benzodiazepines could antagonize the central action of a neuropeptide thus posing the problem of the anxiolytic mechanism of action of benzodiazepines. On the other hand, the fact that an anxiolytic can block the excitatory action of CCK raised the question of whether CCK was not an endogenous anxiogenic agent. Two pilot studies, one in patients with panic disorder and the other in healthy volunteers with no personal or family history of panic attack, were conducted using the CCK tetrapeptide, CCK-4. The decision to administer CCK-4 to patients with panic disorder was based on an anecdotal fact presented at a conference by a biochemist who, while studying the neuroendocrine effects of CCK-4 in healthy volunteers, observed that this substance produced "side effects" such as anxiety, dyspnea and depersonalization [22]. These symptoms were very similar to those encountered by patients during their spontaneous panic attacks.

De Montigny was the first to report that CCK-4 was able to induce panic attacks in the healthy volunteer and that these effects were attenuated by lorazepam [23]. Furthermore, Bradwjen et al. [24] administered CCK-4 to patients with panic disorder according to a double-blind, placebo-controlled method. Intravenous injection of CCK-4 (50 microg) resulted in DSM III R panic attacks in 11 patients, while none of the patients who received placebo had a panic attack. Treatment with CCK-4 induces an average of 12 symptoms per patient, the most common symptoms being: dyspnea, heart palpitations, chest pain, feeling faint or dizzy, paresthesia, flushing, Nausea, abdominal discomfort, anxiety, fear, apprehension and fear of loss of control. Another study showed that the number of symptoms and their intensity were greater when using 50 microg than 25 micrograms [25]. Panic attacks were more prevalent in patients with panic disorder than in healthy volunteers after injection of 25 microg of CCK-4 (91% versus 17%) and 50 microg (100% versus 47%). However, the nature of the symptoms as well as their number or intensity were remarkably identical in patients and healthy volunteers for the dose of 50 microg [26]. These results have been confirmed by studies using pentagastrin, a CCK agonist pentapeptide which has the same amino acid sequence as CCK-4. These authors found that pentagastrin induced panic attacks with a higher rate in patients with panic disorder than in healthy volunteers [27].

On the other hand, patients with panic disorder show a decrease in CCK-8s concentration in their cerebrospinal fluid compared to healthy volunteers [28]. Concentrations of CCK-8s are also decreased in patients' lymphocytes than in healthy volunteers [29]. These data are in favor of CCK system abnormalities due to panic disorder.

Anti-panic drugs, and not the other compounds, block the effects of CCK-4. It has been shown that the panicogenic effects of CCK-4 can be antagonized by chronic treatment with imipramine [30].

Studies using CCK-B receptor antagonists have been conducted [31]. In one study, the pretreatment of patients with a selective CCK-B receptor antagonist, L-365,260, was able to block the effects induced by CCK-4 [32]. In another study of action of another CCK-B antagonist, CI-988 was evaluated; there was a significant decrease in the intensity of the scores and the frequency of panic attacks [33]. These results confirm the role of CCK-B receptors in the panicogenic mechanism of CCK-4. However, a placebo-controlled clinical trial involving L-365,260 showed no improvement in patients with panic disorder. The possible reasons for the lack of activity of this compound in the prevention of spontaneous panic attacks are unclear; however it is possible to explain this failure by poor bioavailability of this compound used in this oral test. Now for years there are animal studies with CCK-B antagonists but there are no new compounds developed in clinical trials so far.

5. Neuroanatomy of Panic Disorder

The panic problem resembles the upper part of the cerebral system of fear [34]. Through various animal models, researchers are beginning to understand the anatomical structures influencing anxiety [35].

5.1. The Amygdala

This complex structure is composed of 13 nuclei receiving afferences from different brain areas and assemblages able to intervene in the rapid acquisition of behaviors based on events having an impact on the organism and an emotional impact. Among these different nuclei, three are more particularly involved in circuits of conditioned fear: the basal nucleus, the lateral nucleus and the central nucleus [36].

The amygdala appears to be heavily involved in managing unpredictable situations, as well as conditioned fear. Sensory information from different cortical areas leads to the lateral nucleus and the basolateral nucleus of the amygdala which in turn project towards the central nucleus of the amygdala [37]. The lateral nucleus appears to be responsible for the consolidation of memory and plasticity in conditioned memory [38].

This set of nuclei forms a complex system regulating fear and involving the expression and acquisition of conditioned fear. The basolateral core also serves as a connection between the lateral core and the central core. The latter projects towards several areas intervening in the expression of anxiety and fear. Moreover, this structure seems to constitute an interface between external sensory stimuli and the motor response necessary for learning and behavioral responses induced by fear. This nucleus therefore appears to be related to the detection and validation of threatening stimuli [39]. Lesions of the lateral or central nucleus may alter the acquisition of conditioned fear, and lesions of the basolateral nucleus may also affect responses of fear, or the sensory aspect of emotionally neutral events [40].

Exposure to a non-predictable auditory stimulus appears to activate the baso-lateral nucleus and trigger an increase in anxiety behaviors in the Rat's EPM [41]. The central and basolateral nucleus appear to be strongly involved in the acquisition and expression of fear of stimuli conditioned by electric shocks [42].

There are many relationships between the amygdala and the systems involved in the reaction to a stimulus triggering fear. Thus, there is a link between the amygdala and the sympathetic nervous system (hypothalamus), hemodynamic parameters (vagus nerve, solitary tract, ventral marrow), respiratory system (parabrachial nucleus) the endocrine system (paraventricular nucleus or terminal stria) [43, 44].

It is important to note that there are direct projections of the amygdala towards the locus coeruleus (noradrenergic system), or indirectly via the serotonergic neurons of the raphe (serotonergic system) involved in motor performance during fear [45]. Finally, there are projections between some areas of the ventral hippocampus (CA1 and the subiculum) and the basolateral and basomedial nuclei of the amygdala.

In conclusion, animal and human studies suggest that the amygdala, which plays a pivotal role in neural network of fear and anxiety, has an important role in the pathogenesis of PD [46].

5.2. The Gray Periaqueductal Substance (PAG)

Numerous studies have demonstrated a major involvement of PAG in anxiety and fear reactions [47, 48].

PAG contains a large amount of GABAergic neurons, which presupposes a role in aversion and anxiety [49]. Injecting antagonists into the BZD site of the GABAA receptors produces an increase in the discharge of neurons from the PAG [50]. In addition, close relationships between the amygdala and PAG were observed in the mechanisms involved in the management of fear-related stimuli [51].

In man, the stimulation of PAG generates fear. It has been suggested that in a dangerous situation, the amygdala regions are activated and stimulate the PAG using their direct projections, a process that leads to defense reactions [52]. Behbehani and his team hypothesized that in the presence of danger signals, amygdala projections activate the ventral region of the PAG, causing a prostration posture [50]. On the other hand, in the presence of an immediate danger (a rat finds itself in front of a cat); it is the lateral region of the PAG that would be activated by the amygdala and produce a leakage reaction often associated with vocalizations.

In summary, data from studies with humans have suggested that abnormalities of midbrain structures, including the periaqueductal gray matter (PAG), could be involved in the neurobiology of panic disorder (PD). The electrical stimulation of the PAG in neurosurgical patients induces panic-like symptoms and the effect of drugs that are effective in the treatment of PD in the simulation of public speaking model of anxiety is in agreement with data from animal models of PD [53].

5.3. The Hippocampus

The hippocampus consists of different regions forming a functionally heterogeneous structure, presumably because of their respective connectivity and narrow interconnections [54]. We can distinguish mainly the horn of Ammon consisting of 3 areas: CA1, CA2 and CA3, as well as the toothed gyrus. Among the numerous connections with other structures, the hippocampus is linked to the amygdala, the nucleus of the raphe and the locus coeruleus [55]. This structure belongs to the neural circuit responsible for the expression of aversive states, proposed by Graeff, with the amygdala, the gray periventricular gray matter and the PAG [56].

It seems, moreover, that there is a close relationship between the hippocampus and the amygdala in tasks of spatial discrimination [57]. Some researchers thus hypothesize that there is competition between the cerebral structures involved in the development of a behavioral response; Such as the hippocampus and the amygdala, in a test for preferential conditioning using spatial indices in the acquisition and processing of external information in relation to the situation [58].

CONCLUSION

Gorman et al. [59] proposed a comprehensive neuroanatomical model of PD, which suggested that fear and anxiety-related responses are mediated by a so-called "fear network" which is centered in the amygdala and includes the hippocampus, thalamus, hypothalamus, periaqueductal gray region, locus coeruleus and other brainstem sites. On the other hand, here are still many uncertainties regarding the neurobiology and neuroanatomy of panic disorder [60].

Donald Klein theorized on the notion of the false alarm of suffocation [61], as if the subject had bad regulation at the respiratory level and suffocated causing a panic attack. Indeed, lactic acidosis, CO2 or even CCK-4 can result from this lack of respiratory regulation and lead to a panic attack. This is the only integrative theory that is, to date, proposed of panic attack.

It would now be necessary to confirm or reject this theory, to integrate all the neurobiological and neuroanatomical data already known.

REFERENCES

[1] Goodwin GM. The overlap between anxiety, depression, and obsessive-compulsive disorder. *Dialogues Clin Neurosci.* (2015) 17(3):249-60.

[2] Meuret AE, Kroll J, Ritz T. Panic Disorder Comorbidity with Medical Conditions and Treatment Implications. *Annu Rev Clin Psychol.* (2017) 13:209-240.

[3] Pitts FM, McClure JM Lactate metabolism in anxiety neurosis. (1967) *N Engl J Med,* 277(25)1329-36.

[4] Kellner M Experimental panic provocation in healthy man-a translational role in anti-panic drug development (2011) *Dialogues Clin Neurosci.* 12(4) 485-493.

[5] Bourin M, Baker GB, Bradwejn J. Neurobiology of panic disorder. *J Psychosom Res.* (1998) 44(1):163-80.

[6] Miles L, Davis M, Walker D. Phasic and sustained fear are pharmacologically dissociable in rats. *Neuropsychopharmacology.* (2011) 36(8):1563-74.

[7] Redmond DE Jr, Huang YH. Current concepts. II. New evidence for a locus coeruleus-norepinephrine connection with anxiety. *Life Sci.* (1979) 25(26): 2149-62.

[8] Charney DS, Woods SW, Goodman WK, Heninger GR. Neurobiological mechanisms of panic anxiety: biochemical and behavioral correlates of yohimbine-induced panic attacks. *Am J Psychiatry.* (1987) 144(8):1030-6.

[9] Valença AM, Nardi AE, Mezzasalma MA, Nascimento I, Lopes FL, Zin WA, Versiani M. Clonidine in respiratory panic disorder subtype. *Arq Neuropsiquiatr.* (2004) 62(2B):396-8.

[10] Charney DS, Redmond DE Jr. Neurobiological mechanisms in human anxiety. Evidence supporting central noradrenergic hyperactivity. *Neuropharmacology.* (1983) 22(12B):1531-6.

[11] Kaplan JS, Arnkoff DB, Glass CR, Tinsley R, Geraci M, Hernandez E, Luckenbaugh D, Drevets WC, Carlson PJ. Avoidant coping in panic disorder: a yohimbine biological challenge study. *Anxiety Stress Coping.* (2012) 25(4):425-42.

[12] Bourin M. Serotoninergic Systems in Anxiety. *JSM Anxiety Depress* 2016 1: 1007.

[13] Chagraoui A, Thibaut F, Skiba M, Thuillez C, Bourin M. 5-HT2C receptors in psychiatric disorders *Prog Neuropsychopharmacol Biol Psychiatry.* (2016) 66:120-35.

[14] Kahn RS, Kalus O, Wetzler S, Cahn W, Asnis GM, van Praag HM. Effects of serotonin antagonists on m-chlorophenylpiperazine-mediated responses in normal subjects. *Psychiatry Res.* (1990) 33(2):189-98.

[15] Mortimore C, Anderson IM. d-Fenfluramine in panic disorder: a dual role for 5-hydroxytryptamine.*Psychopharmacology (Berl).* (2000) 149(3):251-8.

[16] Charney DS, Woods SW, Goodman WK, Heninger GR. Serotonin function in anxiety. II. Effects of the serotonin agonist MCPP in panic disorder patients and healthy subjects. *Psychopharmacology (Berl).* (1987) 92(1):14-24.

[17] Nutt DJ, Glue P, Lawson C, Wilson S. Flumazenil provocation of panic attacks. Evidence for altered benzodiazepine receptor sensitivity in panic disorder. *Arch Gen Psychiatry*. (1990) 47(10):917-25.

[18] Arora DS, Nimitvilai S, Teppen TL, McElvain MA, Sakharkar AJ, You C, Pandey SC, Brodie MS Hyposensitivity to gamma-aminobutyric acid in the ventral tegmental area during alcohol withdrawal: reversal by histone deacetylase inhibitors. *Neuropsychopharmacology*. (2013)38(9):1674-84.

[19] Long Z, Medlock C, Dzemidzic M, Shin YW, Goddard AW, Dydak U. Decreased GABA levels in anterior cingulate cortex/medial prefrontal cortex in panic disorder. *Prog Neuropsychopharmacol Biol Psychiatry*. (2013) 44:131-5.

[20] Bourin M, Dailly E. Cholecystokinin and panic disorder. *Acta Neuropsychiatr*. (2004) 16(2):85-93.

[21] Bradwejn J, de Montigny C. Benzodiazepines antagonize cholecystokinin-induced activation of rat hippocampal neurons. *Nature*. (1984)312(5992):363-4.

[22] Rehfeld JF. Cholecystokinin-From Local Gut Hormone to Ubiquitous Messenger. *Front Endocrinol (Lausanne)* (2017) 8:47.

[23] de Montigny C. Cholecystokinin tetrapeptide induces panic-like attacks in healthy volunteers. Preliminary findings. *Arch Gen Psychiatry*. (1989) 46(6):511-7.

[24] Bradwejn J, Koszycki D, Shriqui C.Enhanced sensitivity to cholecystokinin tetrapeptide in panic disorder. Clinical and behavioral findings. *Arch Gen Psychiatry*. (1991) 48(7):603-10.

[25] Bradwejn J, Koszycki D, Bourin M. Dose ranging study of the effects of cholecystokinin in healthy volunteers. *J Psychiatry Neurosci*. (1991)16(2):91-5.

[26] Bradwejn J, Koszycki D, Payeur R, Bourin M, Borthwick H Replication of action of cholecystokinin tetrapeptide in panic disorder: clinical and behavioral findings. *Am J Psychiatry*. (1992) 149(7):962-4.

[27] van Megen HJ, Westenberg HG, den Boer JA, Haigh JR, Traub M. Pentagastrin induced panic attacks: enhanced sensitivity in panic disorder patients. *Psychopharmacology (Berl).* (1994) 114(3):449-55.

[28] Gunnarsson T, Eklundh T, Eriksson M, Qureshi GA, Sjöberg S, Nordin C. Cholecystokinin peptides in cerebrospinal fluid: a study in healthy male subjects. *Regul Pept.* (1997) 68(1):57-61.

[29] Brambilla F, Bellodi L, Perna G, Garberi A, Panerai A, Sacerdote P. Lymphocyte cholecystokinin concentrations in panic disorder. *Am J Psychiatry.* (1993)15(7):1111-3.

[30] Bradwejn J, Koszycki D. Imipramine antagonism of the panicogenic effects of cholecystokinin tetrapeptide in panic disorder patients. *Am J Psychiatry.* (1994) 151(2):261-3.

[31] Zwanzger P, Domschke K, Bradwejn J. Neuronal network of panic disorder: the role of the neuropeptide cholecystokinin. *Depress Anxiety.* (2012) 29(9):762-74.

[32] Bradwejn J, Koszycki D, Couëtoux du Tertre A, van Megen H, den Boer J, Westenberg H. The panicogenic effects of cholecystokinin-tetrapeptide are antagonized by L-365,260, a central cholecystokinin receptor antagonist, in patients with panic disorder. *Arch Gen Psychiatry.* (1994) 51(6):486-93.

[33] Bradwejn J, Koszycki D, Paradis M, Reece P, Hinton J, Sedman A. Effect of CI-988 on cholecystokinin tetrapeptide-induced panic symptoms in healthy volunteers. *Biol Psychiatry.* (1995) 38(11):742-6.

[34] Duval ER, Javanbakht A, Liberzon I. Neural circuits in anxiety and stress disorders: a focused review. *Ther Clin Risk Manag.* (2015)11:115-26.

[35] Steimer T. The biology of fear- and anxiety-related behaviors. *Dialogues Clin Neurosci.* (2002) 4(3):231-49.

[36] Penzo MA, Robert V, Li B. Fear conditioning potentiates synaptic transmission onto long-range projection neurons in the lateral subdivision of central amygdala. *J Neurosci.* (2014) 34(7):2432-7.

[37] Marek R, Strobel C, Bredy TW, Sah P.The amygdala and medial prefrontal cortex: partners in the fear circuit. *J Physiol.* (2013)591(10):2381-91.

[38] Sears RM, Schiff HC, LeDoux JE.Molecular mechanisms of threat learning in the lateral nucleus of the amygdala. *Prog Mol Biol Transl Sci.* (2014)122:263-304.

[39] Théberge FR, Milton AL, Belin D, Lee JL, Everitt BJ. The basolateral amygdala and nucleus accumbens core mediate dissociable aspects of drug memory reconsolidation. *Learn Mem.* (2010) 17(9):444-53.

[40] Phelps EA, LeDoux JE Contributions of the amygdala to emotion processing: from animal models to human behavior *Neuron.* (2005) 48(2):175-87.

[41] Janak PH, Tye KM. From circuits to behaviour in the amygdala. *Nature.* (2015) 517(7534):284-92.

[42] Kim JJ, Jung MW. Neural circuits and mechanisms involved in Pavlovian fear conditioning: a critical review. *Neurosci Biobehav Rev.* (2006)30(2):188-202.

[43] Frysinger RC, Harper RM. Cardiac and respiratory correlations with unit discharge in human amygdala and hippocampus. *Electroencephalogr Clin Neurophysiol.* (1989)72(6):463-70.

[44] Abelson JL, Khan S, Liberzon I, Young EA HPA axis activity in patients with panic disorder: review and synthesis of four studies. *Depress Anxiety.* (2007) 24(1):66-76.

[45] Ressler KJ. Amygdala activity, fear, and anxiety: modulation by stress. *Biol Psychiatry.* (2010) 67(12):1117-9.

[46] Kim JE, Dager SR, Lyoo IK. The role of the amygdala in the pathophysiology of panic disorder: evidence from neuroimaging studies. *Biol Mood Anxiety Disord.* (2012) 20:2:20.

[47] Graeff FG. Serotonin, the periaqueductal gray and panic. *Neurosci Biobehav Rev.* (2004) 28(3):239-59.

[48] Bertoglio LJ, Anzini C, Lino-de-Oliveira C, Carobrez AP. Enhanced dorsolateral periaqueductal gray activity counteracts the anxiolytic

response to midazolam on the elevated plus-maze Trial 2 in rats. *Behav Brain Res.* (2005) 162(1):99-107.

[49] Li G, Shao C, Chen Q, Wang Q, Yang K Accumulated GABA activates presynaptic GABAB receptors and inhibits both excitatory and inhibitory synaptic transmission in rat midbrain periaqueductal gray. *Neuroreport.* (2017) 28(6):313-318.

[50] Behbehani MM, Jiang MR, Chandler SD, Ennis M.The effect of GABA and its antagonists on midbrain periaqueductal gray neurons in the rat. *Pain.* (1990) 40(2):195-204.

[51] Kim EJ, Horovitz O, Pellman BA, Tan LM, Li Q, Richter-Levin G, Kim JJ. Dorsal periaqueductal gray-amygdala pathway conveys both innate and learned fear responses in rats. *Proc Natl Acad Sci U S A.* (2013) 110(36):14795-800.

[52] Rizvi TA, Ennis M, Behbehani M, Shipley MT Connections between the central nucleus of the amygdala and the midbrain periaqueductal gray: topography and reciprocity. *Journal of Comparative Neurology.* (1991) 303(1): 121-131.

[53] Graeff FG, Del-Ben CM. Neurobiology of panic disorder: from animal models to brain neuroimaging. *Neurosci Biobehav Rev.* (2008) 32(7): 1326-35.

[54] Tau GZ, Peterson BS. Normal development of brain circuits. *Neuropsychopharmacology.* (2010) 35(1):147-68.

[55] McDonald RJ, White NM. A triple dissociation of memory systems: Hippocampus, amygdala, and dorsal striatum. *Behav Neurosci.* (2013) 127(2):835-53.

[56] Waddell J, Morris RW, Bouton ME. Effects of bed nucleus of the stria terminalis lesions on conditioned anxiety: aversive conditioning with long-duration conditional stimuli and reinstatement of extinguished fear. *Behav Neurosci.* (2006) 120(2):324-36.

[57] Gaskin S, White NM. Parallel processing of information about location in the amygdala, entorhinal cortex and hippocampus. *Hippocampus.* (2013) 23(11):1075-83.

[58] Holahan MR. Complementary roles for the amygdala and hippocampus during different phases of appetitive information processing. *Neurobiol Learn Mem*. (2005) 84(2):124-31.
[59] Gorman JM, Kent JM, Sullivan GM, Coplan JD. Neuroanatomical hypothesis of panic disorder, revised. *Am J Psychiatry*. (2000)157(4):493-505.
[60] Sobanski T, Wagner G. Functional neuroanatomy in panic disorder: Status quo of the research. *World J Psychiatry*. (2017) 7(1):12-33.
[61] Klein DF. False suffocation alarms, spontaneous panics, and related conditions. An integrative hypothesis. *Arch Gen Psychiatry*. (1993) 50(4):306-17.

In: Panic Disorder
Editor: Yong-Ku Kim

ISBN: 978-1-53613-001-0

Chapter 10

Pharmacological and Non-Pharmacological Approaches for Treatment-Resistant Panic Disorder

Rafael C. Freire**, *Morena M. Zugliani, Rafael F. Garcia and Antonio E. Nardi

Laboratory of Panic and Respiration, Institute of Psychiatry, Federal University of Rio de Janeiro, Rio de Janeiro, Brazil

Abstract

Panic disorder (PD) is an anxiety disorder with a high prevalence in the world population, and it is likely to bring about high unemployment rates, work impairment and treatment-seeking behavior. The most effective treatments for this disorder are the psychological and pharmacological ones. However, these treatments are effective only to 70% of the patients; thus, one third of all PD patients do not achieve remission after treatment, and keep on presenting persistent panic attacks

* Corresponding author. E-mail: rafaelcrfreire@gmail.com.

and other panic symptoms throughout their lives. In this chapter, we review the evidences regarding alternative treatments for adult patients with treatment-resistant PD. There are not enough articles addressing refractory PD, most of them being open studies. Long-term clinical trials for these patients are needed. Monotherapy with reboxetine or olanzapine, as well as augmentation with pindolol, divalproex sodium, aripiprazole, olanzapine, risperidone or sulpiride may be effective for patients with treatment-resistant PD. Augmentation with quetiapine was not effective in these patients. Augmentation of the pharmacological treatment with cognitive-behavioral therapy may also be an effective strategy for refractory PD.

Keywords: agoraphobia, clinical trial, cognitive-behavioral therapy, panic attack, anxiety

1. Introduction

The 12-month prevalence of anxiety disorders ranges from 14.0% to 19.9% in the general population [1, 2] and these disorders are the most important causes of disability and work impairment, along with chronic pain and mood disorders. [3-5] In the general population, the 12-month prevalence of panic disorder (PD) ranges from 1.1% to 2.8% and for agoraphobia from 0.8% to 2.0%. [1, 2, 5, 6] The lifetime prevalence is even higher, 7.2% - 28.3% for panic attacks, 3.4% - 4.7% for panic disorder and 1.9% for agoraphobia. [5, 6] Patients with PD have high unemployment rates, show significant work impairment, seek medical treatment more frequently and have more hospitalizations than people without PD symptoms. In addition, subthreshold PD is also associated to the same problems, [7] indicating that the treatment should always aim at achieving full remission of panic symptoms.

It was hypothesized that panic attacks are acute anxiety and fear episodes with somatic symptoms, which occur in subjects with abnormally sensitive fear networks, such as PD patients. In this network, the central nucleus of the amygdala gathers information from different brain regions and coordinates autonomic and behavioral responses. If there is a deficiency in the coordination of stimuli from the cortex and brainstem, an abnormal activation of the amygdala may be triggered, with behavioral, autonomic, and neuroendocrine activation. Compounds that increase the transmission in the serotonin or γ-aminobutyric-acid (GABA) systems have an inhibitory effect on the amygdala and on the fear-related structures. Some antidepressants increase noradrenergic activity and modulate the noradrenaline releases related to stressful situations, acting in the central nucleus of the amygdala and its projections by decreasing the sensitivity of the fear network, thus reducing the severity and frequency of panic attacks. [8, 9]

Guidelines, meta-analysis and other review studies indicate that several medications are effective in the treatment of PD, including antidepressants, benzodiazepines, and other classes of drugs. [2, 10-12] However, many PD patients do not respond adequately to treatment with these drugs. In clinical trials with fluvoxamine, sertraline, citalopram, escitalopram, paroxetine and clonazepam, with duration of eight to twelve weeks, 17% to 61% of the PD patients did not respond to treatment. [13, 14] In clinical trials with venlafaxine, the response rates were somew hat higher, from 68% to 89%, but 49% to 64% of the patients did not achieve remission after ten to twelve weeks of treatment. [15] In the general population, almost one half of PD patients do not achieve remission in the first year of treatment, and even after two years of treatment more than one third of the patients still have PD symptoms. [16]

In this chapter, we summarize and discuss all psychopharmacological agents which have demonstrated efficacy in the treatment of refractory PD. The authors analyzed studies with a broad spectrum of experimental designs and performed a qualitative systematic review of the evidence.

There is no consensus about the criteria for what is considered treatment-resistant PD. Some authors define treatment-resistance when patients do not respond to at least one [17, 18] or two [19-21] adequate 8-week treatment trials with drugs recognized as effective for PD or a standard course of cognitive-behavioral therapy (CBT). However, other authors consider treatment resistance when patients do not respond to at least one [22] or two [23] 6-week clinical trials. Another criterion for treatment-resistance used by some researchers is when patients show an incomplete response after three to four months of treatment. [24-27]

The drugs considered for this study were paroxetine, sertraline, escitalopram, fluoxetine, imipramine, trimipramine, moclobemide, reboxetine, aripiprazole, olanzapine, quetiapine, ziprasidone, sulpiride, sodium valproate, alprazolam, clonazepam, lithium, tiagabine, pindolol and d-fenfluramine.

2. Antidepressants

The augmentation of CBT with paroxetine was effective for treatment-resistant PD patients. [28] Forty-three patients who did not respond to 15 sessions of CBT were included in a randomized double blind controlled trial. During this 8-week trial, patients received paroxetine 40 mg/day or placebo, and all of them had four more sessions of CBT. In the CBT + paroxetine group, 74% of the patients became panic-free, while in the CBT + placebo group only 47% of them became panic free. There were improvements in all scales in both groups. The score change for the active drug was larger than the one for the placebo group in the Mobility Inventory (MI), but not in the Agoraphobic Cognitions Questionnaire (ACQ).

In a study from Simon et al., [22] patients who tolerated sertraline 100 mg/day or escitalopram 15 mg/day but did not achieve remission after 6 weeks of treatment were included in the next phase of this study. In the second phase, patients were randomized in double-blind fashion either to receive a higher dose of selective serotonin reuptake inhibitor (SSRI) or to remain in the same dose. Both groups had a decrease in the Panic Disorder Severity Scale (PDSS) scores, and there were no differences regarding other anxiety and depression scales. The high SSRI dose group failed to show differences compared to the low dose group.

The noradrenaline reuptake inhibitor reboxetine was administered to refractory PD patients in an open study from Dannon et al. [19] Washout of previous medications was performed, and then reboxetine 2 - 8 mg/day was started. After six weeks of treatment, the Panic Self-Questionnaire (PSQ) scores decreased 90%. Besides, panic symptoms, general anxiety and impairment also improved significantly.

Case reports indicate that the associations fluoxetine + tricyclic antidepressants (TCA), [29] imipramine + moclobemide + CBT, [30] or trimipramine + alprazolam [31] may also be effective for a number of patients.

3. Atypical Antipsychotics

One randomized double blind controlled study did not demonstrate efficacy of augmentation with quetiapine extended release in treatment-resistant PD. [32] Patients who did not respond or had a poor response to a 8-week trial with a SSRI or a serotonin and noradrenaline reuptake inhibitor (SNRI) were considered resistant to treatment. They were randomized to receive quetiapine flexible dose (50-400 mg/day) or placebo. After 8 weeks of treatment, both groups had improvements; 31% of the patients who received the active drug and 23% of the patients who received placebo achieved remission. There were no significant differences between both groups regarding primary and secondary measures.

In open studies, olanzapine and sulpiride showed efficacy for treatment-resistant PD as monotherapy. [20, 33] In the first study, [20] washout of previous medications was performed, and then olanzapine 2.5 - 20 mg/day was started. After an 8-week trial, panic attacks, anticipatory anxiety, phobic avoidance and impairment were significantly improved. In the second study, [33] sulpiride 100 mg/day, 150 mg/day or 200 mg/day was administered for 8 weeks, and there were substantial improvements in the number of panic attacks, Clinical Global Impression - Severity scale (CGI-S) scores and Hamilton Anxiety Rating Scale (HAM-A) scores. More than 60% of the patients achieved remission.

Atypical antipsychotics were used as augmentation of antidepressants and benzodiazepines in three open studies. In the first study, [18] aripiprazole 5 - 30 mg/day was administered for 8 weeks, and there was a significant reduction of CGI-S scores, but the decrease in the Panic Disorder Severity Scale (PDSS) scores was not statistically significant. In the second study, [23] in which olanzapine 5 mg/day was administered for 8 weeks, panic and anxiety symptoms were significantly reduced. In addition, 81% of the patients responded to this augmentation strategy and 58% achieved remission. In the third study, [34] augmentation with risperidone was effective for treatment-resistant anxiety disorder patients. Thirty patients with generalized anxiety disorder, social anxiety disorder or PD received risperidone 0.25 to 3.00 mg/day for 8 weeks and had significant improvements in the HAM-A and CGI-S scores. The 7 PD patients enrolled in this study also had significant decreases in the PDSS scores.

Case reports showed positive results with olanzapine, [35, 36] aripiprazole [37] and ziprasidone. [38] Ziprasidone had positive results as monotherapy or augmentation strategy in doses ranging from 40 to 80 mg/day. [38]

4. Mood Stabilizers

In refractory PD patients, the augmentation with divalproex sodium proved effective. In an open trial from Baetz et al., [17] divalproex sodium was administered for 8 weeks and the dose was adjusted to achieve serum levels between 45 and 90 μg/mL. Beside the improvement of anxiety and panic symptoms, there was also improvement of depressive and mood instability symptoms. Only patients with comorbid mood disorder and self-reported "mood instability" were included. Forty percent of the patients had concurrent use of antidepressants, benzodiazepines or both.

In a case series report, the association of sodium valproate and clonazepam showed positive results for four treatment-resistant PD patients. [39]

Table 1. Pharmacological studies

Trial	TRPD criteria	Number of patients (completed)	Type	Treatment	Dose	Trial duration (in weeks)	Outcome	Other information
Goddard et al. 2015	Previous treatment with one SSRI or SNRI in sufficient dose and poor response (CGI-I ≥ 3) after a 8-week trial.	27 (21)	RCDBCT - Aug	SSRI/SNRI + quetiapine XR OR SSRI/SNRI + PBO	SSRI/SRRI stable dose; quetiapine XR 50 - 400 mg/day	8	Not superior to PBO. Response (active/PBO): 46%/38%; Remission (active/PBO): 31%/23% ‡	Both groups improved over time.
Hirschmann et al. 2000	Previous treatment with at least two antidepressants and no response after a 8-week trial with fluoxetine 20 mg/day	26 (25)	RCDBCT - Aug	fluoxetine + pindolol OR fluoxetine + PBO	fluoxetine 20 mg/day; pindolol 7,5 mg/day	4	Superior to PBO; significant differences in PSQ (ES: 2.72), CGI-I (ES: 4.00), HAM-A, CAS+PA and NIMH Anxiety Scale **	The clinical changes noted with pindolol were evident by the second week of the study
Simon et al. 2009 – phase II	No response after 6-week trial with sertraline (up to 100 mg/day) or escitalopram (up to 15 mg/day)	24 (19)	RCDBCT - Aug	sertraline or escitalopram high dose OR PBO (no dose increase)	high dose – sertraline 150-200 mg/day; escitalopram 20-30 mg/day	6	Not superior to PBO, no significant differences in CGI-S (ES: 0.16) and PDSS (ES: 0.01); Significant improvement in PDSS in both groups †	

Table 1. (Continued)

Trial	TRPD criteria	Number of patients (completed)	Type	Treatment	Dose	Trial duration (in weeks)	Outcome	Other information
Baetz and Bowen 1998*	Not respond to one trial with CBT and medication (benzodiazepines or antidepressants)	13(10)	OS - Aug 40% of subjects using concurrent benzo-diazepines, antidepressants or both	divalproex sodium	minimum 500 mg/day; serum level 45-90 μg/mL	8	Significant improvement in PA (65% decrease in frequency), HAM-A, BAI, PGI (70% much or very much improved) and CGI-I (90% much or very much improved) scores **	
Dannon et al. 2002	Not respond to two adequate trials with SSRI (paroxetine 40 mg/day and fluoxetine 40mg/day, duration 8.4±4.3 weeks)	29(24)	OS	reboxetine	2 - 8 mg/day	6	Significant improvement in PSQ (90% decrease), HAM-A and GAF scores in patients with and without agoraphobia **	Short washout (paroxetine - 4 days; fluoxetine - 21 days) before study
Hoge et al. 2008	Not respond to one 8-week adequate trial (SSRI, SNRI, benzodiazepines, trazodone or bupropion)	10(7)	OS - Aug Concurrent use of antidepressant, benzo-diazepine or both	aripiprazole	5 - 30 mg/day	8	Significant improvement in CGI-S scores (17% decrease); no difference in PDSS scores (14% decrease); 10% achieved remission ***	Significant improvement in CGI-S and HAM-A in the combined group (PD and GAD)

Trial	TRPD criteria	Number of patients (completed)	Type	Treatment	Dose	Trial duration (in weeks)	Outcome	Other information
Hollifield et al. 2005	Not respond to two 8-week adequate trials (medication or CBT)	15(10)	OS	olanzapine	2.5 - 20 mg/day	8	Significant improvement in PAI - PA frequency (ES: 1.83), intensity (ES: 1.36) and anticipatory anxiety (ES: 1.18); Significant improvement in PPPDS - anticipatory anxiety (ES: 3.65), phobic avoidance (ES: 2.59) and impairment (ES: 2.18); Significant improvement in CGI-S scores (ES: 2.61) **	
Kampman et al. 2002	Not respond to 15 sessions of CBT	43 (38)	RCDBCT - Aug	CBT + paroxetine OR CBT + PBO	CBT 4 sessions; paroxetine 40 mg/day	8	Superior to PBO; significant differences in the MI, but not in ACQ; Remission (active/PBO): 74%/47% Δ	
Nunes et al. 2012	Not respond to two 8-week adequate pharmacological trials	19	OS	sulpiride	100 - 200 mg/day	8	Significant improvement in number of PA (ES: 2.76), CGI-S (ES: 6.88) and HAM-A (ES: 1.64). Remission: 63.2% Δ	

Table 1. (Continued)

Trial	TRPD criteria	Number of patients (completed)	Type	Treatment	Dose	Trial duration (in weeks)	Outcome	Other information
Sepede et al. 2006	Not responded previously to adequate therapeutic trials of either medication or CBT and not responded to current treatment (at least 6 weeks with paroxetine 40 mg/day or sertraline 150 mg/day)	31 (26)	OS - Aug Concurrent use of paroxetine 40 mg/day or sertraline 150 mg/day	olanzapine	5.0 mg/day	12	Significant improvement in PAAAS –PA frequency (ES: 2.36), PA duration (ES: 3.35) and anticipatory anxiety (ES: 3.74); Significant improvement in ACQ and HAM-A scores; Response 81%; Remission 58% ****	Improvements in HAM-D and GAF scales; significant and similar improvement in patients with or without agoraphobia
Simon et al. 2006	Previous treatment with one SSRI or SNRI or benzodiazepine in sufficient dose and no response after a 8-week trial.	30 (21)	OS - Aug Concurrent use of SSRI, SNRI or benzodiazepine	risperidone	0.25 - 3.00 mg/day	8	**Full sample** - significant improvement of HAM-A (ES: 0.87) and CGI-S (ES: 1.25) **PD subsample** - significant improvement of PDSS (ES: 1.00) **	Mixed sample (PD, GAD and SAD patients) with only 7 PD patients.

CAS+PA = Clinical Anxiety Scale with Panic Attacks; NIMH = National Institute of Mental Health; PBO = placebo; RCDBCT = Randomized controlled double-blind clinical trial; OS = Open study; Aug = Augmentation; ACQ = Agoraphobic Cognitions Questionnaire; BAI = Beck Anxiety Inventory; CBT = cognitive-behavioral therapy; CGI-I = Clinical Global Impression – Improvement; CGI-S = Clinical Global Impression – Severity; ES = effect size compared to baseline scores, Cohen's d; GAD = generalized anxiety disorder; GAF = Global Assessment of Functioning; HAM-A = Hamilton Rating Scale for Anxiety; HAM-D = Hamilton Rating Scale for Depression; MI = Mobility Inventory; PA = panic attack; PAAAS = Panic Attack and Anticipatory

Anxiety Scale; PAI = Panic Attack Inventory; PDSS = Panic Disorder Severity Scale; PGI = Patient Global Impression; PPPDS = Physicians Panic and Phobic Disorders Scale; PSQ = Panic Self-Questionnaire; SSRI = selective serotonin reuptake inhibitor; TRPD = treatment-resistant panic disorder.

* Subsample of patients with comorbid mood disorder and self-reported "mood instability".

** Response and remission were not defined in this study.

*** Remission criteria: CGI-S score of 1 or 2.

**** Response criteria: 50% decrease in number of panic attacks and CGI-I score of 1 or 2; remission criteria: no panic attacks and HAM-A score ≤ 7.

† Remission status: zero panic attacks for at least one week and a CGI-S score of 1 or 2.

‡ Response criterion: 50% decrease in PDSS scores; remission criterion: PDSS ≤ 4 at endpoint.

Δ Remission criterion: zero panic attacks for at least one week.

Table 2. Cognitive-behavioral therapy studies

Trial	TRPD criteria	Number of patients (completed)	Type	Number/type of sessions	Comparison	Trial duration (in weeks)	Outcome	Other information
Heldt et al. 2003	Residual symptoms of panic attacks, anticipatory anxiety and phobic avoidance after adequate trial with SSRI; on SSRI for four months	32(29)	OS - Aug Concurrent use of antianxiety or antidepressant medications	12 group sessions	no	16	Significant improvement in CGI-S (ES: 1.5), PA frequency (ES: 1.0), PA intensity (ES: 1.0), agoraphobia (PI) (ES: 1.5), anticipatory anxiety (PI) (ES: 1.0) and HAM-A scores (ES: 1.3); No PA 81%	Decrease in use of benzodia-zepines
Heldt et al. 2006(1)	Residual symptoms of panic attacks, anticipatory anxiety and phobic avoidance after adequate trial with SSRI; on SSRI for four months	71(64)	OS - Aug Concurrent use of antianxiety or antidepressant medications	12 group sessions	no	16	Significant improvement in CGI-S (ES: 2.2), PA (ES: 0.6), agoraphobia (ES: 1.3) (PI), anticipatory anxiety (ES: 1.1) (PI) and HAM-A scores (ES: 1.3); No PA 81%; Remission 64% *	Decrease in use of benzodia-zepines and antidepressants
Heldt et al. 2006(2)	Residual symptoms of panic attacks, anticipatory anxiety and phobic avoidance after adequate trial with SSRI; on SSRI for four months	36(32)	OS - Aug Concurrent use of antianxiety, antidepressant medications or lithium	12 group sessions	no	16	Significant improvement in CGI-S (ES: 2.3), PA (ES: 0.5), agoraphobia (ES: 1.0) (PI), anticipatory anxiety (ES: 0.9)(PI), HAM-A (ES: 1.1) and quality of life scores (ES: 0.9) (WHOQOL); No PA 75%; Remission 44% **	

Trial	TRPD criteria	Number of patients (completed)	Type	Number/type of sessions	Comparison	Trial duration (in weeks)	Outcome	Other information
Otto et al. 1999 †	Incomplete response after adequate 2-month trial with medication (SSRI, TCA, MAOI or benzodiazepine)	10(10)	OS - Aug Concurrent use of SSRI, TCA, MAOI or benzodiazepine	12 group sessions	no	12	Significant improvement in CGI-S (ES: 3.1) and PDSS (ES: 1.7); Remission 60% ***	
Pollack et al. 1994	Incomplete response after adequate 12-week trial with medication (imipramine, fluoxetine, phenelzine, clonazepam or alprazolam)	18(15)	OS - Aug Concurrent use of clonazepam, alprazolam, fluoxetine, TCA or lithium.	12 group sessions	no	12	Significant improvement in PA (ES:0.5) and CGI-S (ES: 1.6); Remission 40% ***	Persistent improvement after 1-8 months of follow-up
Simon et al. 2009 – phase III	No response after 12-week trial with sertraline (up to 200 mg/day) or escitalopram (up to 30 mg/day)	19(17)	HHRCT - Aug Concurrent use of escitalopram (15-30 mg/day) or sertraline (100-200 mg/day)	12 group sessions	CLZ 0.5 - 4.0 mg/day	12	No significant difference between the two treatments; Significant improvement in CGI-S (ES: 1.0) and PDSS (ES: 0.6); Remission CLZ 11%, CBT 10% **	

Aug = Augmentation; OS = Open study; HHRCT = Head-to-head randomized clinical trial; CBT = Cognitive-behavioral therapy; CGI-S = Clinical Global Impression – Severity; CLZ = clonazepam; ES = effect size compared to baseline scores, Cohen's d; HAM-A = Hamilton Rating Scale for Anxiety; MAOI = monoamine oxidase inhibitor; PA = panic attack; PDSS = Panic Disorder Severity Scale; PI = Panic Inventory; SSRI = selective serotonin reuptake inhibitor; TCA = tricyclic antidepressant; TRPD = treatment-resistant panic disorder; WHOQOL = World Health Organization Quality of Life Instrument – Short Version.

* Remission was defined by no panic attacks and CGI-S < 3 for at least two months (evaluation made 12 months after the end of the treatment).

** Remission was defined as the absence of PA and CGI-S < 3.

*** Remission was defined as CGI-S < 3.

† Only the results referring to treatment-resistant PD patients were included in this table.

5. Other Drugs

In a double-blind controlled randomized trial from Hirschmann et al. [21] pindolol 7.5 mg/day or placebo were added to fluoxetine 20 mg/day in a 4-week clinical trial. Patients on pindolol and fluoxetine had significant improvements in PSQ (Cohen's d = 2.72) and Clinical Global Impression – Improvement scale (CGI-I) (Cohen's d = 4.00), compared to patients taking fluoxetine monotherapy. There were significant improvements in other panic and anxiety scales, although but no differences regarding depression symptoms showed up. There were significant improvements in anxiety symptoms after two weeks of treatment.

Case reports indicated that tiagabine, [40, 41] clonazepam, [42] d-fenfluramine, [43] and lithium [44] could also be effective for at least some of the treatment-resistant PD patients.

6. Cognitive Behavioral-Therapy

Five CBT trials [24-27, 45] did not include comparisons to placebo, wait list or other treatments. In one randomized trial, [22] CBT and clonazepam were compared as augmentation to SSRI and both treatments were equally effective. All studies had limitations regarding the treatment-resistance criteria and concurrent use of multiple pharmacological agents such as antidepressants, benzodiazepines and lithium.

All protocols [22, 24-27, 45] included 12 sessions of group therapy. CBT was effective as an augmentation in all six trials, with improvements in panic attacks, anticipatory anxiety, agoraphobia, other panic symptoms, general anxiety and quality of life. A decrease in the use of medications was also observed. [26, 27] The improvement of panic symptoms persisted for at least a couple of months after the end of the CBT. [24] PD patients who were treated inadequately with antidepressants and benzodiazepines for at least two months were compared to treatment-resistant patients, and the authors [45] found that both groups had significant and similar improvements with the add-on CBT.

7. Other Treatments

Among the biological non-pharmacological treatments, repetitive transcranial magnetic stimulation (TMS) is the only one tested in treatment-resistant PD patients. [46] This treatment consists of an electrical current running through a coil, producing an electromagnetic field over the skull of the patient, and therefore depolarizing superficial brain neurons. It was demonstrated that there is a decrease in glucose metabolism in the cortical and subcortical regions immediately after the application of low frequency stimulation. However, it is still not completely clear how TMS works in neuropsychiatric disorders. [46]

In one randomized double blind controlled study, [46] TMS was not superior to the sham TMS as an augmentation treatment for treatment-resistant PD patients. They received ten 30-minute sessions of sham TMS or 1 Hz TMS at 110% of the motor threshold in the right dorsolateral prefrontal cortex. All 15 patients were on stable doses of SSRI during the trial. There were significant improvements in several scales, including CGI-S and PDSS, but there were no significant differences between the two groups.

8. Discussion

The lifetime prevalence of PD in the population is high. [5, 6] Among these patients, approximately 30% of them have persistent panic symptoms despite pharmacological and psychological treatment. [16, 47] Improving the treatments for PD and finding alternatives for patients who do not respond to conventional treatments is a matter of public health and of crucial importance.

There is no consensus about what is considered treatment-resistant PD, and currently there are no operational criteria for classifying the patients. The authors believe that the best criteria for treatment-resistant PD were those used by Dannon et al. [19] and Hollifield et al. [20] : patients who do not respond to at least two adequate 8-week treatment trials with drugs recognized as effective for PD in adequate doses or standard course of CBT. Patients who have a poor response to the first medication trial, might respond very well in a second trial; therefore, they should not be considered treatment-resistant. Similarly, patients who take small doses of medication and have a poor response after 6 weeks of treatment should not be initially regarded as treatment-resistant, as they might improve if the doses were increased and the trial prolonged.

Treatment-resistance in PD may be the consequence of untreated comorbid disorders, and these patients could benefit from treatments targeted to the original causes. Patients with comorbid bipolar spectrum disorders would probably benefit from mood stabilizers and antipsychotics. Switching the antidepressant – including TCA and monoamine oxidase inhibitors (MAOI) in the treatment options – or combining two antidepressants could be a good strategy for patients with comorbid major depressive disorder. Psychotherapy would probably be the best augmentation strategy for patients with treatment-resistant PD and comorbid avoidant or dependent personality disorders, agoraphobia or other phobias.

Antidepressants, particularly SSRI and SNRI, are highly recommended by current guidelines [2, 11, 12] among the pharmacological agents used in the treatment of PD. Due to their high efficacy and low risk of adverse reactions the SSRI escitalopram, citalopram, sertraline, fluoxetine, paroxetine, fluvoxamine and the SNRI venlafaxine have the highest recommendation grades. The NRI reboxetine, the MAOI phenelzine, and the TCA clomipramine, desipramine, imipramine and lofepramine are effective, but they have a less favorable side-effects profile. Reboxetine, moclobemide, duloxetine, milnacipran, nefazodone and mirtazapine also have some evidence of efficacy in the treatment of PD. [2, 10] Kampman et al. [28] demonstrated that an augmentation with paroxetine can be effective for patients who do not respond to CBT. Treatment-resistant patients may also benefit from augmentation with reboxetine. [19] Other strategies for treatment-resistant PD with antidepressants, such as combining two antidepressants, or switching the antidepressant to TCA or MAOI, are used in clinical practice but have not been systematically studied. There is preliminary evidence indicating that escitalopram and venlafaxine are more effective in the treatment of PD than citalopram and paroxetine, respectively. [2, 13] These evidences make these antidepressants good drug recommendations to treat treatment-resistant PD, but there are still no clinical trials with these drugs for treatment-resistant PD.

Atypical antipsychotics are not recommended by the current guidelines [2, 11, 12] as first-line agents for the treatment of PD. However, aripiprazole, olanzapine, risperidone and sulpiride have demonstrated relative efficacy in refractory and non-refractory PD. [10] Quetiapine showed anxiolytic properties in several studies and is used in mood disorders with good results, [48, 49] but it did not present efficacy in treatment-resistant PD. [32] The risks and benefits of atypical antipsychotics should be weighted in treatment-resistant PD patients because these agents are associated to increased appetite, weight gain, metabolic abnormalities, amenorrhea/galactorrhea, somnolence, sialorrhea, sexual dysfunction, somnolence, blurred vision, headache, dizziness, akathisia, insomnia, tremor and other side effects. [10, 50] Besides, increased appetite, weight gain, metabolic abnormalities and sexual dysfunction are also associated to antidepressants and, combining these two compounds can further increase the risk of the mentioned side effects.

There are some evidences of efficacy of sodium valproate in treatment-resistant PD, especially in patients with bipolar disorders. Patients with bipolar disorder type I and PD would probably benefit from sodium valproate, benzodiazepines or atypical antipsychotics due to the restrictions regarding antidepressant use. The association of sodium valproate and clonazepam may be beneficial for some patients.

The benzodiazepines alprazolam, clonazepam, diazepam and lorazepam are effective in acute treatment of PD, but have lower recommendation grades due to side effects and risks. [2, 11, 12] Even though benzodiazepines are frequently combined to antidepressants in clinical practice, there are no randomized double-blind controlled trials with benzodiazepines as monotherapy or augmentation for treatment-resistant PD.

Guidelines do not recommend lithium, tiagabine, pindolol or d-fenfluramine for the treatment of PD, but they have been studied in treatment-resistant PD. On the one hand, augmentation with pindolol has a high level of evidence and is considered a good alternative for these patients. On the other hand, lithium, tiagabine and d-fenfluramine have a very low level of evidence and should not be prescribed for treatment-resistant PD. Structured clinical trials are still needed to ascertain the efficacy of these compounds.

According to the guidelines, the best treatments for PD are pharmacological, psychological or a combination of both. [2] Among psychological treatments for PD, CBT has the highest level of evidence. Several studies demonstrated that augmentation with CBT is also effective for patients who do not respond well to pharmacological treatment. [24-27, 45] In most protocols, there are 8-12 weekly sessions, but short term CBT programs with only five sessions may also be effective if combined with the CBT adjuvant D-cycloserine. [10, 51] Presently, the CBT adjuvants have a low level of evidence and are not indicated for the treatment of PD, [51] but they are promising compounds for PD and treatment-resistant PD.

TMS and other neurostimulation techniques have had significant developments in the last decade. [52, 53] However, in the only study [46] with treatment-resistant PD, TMS was not superior to the sham TMS. The authors believe that new TMS protocols could increase its efficacy in the treatment of PD and other anxiety disorders.

Currently there are few studies addressing the treatment-resistant PD, most of them low-quality open studies with very small samples of PD patients. Well-designed, double blind, randomized and controlled studies with sufficient number of subjects are needed to shed light on this subject.

Conclusion

Clinical trials with treatment-resistant PD are scant and quality studies regarding this subject are exiguous. Regarding the pharmacological treatment, there is preliminary evidence of efficacy of monotherapy with reboxetine and olanzapine in treatment-resistant PD. The augmentation of antidepressants, anxiolytics and other drugs with CBT, pindolol, divalproex sodium, aripiprazole, olanzapine, risperidone and sulpiride could be effective. Augmentation of CBT with paroxetine may also be effective for treatment-resistant patients. It was observed that dose escalation after initial lack of response may produce little improvement or no improvement at all. More randomized, controlled, and blind clinical trials are definitely needed to ascertain adequate strategies for treatment-resistant PD.

REFERENCES

[1] Andrade LH, Wang YP, Andreoni S, Silveira CM, Alexandrino-Silva C, Siu ER, et al. Mental disorders in megacities: findings from the Sao Paulo megacity mental health survey, Brazil. *PloS One.* 2012;7(2).

[2] Baldwin DS, Anderson IM, Nutt DJ, Allgulander C, Bandelow B, den Boer JA, et al. Evidence-based pharmacological treatment of anxiety disorders, post-traumatic stress disorder and obsessive-compulsive disorder: A revision of the 2005 guidelines from the British Association for Psychopharmacology. *J Psychopharmacol.* 2014;28(5):403-39.

[3] Andrade LH, Baptista MC, Alonso J, Petukhova M, Bruffaerts R, Kessler RC, et al. Days out-of-role due to common physical and mental health problems: results from the Sao Paulo Megacity Mental Health Survey, Brazil. *Clinics*. 2013;68(11):1392-9.

[4] Lepine JP. Epidemiology, burden, and disability in depression and anxiety. *J Clin Psychiatry*. 2001;62(Suppl 13):4-10.

[5] Roy-Byrne PP, Stang P, Wittchen HU, Ustun B, Walters EE, Kessler RC. Lifetime panic-depression comorbidity in the National Comorbidity Survey. Association with symptoms, impairment, course and help-seeking. *Br J Psychiatry*. 2000;176:229-35.

[6] Kessler RC, Chiu WT, Jin R, Ruscio AM, Shear K, Walters EE. The epidemiology of panic attacks, panic disorder, and agoraphobia in the National Comorbidity Survey Replication. *Arch Gen Psychiatry.* 2006;63(4):415-24.

[7] Bystritsky A, Kerwin L, Niv N, Natoli JL, Abrahami N, Klap R, et al. Clinical and subthreshold panic disorder. *Depress Anxiety.* 2010;27(4):381-9.

[8] Gorman JM, Kent JM, Sullivan GM, Coplan JD. Neuroanatomical hypothesis of panic disorder, revised. *Am J Psychiatry.* 2000;157(4):493-505.

[9] Nardi AE, Freire RC, Zin WA. Panic disorder and control of breathing. *Respir Physiol Neurobiol.* 2009;167(1):133-43.

[10] Freire RC, Machado S, Arias-Carrion O, Nardi AE. Current pharmacological interventions in panic disorder. *CNS Neurol Disord Drug Targets.* 2014;13(6):1057-65.

[11] Bandelow B, Zohar J, Hollander E, Kasper S, Moller HJ, Zohar J, et al. World Federation of Societies of Biological Psychiatry (WFSBP) guidelines for the pharmacological treatment of anxiety, obsessive-compulsive and post-traumatic stress disorders - first revision. *World J Biol Psychiatry.* 2008;9(4):248-312.

[12] Katzman MA, Bleau P, Blier P, Chokka P, Kjernisted K, Van Ameringen M, et al. Canadian clinical practice guidelines for the management of anxiety, posttraumatic stress and obsessive-compulsive disorders. *BMC Psychiatry.* 2014;14 Suppl 1:S1.

[13] Freire RC, Hallak JE, Crippa JA, Nardi AE. New treatment options for panic disorder: clinical trials from 2000 to 2010. *Expert Opin Pharmacother.* 2011;12(9):1419-28.

[14] Bandelow B, Behnke K, Lenoir S, Hendriks GJ, Alkin T, Goebel C, et al. Sertraline versus paroxetine in the treatment of panic disorder: an acute, double-blind noninferiority comparison. *J Clin Psychiatry.* 2004;65(3):405-13.

[15] Kjernisted K, McIntosh D. Venlafaxine extended release (XR) in the treatment of panic disorder. *Ther Clin Risk Manag.* 2007;3(1):59-69.

[16] Batelaan NM, de Graaf R, Penninx BW, van Balkom AJ, Vollebergh WA, Beekman AT. The 2-year prognosis of panic episodes in the general population. *Psychol Med.* 2010;40(1):147-57.

[17] Baetz M, Bowen RC. Efficacy of divalproex sodium in patients with panic disorder and mood instability who have not responded to conventional therapy. *Can J Psychiatry.* 1998;43(1):73-7.

[18] Hoge EA, Worthington III JJ, Kaufman RE, Delong HR, Pollack MH, Simon NM. Aripiprazole as augmentation treatment of refractory generalized anxiety disorder and panic disorder. CNS Spectr. 2008;13(6):522-7.

[19] Dannon PN, Iancu I, Grunhaus L. The efficacy of reboxetine in the treatment-refractory patients with panic disorder: An open-label study. *Hum Psychopharmacol.* 2002;17(7):329-33.

[20] Hollifield M, Thompson PM, Ruiz JE, Uhlenhuth EH. Potential effectiveness and safety of olanzapine in refractory panic disorder. *Depress Anxiety* [Internet]. 2005; 21(1):[33-40 pp.]. Available from: http://onlinelibrary.wiley.com/o/cochrane/clcentral/articles/238/CN-00521238/frame.htmlhttp://onlinelibrary.wiley.com/store/10.1002/da.20050/asset/20050_ftp.pdf?v=1&t=i5xyyimo&s=876ac8523cb59d18c4ecb2473ea21219d36b92e1.

[21] Hirschmann S, Dannon PN, Iancu I, Dolberg OT, Zohar J, Grunhaus L. Pindolol augmentation in patients with treatment-resistant panic disorder: A double-blind, placebo-controlled trial. *J Clin Psychopharmacol.* 2000;20(5):556-9.

[22] Simon NM, Otto MW, Worthington JJ, Hoge EA, Thompson EH, Lebeau RT, et al. Next-step strategies for panic disorder refractory to initial pharmacotherapy: a 3-phase randomized clinical trial. *J Clin Psychiatry.* 2009;70(11):1563-70.

[23] Sepede G, De Berardis D, Gambi F, Campanella D, La Rovere R, D'Amico M, et al. Olanzapine augmentation in treatment-resistant panic disorder: a 12-week, fixed-dose, open-label trial. *J Clin Psychopharmacol.* 2006;26(1):45-9.

[24] Pollack MH, Otto MW, Kaspi SP, Hammerness PG, Rosenbaum JF. Cognitive behavior therapy for treatment-refractory panic disorder. *J Clin Psychiatry.* 1994;55(5):200-5.

[25] Heldt E, Blaya C, Isolan L, Kipper L, Teruchkin B, Otto MW, et al. Quality of life and treatment outcome in panic disorder: cognitive behavior group therapy effects in patients refractory to medication treatment. *Psychother Psychosom.* 2006;75(3):183-6.

[26] Heldt E, Manfro GG, Kipper L, Blaya C, Isolan L, Otto MW. One-year follow-up of pharmacotherapy-resistant patients with panic disorder treated with cognitive-behavior therapy: Outcome and predictors of remission. *Behav Res Ther.* 2006;44(5):657-65.

[27] Heldt E, Manfro GG, Kipper L, Blaya C, Maltz S, Isolan L, et al. Treating medication-resistant panic disorder: predictors and outcome of cognitive-behavior therapy in a Brazilian public hospital. *Psychother Psychosom.* 2003;72(1):43-8.

[28] Kampman M, Keijsers GP, Hoogduin CA, Hendriks GJ. A randomized, double-blind, placebo-controlled study of the effects of adjunctive paroxetine in panic disorder patients unsuccessfully treated with cognitive-behavioral therapy alone. *J Clin Psychiatry.* 2002;63(9):772-7.

[29] Tiffon L, Coplan JD, Papp LA, Gorman JM. Augmentation strategies with tricyclic or fluoxetine treatment in seven partially responsive panic disorder patients. *J Clin Psychiatry.* 1994;55(2): 66-9.

[30] Boerner RJ. [Treatment refractory panic disorder--success of a combined treatment with imipramine, moclobemide and behavior therapy]. *Psychiatr Prax.* 1995;22(1):30-2.

[31] Cerra D. Trimipramine for refractory panic attacks. *Am J Psychiatry.* 2006;163(3):548.

[32] Goddard AW, Mahmud W, Medlock C, Shin YW, Shekhar A. A controlled trial of quetiapine XR coadministration treatment of SSRI-resistant panic disorder. *Ann Gen Psychiatry.* 2015;14:26.

[33] Nunes EA, Freire RC, dos Reis M, de Oliveira e Silva AC, Machado S, Crippa JAS, et al. Sulpiride and refractory panic disorder. *Psychopharmacology.* 2012;223(2):247-9.

[34] Simon NM, Hoge EA, Fischmann D, Worthington Iii JJ, Christian KM, Kinrys G, et al. An Open-Label Trial of Risperidone Augmentation for Refractory Anxiety Disorders. *Journal of Clinical Psychiatry.* 2006;67(3):381-5.

[35] Khaldi S, Kornreich C, Dan B, Pelc I. Usefulness of olanzapine in refractory panic attacks. *J Clin Psychopharmacol.* 2003;23(1):100-1.

[36] Etxebeste M, Aragues E, Malo P, Pacheco L. Olanzapine and panic attacks. *Am J Psychiatry.* 2000;157(4):659-60.

[37] Worthington Iii JJ, Kinrys G, Wygant LE, Pollack MH. Aripiprazole as an augmentor of selective serotonin reuptake inhibitors in depression and anxiety disorder patients. *International Clinical Psychopharmacology.* 2005;20(1):9-11.

[38] Crane DL. Ziprasidone as an Augmenting Agent in the Treatment of Anxiety-Spectrum Disorders. *CNS Spectr.* 2005;10(3):176-9.

[39] Ontiveros A, Fontaine R. Sodium valproate and clonazepam for treatment-resistant panic disorder. *Journal of Psychiatry & Neuroscience.* 1992;17(2):78-80.

[40] Zwanzger P, Baghai TC, Schule C, Minov C, Padberg F, Moller HJ, et al. Tiagabine improves panic and agoraphobia in panic disorder patients. *J Clin Psychiatry.* 2001;62(8):656-7.

[41] Schwartz TL. The use of tiagabine augmentation for treatment-resistant anxiety disorders: a case series. *Psychopharmacol Bull.* 2002;36(2):53-7.

[42] Tesar GE, Rosenbaum JF. Successful use of clonazepam in patients with treatment-resistant panic disorder. *Journal of Nervous and Mental Disease.* 1986;174(8):477-82.

[43] Hetem LA. Addition of d-fenfluramine to benzodiazepines produces a marked improvement in refractory panic disorder--a case report. *J Clin Psychopharmacol.* 1996;16(1):77-8.

[44] Cournoyer J. Response rapid a l'addition du carbonate de lithium d'un trouble: panique resistant aux antidepresseurs tricycliques [Rapid response of a disorder to the addition of lithium carbonate: panic resistant to tricyclic antidepressants]. *Can J Psychiatry.* 1986;31(4):335-8.

[45] Otto MW, Pollack MH, Penava SJ, Zucker BG. Group cognitive-behavior therapy for patients failing to respond to pharmacotherapy for panic disorder: a clinical case series. *Behav Res Ther.* 1999;37(8):763-70.

[46] Prasko J, Zalesky R, Bares M, Horacek J, Kopecek M, Novak T, et al. The effect of repetitive transcranial magnetic stimulation (rTMS) add on serotonin reuptake inhibitors in patients with panic disorder: a randomized, double blind sham controlled study. *Neuro Endocrinol Lett.* 2007;28(1):33-8.

[47] Bandelow B, Rüther E. Treatment-Resistant Panic Disorder. *CNS Spectr.* 2004;9(10):725-39.

[48] Gao K, Wu R, Kemp DE, Chen J, Karberg E, Conroy C, et al. Efficacy and safety of quetiapine-XR as monotherapy or adjunctive therapy to a mood stabilizer in acute bipolar depression with generalized anxiety disorder and other comorbidities: a randomized, placebo-controlled trial. *J Clin Psychiatry.* 2014;75(10):1062-8.

[49] Chen YC, Chen CK, Wang LJ. Quetiapine fumarate augmentation for patients with a primary anxiety disorder or a mood disorder: a pilot study. *BMC Psychiatry.* 2012;12:162.

[50] Hershenberg R, Gros DF, Brawman-Mintzer O. Role of atypical antipsychotics in the treatment of generalized anxiety disorder. *CNS Drugs.* 2014;28(6):519-33.

[51] Ori R, Amos T, Bergman H, Soares-Weiser K, Ipser JC, Stein DJ. Augmentation of cognitive and behavioural therapies (CBT) with d-cycloserine for anxiety and related disorders. *Cochrane Database Syst Rev.* 2015(5):CD007803.

[52] George MS, Padberg F, Schlaepfer TE, O'Reardon JP, Fitzgerald PB, Nahas ZH, et al. Controversy: Repetitive transcranial magnetic stimulation or transcranial direct current stimulation shows efficacy in treating psychiatric diseases (depression, mania, schizophrenia, obsessive-complusive disorder, panic, posttraumatic stress disorder). *Brain Stimul.* 2009;2(1):14-21.

[53] Cristancho MA, Cristancho P, O'Reardon JP. Other therapeutic psychiatric uses of superficial brain stimulation. *Handb Clin Neurol.* 2013;116:415-22.

In: Panic Disorder
Editor: Yong-Ku Kim
ISBN: 978-1-53613-001-0

Chapter 11

PSYCHOTHERAPIES OF PANIC DISORDER

Min-Kyu Song and Won Kim*

Department of Psychiatry, College of Medicine, Inje University, Seoul Paik Hospital, Republic of Korea

ABSTRACT

This chapter will introduce psychological treatment options for panic disorder. According to the current available evidence, the most commonly indicated psychological treatment for the panic disorder is cognitive-behavioral therapy (CBT). CBT for panic disorder has proved efficacy in many controlled trials. CBT is effective when conducted both individually and in a group format. The efficacy of Panic-focused psychodynamic psychotherapy (PFPP) for panic disorder also has been tested. PFPP can be indicated as a psychological treatment for panic disorder in specific clinical situations (e.g., patient who is motivated for psychoanalysis and able to engage in psychodynamic psychotherapy). Other psychological treatments have been applied to panic disorder, but certain forms of psychodynamic psychotherapy have not been formally tested for panic disorder, and eye movement desensitization and reprocessing (EMDR) and emotion-focused therapy (EFT) have proven ineffective or inferior to evidence-based treatments for panic disorder such as CBT.

---

* Corresponding author E-mail: phrenie@naver.com.

1. Cognitive-Behavioral Therapy of Panic Disorder

1.1. The Cognitive-Behavioral Model in Panic Disorder

The use of CBT for panic disorder is based on the assumption that maladaptive patterns of cognitive interpretation and behavior maintain the symptoms of panic disorder. Cognitive-behavioral therapy primarily aims more at these maintaining factors than the origin of panic disorder for a particular patient. According to the cognitive-behavioral models, panic attacks are developed mainly by a distorted and catastrophic interpretations of somatic sensation [1]. For example, dizziness or heart palpitations can be interpreted as impending myocardial infarction or stroke. Such interpretations increase the alertness and amplify somatic symptoms to the imminent "danger" and causes a sudden spiral of more catastrophic interpretations and anxiety [2]. According to Barlow's cognitive-behavioral model, the first panic attack represents a "false alarm" where too much anxiety is signaled, often in response of life stress. The stressors reported by the patient include negative life events such as intimidation or interpersonal difficulties, as well as threatening loss or serious illness to oneself or loved ones [3]. This "alarm response" is assumed to exist more in individuals who are biologically or psychologically vulnerable. After the first attack, patients with panic disorder are anxious about new attacks and fear of bodily sensations related to autonomic arousal. The repetition of attacks is assumed to make individuals more sensitive to internal stimuli and to the situations in which the attack occurred, and to strengthen the vigilance of physical sensations. The fear of having another attacks and catastrophic interpretations of symptoms are combined when panic attacks occur [4, 5]. The individual's reaction to such fear include the avoidance of all the situations associated with previous attacks (agoraphobia) [3]. As a consequence, patients begin to have substantial limitations in their daily lives [4]. Therefore the therapeutic goal of CBT is to remove the hypervigilance to symptoms, modify distorted interpretations and beliefs, and eliminate the agoraphobia.

1.2. Elements of CBT

CBT is typically a brief treatment, between 10 and 20 structured sessions, with clear objectives to be achieved. It aims to correct catastrophic interpretations and conditioned fears of body sensations and avoidances. It is practical and task-based. Both the patient's and therapist's roles are active and cooperative. CBT can be conducted individually or as a groups [2]. Despite many studies suggesting that CBT should be brief, recent treatment data indicated that higher number of sessions, either face-to-face or telephone counseling sessions, is associated with better response to CBT in panic disorder [6]. Nevertheless, there have been reports of positive results regarding the application of very short treatments (6 sessions) provided in clinic and the primary care settings [7-9]. CBT can be introduced at any stage of treatment, including primary prevention and interventions to patients with refractory to other treatments [4]. It can be also started with medications [4, 5, 10]. The standard form of CBT for panic disorder is comprised of psychoeducation, anxiety coping techniques (muscle relaxation and abdominal or diaphragmatic breathing), cognitive restructuring, interoceptive exposure and *in vivo* exposure [2, 4]. In a study of 76 panic patients with or without agoraphobia, a combination of cognitive (psychoeducation, cognitive restructuring, and problem solving skills) and behavioral (interceroceptive and *in vivo* exposure) techniques showed significant efficacy in the remission of acute symptoms and in the maintenance of gains in the follow-up until 6 months after CBT [11].

1.2.1. Psychoeducation

Psychoeducation consists of a description of the nature of the patient's illness and an explanation of the management methods available for disorder. This can be particularly important in panic disorder, where the patient's cognitive coping mechanisms are compromised and anticipatory anxiety can cause additional attacks. Nowadays the role of psychoeducation in anxiety disorders has attracted the more attention of clinicians and consumers than before [12].

Psychoeducation for panic disorder breaks the cascade of anxiety and panic reactions into component elements, and provides the rationale for subsequent treatment interventions. It focuses on defining and clarifying the source of anxiety and panic symptoms, introducing the role of thoughts in maintaining fear and anxiety, and the role of avoidance and escape behaviors in maintaining fears and perpetuating the disorder [2]. Psychoeducation is performed during the initial sessions and can be repeated at any time during the treatment. Psychoeducation also have the important role for motivating the patient to take an exposure exercise.

1.2.2. Anxiety Coping Skills

Improper breathing patterns may cause hyperventilation and physiological symptoms such as dizziness, suffocation, and tachycardia due to significant increase in blood oxygenation. Muscle tensions also increase anxiety and can also cause physical reactions such as pain and sensory abnormalities. These sensations are very similar to panic attacks and can be reduced by using proper breathing techniques and muscle relaxation. Diaphragmatic breathing is a technique to regulate breathing by controlling abdominal muscles. Progressive muscle relaxation (PMR), developed by Edmund Jacobson [13], is the exercise involving the practice of tension and relaxation of the main muscle groups. Both skills (relaxation and abdominal breathing) can be practiced sequentially or independently, and is helpful especially for anticipatory anxiety [2]. However there is some arguments that this anxiety coping technique is not an essential part of therapy [14]. Moreover, there is a concern that these techniques can lead to a desperate attempt to control the patient's anxiety rather than eliminate fears of these symptoms.

1.2.3. Cognitive Techniques

Distorted and catastrophic interpretations of physical sensations of anxiety are common in panic disorder. These cognitive errors are found in the patient's beliefs about hopelessness and inability to manage anxiety and panic. Cognitive techniques aim to restructure such catastrophic thoughts. To do so, the patients need to know the cognitive model and the underlying assumptions of cognitive therapy: that thoughts influence emotions and behavior, and that, in the case of panic disorder, anxiety and panic can be a consequence of distorted interpretations of physical sensations [2]. In therapy, the patient must consider his or her thoughts as hypotheses or "guesses" about the world. Training is conducted to identify automatic catastrophic thoughts related to anxiety and panic [2]. After identifying these thoughts in the session, the patient is asked to monitor his/her thoughts, identify logical errors inherent in the catastrophic interpretation, and produce a more adaptive thought. In the anxiety disorders, the treatment focuses on patient's overestimation of negative outcome as well as overestimation of the degree of catastrophe of those outcomes. These negative thoughts are frequently challenged through logical Socratic Questioning, or, in the form of specific behavioral experiments designed to help the patient to check the accuracy of their anxiogenic predictions in real situations [2].

1.2.4. Exposure Techniques

Interoceptive Exposure

Interoceptive exposure aims to correct the catastrophic interpretation of the physical sensations that patients feel as part of anticipatory anxiety or panic attack. Interoceptive exposure gives patients a step-by-step experience to familiarize themselves with the sensations. Such exposure is accomplished by intentionally inducing symptoms using physical exercises. For example, by spinning in a swivel chair, dizziness can be induced. Paresthesia, derealization and dizziness can also be induced with only a minute of hyperventilation. In addition to direct training to get used to these sensations (where the patient learns to experience strange or uncomfortable rather than fear), interoceptive exposure can also be used to identify automatic thoughts and catastrophic interpretations linked to physical sensations and correct them. Interoceptive exposure exercises can work as a preparation for *in vivo* exposure [2]. Interoceptive exposure is typically introduced in the session when helping the patient without trying to control or minimize the sensations. A homework with this exercise is then assigned for the patient to feel "bored" until the next week session. Finally, the patient is asked to complete an interoceptive exposure during a session. Therefore the comfort with the sensations can be acquired in that context.

In Vivo Exposure

In vivo exposure is a key intervention applied to overcome agoraphobic avoidance. To plan an *in vivo* exposure, the patient should make a list of places or situations that avoided because of fear and record the levels of anxiety and automatic thoughts that occur in these situations [2]. This list should be arranged in hierarchically according to the level of difficulty to face the places and situations. *In vivo* exposure exercise is initiated by situations considered less anxiogenic and that the patient is willing to confront. To be effective, exposure should consume enough time (stay in a given situation for about twice the amount of time it takes to get comfortable in that situation). Moreover *in vivo* exposure exercise should be frequently repeated and the anxiety level should be sufficient for patient to feel anxious and uncomfortable during the task.

Dependence on Relatives

Dependence on relatives is a very common problem in panic disorder, and the result is loss of autonomy of the patient in addition to impaired performance and reduced self-esteem. Relatives can often participate in certain stage of treatment to help with exposure tasks. However, treatment should encourage the patient to go to a place where he or she has not used to go alone to recover the lost autonomy [2].

1.2.5. CBT Sessions

CBT sessions of panic disorder are structured according to the basic model proposed by Beck [15]. Barlow and Craske developed Panic Control Treatment by inheriting and modifying Beck's model [16]. In initial sessions, the therapist devote for patient assessment, psychoeducation, and training of anxiety coping skills including diaphragmatic breathing and progressive muscle relaxation. As sessions progress, more attention is paid to cognitive restructuring, interoceptive exposure, and *in vivo* exposure interventions. Final sessions are dedicated to strengthening profits and preventing relapse. Prevention of relapse is assisted by full practice of interoceptive exposure in a variety of situations, ensuring that patients do not avoid full exposures in feared situations. Also, rehearsal and appropriate coping skills for expecting future difficulties, along with strategies that the patient found to be helpful in the past, provided additional elements of relapse preventive effort [2, 3]. Wade et al. found that chronic stress predicts worse outcomes in patients with agoraphobia at the time of 12 weeks after CBT, as well as in a 2-year follow-up assessment [17]. It is therefore important to identify situations that predispose to a higher psychological vulnerability to prevent relapses and chronicity [18].

1.3. Effectiveness of CBT

There are numerous controlled trials demonstrating the efficacy of CBT for panic disorder [19-29], although specific CBT protocols used in clinical trials vary in their emphasis on different treatment components. Meta-analyses of clinical trials have concluded the effects of CBT for panic disorder are strong and durable [30-33]. CBT also have strong cost-efficacy in treatment of panic disorder [34]. There is also evidence that CBT can be effective for PD patients refractory to drug treatment [35, 36].

Some researches suggest at least minimal additive treatment effects when CBT and medications are combined [37]. Moreover, if patients have been started on medication and are subsequently offered CBT, there is evidence that medication can be tapered successfully during the course of CBT, with strong maintenance of treatment gains [14, 38, 39].

There is promising evidence for a new combined strategy for the anxiety disorders. This strategy is focused on promoting the learning process of brain in therapy sessions, and is based on the basic research of the neural circuits underlying fear extinction [40]. D-cycloserine (DCS), a partial NMDA agonist, appears to augment learning process of extinction in animal studies [41]. However, until now DCS does not improve but slightly speed up the outcome of in-vivo exposure therapy in patients with panic disorder in randomized clinical trials [42, 43].

New delivering approaches, such as Internet-based CBT [44, 45] and two-days intensive CBT have been tested in panic disorder with favorable outcomes [46], especially in patients with milder symptoms and low functional impairment [47]. More researches are needed to assess the efficacy of this combined treatments, and the role of coexisting illnesses and stressful life events in the treatment refractoriness and relapses in panic disorder.

2. Psychodynamic Psychotherapy

Psychodynamic therapists view panic attacks as a signal anxiety caused by unconsciously unresolved past conflicts involving aggression, anger, separation and dependency. Thus psychodynamic psychotherapy aims to relieve symptoms of panic disorder through a therapeutic process that encourages exploration of past and present traumatic experiences. The core principles of psychodynamic psychotherapy are 1) the appreciation that much of mental life is unconscious, 2) childhood experiences in concert with genetic and constitutional factors shape adult personality, and 3) individual symptoms and behaviors may serve multiple functions [48]. Many studies suggest that an acute stressor or life event occurs just before the onset of panic disorder [49-51]. According to psychodynamic theories, the psychological meaning of these events, as well as their symptoms, behaviors and coping styles, is determined by complex forces that may be unavailable to the patient's conscious awareness [52-54]. In the case of patients with panic disorder, one of the goals of psychodynamic psychotherapy is to uncover and understand the thoughts and feelings associated with panic symptoms as well as the unconscious psychological meanings of these panic symptoms, and those of the issues that are theorized to be related to separation, autonomy, self-esteem, anger, or aggression [55]. Understanding of transference and interpretation is used to clarify these issues as well as related interpersonal conflicts. The therapist also tries to identify and alter core conflicts for reducing vulnerability to future panic symptoms [56]. Given the highly individualized nature of these thoughts, feelings, and conflicts, the duration and frequency of most psychodynamic psychotherapy also tend to be individualized. In psychodynamic psychotherapy, symptom relief or resolution is theorized by emotional growth and understanding of the various developmental and psychological issues associated with the patient's symptoms. There are both conscious and unconscious problems, such as self-esteem and self-cohesion, unresolved developmental trauma, and psychic conflict including unacceptable impulses, unrealistic or harsh issues of self-esteem and conscience, maladaptive psychological defenses. The therapist presents the current symptoms in the context of the patient's life history and current realities. The relationship between the therapist and the patient is often used as a means of gaining an insightful awareness by bringing the unconscious into consciousness, as well as to promote intrapsychic growth. Because psychodynamic therapies are rooted in various psychoanalytic and psychodynamic theoretical models, there are a various ways to conduct psychodynamic psychotherapy.

Panic-focused psychodynamic psychotherapy (PFPP) is a twice weekly, 12 weeks, total 24-session manualized psychoanalytic psychotherapy developed by Milrod [57]. PFPP is conducted in three phases. Phase 1 focuses on acute panic. Phase 2 of PFPP deals with on lessening vulnerability to panic reactions through the understanding and alteration of core unconscious conflicts. Phase 3 of PFPP occurs the last third of the sessions and focuses on termination [58]. PFPP has demonstrated its efficacy for panic symptoms and psychosocial function in a randomized controlled trial [59]. But, other large randomized controlled comparison of PFPP and CBT for panic disorder showed site-by-treatment interactions that complicated interpretation of results [60]. In this study, PFPP and CBT showed the same overall efficacy. However, CBT showed similar efficacy in both sites, and PFPP had a large variation. PFPP is more symptom-focused than most dynamic therapies and requires a shift in focus particularly for some experienced dynamic therapists. It focuses on the underlying psychological meanings of panic symptoms and current social and emotional functioning. PFPP is based on the assumption that panic symptoms have certain emotional significance that the patient must confront before relief of panic symptoms can occur. According to this theoretical model, a patients with panic disorder has the concept that it is difficult to separate himself from important attachment figures and to perceive themselves as autonomous. This is thought to lead agoraphobic avoidance [58]. The combination of perceiving their environment and relationships as overly dangerous and themselves as inadequate and lacking autonomy may trigger high levels of anxiety that keeps panic and agoraphobic avoidance. Panic symptoms in turn are believed to reinforce conflicted interpersonal relationships in which the patient relies heavily on others who are important and afraid to lose them. PFPP focuses on the transference as a mutative therapeutic agent and does not require behavioral exposure to agoraphobic situations. It helps patients to confront the emotional importance of their physical symptoms and recognize that their fears of expecting catastrophe reflect inner emotional state rather than reality. These techniques allows PFPP to make patients more autonomous, to increase personal efficacy of patients with panic disorder, and to improve function and symptom relief. Compared to PFPP, other psychodynamic approaches often focus more on other psychological and interpersonal issues in the patient's life [58]. These approaches have not been the subject of rigorous research studies. As a result, the evidence of the use of other psychodynamic therapies in panic disorder is limited to case reports and comments from psychodynamic psychotherapists. There are no studies comparing the efficacy of the different psychodynamic psychotherapy approaches or comparing psychodynamic psychotherapy with other psychosocial treatments in patients with panic disorder. As with other psychiatric treatments, psychodynamic psychotherapy (including PFPP) should be conducted by a suitably trained therapist and the patients must understand the basis, goals, and potential risks and benefits of the treatment. The exploration of memories and important conflicted relationships and the rising of unconscious material may sometimes be associated with powerful influences and temporary confusion in therapy and other relationships. These events tend to decrease both frequency and intensity as the patient experiences how they relate to. It also helps to resolve the symptoms and problems that brought the patient to treatment. Many patients with panic disorder have complicating co-occurring psychiatric conditions. The broad focus of some forms of psychodynamic psychotherapy may be useful in reducing symptoms or maladaptive behaviors in these related conditions. For example, some preliminary studies have shown that PFPP is superior to applied relaxation therapy for patients with Cluster C personality disorders, compared to patients without Cluster C personality disorder [61]. Although evidence is limited, psychodynamic therapies have been used with medication or CBT element [62]. For example, a patient with agoraphobic avoidance can be encouraged to expose himself to fearful situations and explore feelings to gain deeper understanding of the conflicts surrounding the awful situation. In fact, psychodynamic therapies are supplemented with medications to help relieve panic symptoms [63].

3. Eye Movement Desensitization and Reprocessing

Eye movement desensitization and reprocessing (EMDR) was originally developed as a treatment for traumatic memories [64], but it has been rapidly adopted for a wide variety of problems, especially in anxiety disorders other than posttraumatic stress disorder. EMDR involves reprocessing distressing memories while engaging in guided eye movement. Like traumatic events that cause PTSD, panic attacks are frequently perceived as sudden, unpredictable, and life threatening [65], and the subsequent symptoms of panic disorder are similar to those associated with PTSD in some ways. Therefore, panic disorder may be well-suited by EMDR [66]. When applied to panic disorder, EMDR aims at miserable memories such as the first panic attack and life events associated with panic disorder [66]. There is limited empirical data on the use of EMDR in the treatment of panic disorder. In one trial, six sessions of EMDR were superior to a waiting-list control at posttreatment [66]. Another study for 20 subjects showed EMDR to be equivalent in the therapuetic efficacy to CBT in panic disorder [67]. More researches of EMDR for the treatment of panic disorder are needed. EMDR seems to be applicable to patients with traumatic memories.

4. Emotion-Focused Therapy

A primary goal of emotion-focused therapy (EFT) is to ensure that the patient identifies and accepts emotional reactions and can cope with them effectively. EFT for patient with panic disorder is developed by Shear et el. [62] They modified Rice and Saperina's five-step procedure [68] for evocative unfolding to develop the six-steps of the focused unfolding process. 1) Reflect the primary reaction, 2) Encourage the patient to recall and envision the scene in which the reaction occurred, 3) Elicit detailed descriptions of the quality of the internal emotional reaction and the nature of the eliciting stimulus, 4) Identify idiosyncratic personal meanings of the stimulus and qualities of familiarity and repetitiveness of the response, 5) Explore the generalizability of the stimulus-response paradigm and consider its importance, 6) Explore strategies for managing the emotional response [62]. EFT involves a psychoeducational component similar to that of other effective therapies and includes everyday monitoring of panic symptoms. However, EFT differs from CBT in several ways. EFT is less structured and focusing on emotionally relevant material identified by the therapist according to symptoms and other problems of patient's report. Treatment also treats broadly defined emotional reactions rather than specific mechanisms inducing panic. One controlled study compared the efficacy of EFT, CBT, imipramine, and pill placebo in patients with panic disorder [69]. Results showed that EFT was less effective than CBT and imipramine in treatment of panic disorder and that its effect was about equivalent to that of placebo.

5. Acceptance and Commitment Therapy

ACT is developed within a pragmatic philosophy called functional contextualism. ACT is based on relational frame theory (RFT), a comprehensive theory of language and cognition that is an offshoot of behavior analysis. ACT differs from traditional cognitive behavioral therapy (CBT) in that rather than trying to teach people to better control their thoughts, feelings, sensations, memories and other private events, ACT teaches them to "just notice," accept, and embrace their private events, especially previously unwanted ones [70].

ACT helps the individual get in contact with a transcendent sense of self known as "self-as-context" that is always there observing and experiencing and yet distinct from one's thoughts, feelings, sensations, and memories. ACT aims to help the individual clarify their personal values and take action on them, bringing more vitality and meaning to their life in the process, increasing their psychological flexibility [71].

While Western psychology has been typically operated under the "healthy normality" assumption which states that by their nature, humans are psychologically healthy, ACT assumes, rather, that psychological processes of a normal human mind are often destructive [72]. The core conception of ACT is that psychological suffering is usually caused by experiential avoidance, cognitive entanglement, and resulting psychological rigidity that leads to a failure to take needed behavioral steps in accord with core values. As a simple way to summarize the model, ACT views the core of many problems to be due to the concepts represented in the acronym, FEAR: Fusion with your thoughts, Evaluation of experience, Avoidance of your experience, Reason-giving for your behavior. And the healthy alternative represented in the acronym, ACT: Accept your reactions and be present, Choose a valued direction, Take action.

ACT commonly employs six core principles to help clients develop psychological flexibility [72]. 1) Cognitive defusion: Learning methods to reduce the tendency to reify thoughts, images, emotions, and memories. 2) Acceptance: Allowing thoughts to come and go without struggling with them. 3) Contact with the present moment: Awareness of the here and now, experienced with openness, interest, and receptiveness. 4) Observing the self: Accessing a transcendent sense of self, a continuity of consciousness which is unchanging. 5) Values: Discovering what is most important to one's true self. 6) Committed action: Setting goals according to values and carrying them out responsibly. Applied to panic disorder, the FEAR algorithm depicts a person who is involved in a process of experienctial aviodance characterized by 1) constant evaluation of the physical sensations and situations in which they occur (hyperventilating is bad, dangerous; going out is risky, it will kill me, etc.); 2) literal behavior with regard to the contents of such evaluations, that is, systematic efforts to avoid, escape and control the feared situations as much as possible (hyperventilating and going out will make me die, therefore I will stay home); 3) justifying the avoidance and escape behaviors as well as their results (I cannot go out because otherwise I will die; with such strong physiological reactions I cannot do anything); 4) deliberate efforts to control panic attacks, which are incompatible with valued living.

The ACT therapists defines that the symptoms of panic disorder might be divided into three classes according to functional criteria: 1) avoidance and escape from the own experience of panic (hyperventilation, relaxation, distraction, etc.); 2) efforts to control the situations eliciting panic responses (safety behaviors, efforts to suppress thoughts and memories); and 3) functional detach from the own personal values [73]. The therapeutic intervention is aimed at replacing the FEAR functioning which is present in all forms of experiential avoidance including panic disorder, with the ACT functioning (Accept, Choose, and Take action; [50]), which is more flexible and adaptive, and allows the person keeping the commitment with his/her personal values.

Experiential Avoidance (EA) occurs when an individual is not willing to stay in contact with a variety of private events which are experienced as aversive (pain, fears, feelings of loneliness, insecurity, anxiety, traumatic memories, etc.) and makes diverse deliberate efforts to alter the form and frequency of those events and the contexts that occasion them [74, 75]. The immediate consequence of these varied efforts is the momentary relief from the aversive state the individual was experiencing, which turns into a potent negative reinforcement for avoiding. However, in the long run, the intensity and frequency of those private events experienced as aversive increase to the point that the individual restricts his life to do whatever it takes to get rid of the suffering, abandoning the valuable and meaningful directions in his life.

The maintenance of the rigid pattern of EA is related to four verbal context potentiated by the verbal community: Literality, Evaluation, Reasons-giving, and Control of Causes [70]. EA becomes a problem when the inflexible patterns of avoidance restricts the life of the individuals to the point of abandoning the trajectories that give meaning or value to their lives according to personal standards. Within this perspective, panic disorder would be a case of rigid verbal regulation controlled by the necessity of getting rid of the symptoms of a panic attack, the fears of the symptoms of a panic attack, memories, self-attributions, disturbing feelings, etc. prior to engaging in personal valuable trajectories or directions. Depending on the consequences that control this type of destructive verbal regulation, panic disorder may be an instance of generalized pliance-which interferes with the sensitivity to the direct consequences of the action, or overextended tracking-reacting to private events in a way which is not useful to long term goals, or the type of augmenting which transform private events into barriers for action and promote the control rules [76]. The goal of ACT is then to undermine private events as barriers for action and to promote flexibility in the reaction to those private events so as to facilitate the occurrence of behavior in valued trajectories. Moreover, a review found that ACT was better for anxiety disorders than placebo [77]. In the same study, ACT was found to be more effective than typical treatment consisting of medication, psychoeducation and counselling in anxiety disorders. The effectiveness of ACT was similar to traditional treatments like CBT [77].

6. Mindfulness-Based Cognitive Therapy

Mindfulness-based cognitive therapy (MBCT) is a psychological therapy designed to aid in preventing the relapse of depression, specifically in individuals with major depressive disorder [78]. But, recently, MBCT has shown its effectiveness in panic disorder [79]. MBCT uses traditional CBT methods and newer psychological strategies such as mindfulness and mindfulness meditation. Mindfulness and mindfulness meditation focus on becoming aware of all incoming thoughts and feelings and accepting them, but not attaching or reacting to them [80]. This process is known as "decentering" and aids in disengaging from self-criticism, rumination, and dysphoric mood that can arise when reacting to negative thinking patterns [81].

In 1991 Philip Barnard and John Teasdale created a multilevel concept of the mind called "Interacting Cognitive Subsystems" (ICS). The ICS model is based on Barnard and Teasdale's concept that the mind has multiple modes that are responsible for receiving and processing new information cognitively and emotionally [82]. Barnard and Teasdale's concept associates an individual's psychological vulnerability with the degree to which he/she relies on only one of the modes of mind, inadvertently blocking the other modes. The two main modes of mind include the "doing" mode and "being" mode. "Doing" mode is goal-oriented and triggered when the mind develops a discrepancy between how things are versus how the mind wishes things to be. "Being" mode is not focused on achieving specific goals, instead the emphasis is on "accepting and allowing what is," without any immediate pressure to change it [83]. Therefore, individuals that are able to flexibly move between the modes of mind based on the conditions in the environment are in the most favorable state. The ICS model theorizes that the "being" mode is the most likely mode of mind that will lead to lasting emotional changes.

It is theoretically possible that panic disorder may include cognitive components such as lower self-efficacy, high anxiety sensitivity, and cognitive misinterpretation with or without phobic avoidance [84, 85]. The main construct of MBCT, mindfulness, has been associated with improvements in the self-regulation of attention, which has been suggested to allow for increasing self-efficacy allowing individuals to encounter anxiety-producing situations more effectively rather than being preoccupied with fearful thoughts [79]. Through the adoption of a decentered perspective on experiences in mindfulness training [86], it is possible that decreased levels of anxiety sensitivity can be achieved by virtue of an increased level of tolerance for anxiety, especially given that it is possible to become very aware of thoughts, feelings, and body sensations just as it is. Also, it has been suggested that mindfulness may include an active process of relating openly with experience [73], something that can be associated with a different relationship with an individual's own thoughts as an alternative viewpoint against cognitive misinterpretation as experienced in panic disorder.

MBCT was effective as an adjunct to pharmacotherapy in the treatment of patients with panic disorder [79]. And the comorbid personality disorders of participants could be a potential predictor of MBCT non-completion. Furthermore, anxiety sensitivity improvement after MBCT may predict treatment response and remission after MBCT for PD [87].

7. Group Therapy

Clinical experience suggests that possible benefits of a group format for treating panic disorder include 1) reducing shame and stigma by experiencing similar symptoms and difficulties with others; 2) providing opportunities for modeling, inspiration, and reinforcement of other group members; and 3) providing a natural exposure to patients who are afraid of panic symptoms in social situations. Group CBT for panic disorder has been shown to be effective in controlled studies and therefore can be recommended with confidence as a treatment for panic disorder [23, 88]. The advantages of a CBT group are also having greater opportunities for role modeling, practicing new behaviors in the group before testing them in the world outside. The patients can get peer feedback from others with similar anxieties and can be reinforcement positively from many persons including therapist.

When a patient is considered to be in the CBT group, the therapist should consider the severity of the patient's panic symptoms, concomitant disorders, insight, interpersonal skills, and preference for a group versus individual format. There is limited evidence from small uncontrolled experiments on the effect of group mindfulness-based stress reduction on patients with panic disorder [89, 90].

8. Summary of the Psychotherapies of Panic Disorder

We reviewed CBT, psychodynamic psychotherapy, EMDR, EFT, ACT and MBCT for the psychotherapy for panic disorder. We discussed the pros and cons of psychotherapy in group form, and the points that the therapist should take. To date, the most widespread and effective treatment for panic disorder is cognitive-behavioral therapy. Recently, it has been proved its effectiveness on group or other forms of CBT. PFPP is a form of psychodynamic psychotherapy specialized for panic disorder, and it can be expected to improve the symptoms by finding the psychological meanings of panic symptoms through the discovering underlying unconscious conflicts. In some cases, such as those with severe traumatic memory, EMDR and othe forms of psychotherapies may be effective in treating panic disorder. Finally, Acceptance and Commitment Therapy (ACT) and mindfulness-based cognitive therapy (MBCT) are proving very useful in the treatment of a broad range of psychological problems including panic disorder.

References

[1] Clark, DM. A cognitive approach to panic. *Behav Res Ther*, 1986, 24(4), p. 461-70.

[2] Manfro, GG; et al., [Cognitive-behavioral therapy in panic disorder]. *Rev Bras Psiquiatr*, 2008, 30 Suppl 2, p. s81-7.

[3] Barlow, D. *Anxiety and its disorders: the nature and treatment of anxiety and panic.*, 1988, New York: Guilford Press.

[4] Otto, MW; Deveney, C. Cognitive-behavioral therapy and the treatment of panic disorder: efficacy and strategies. *J Clin Psychiatry*, 2005, 66 Suppl 4, p. 28-32.

[5] Otto, MW; Whittal, ML. Cognitive-behavior therapy and the longitudinal course of panic disorder. *Psychiatr Clin North Am*, 1995, 18(4), p. 803-20.

[6] Craske, MG; et al., CBT intensity and outcome for panic disorder in a primary care setting. *Behav Ther*, 2006, 37(2), p. 112-9.

[7] Clark, DM; et al., Brief cognitive therapy for panic disorder: a randomized controlled trial. *J Consult Clin Psychol*, 1999, 67(4), p. 583-9.

[8] Craske, MG; Maidenberg, E; Bystritsky, A. Brief cognitive-behavioral versus nondirective therapy for panic disorder. *J Behav Ther Exp Psychiatry*, 1995, 26(2), p. 113-20.

[9] Roy-Byrne, PP; et al., A randomized effectiveness trial of cognitive-behavioral therapy and medication for primary care panic disorder. *Arch Gen Psychiatry*, 2005, 62(3), p. 290-8.

[10] Heldt, E; et al., Treating medication-resistant panic disorder: predictors and outcome of cognitive-behavior therapy in a Brazilian public hospital. *Psychother Psychosom*, 2003, 72(1), p. 43-8.

[11] Galassi, F; et al., Cognitive-behavioral group treatment for panic disorder with agoraphobia. *J Clin Psychol*, 2007, 63(4), p. 409-16.

[12] Dannon, PN; Iancu, I; Grunhaus, L. Psychoeducation in panic disorder patients: effect of a self-information booklet in a randomized, masked-rater study. *Depress Anxiety*, 2002, 16(2), p. 71-6.

[13] Jacobson, E. Relaxation methods in labor; a critique of current techniques in natural childbirth. *Am J Obstet Gynecol*, 1954, 67(5), p. 1035-48.

[14] Schmidt, NB; et al., Antidepressant discontinuation in the context of cognitive behavioral treatment for panic disorder. *Behav Res Ther*, 2002, 40(1), p. 67-73.

[15] Beck, AT. Psychiatry: cognitive therapy for depression and panic disorder. *West J Med*, 1989, 151(3), p. 311.

[16] Barlow, D; Craske, MG. *Mastery of your anxiety and panic.*, 2000, San Antonio: Graywind Publications/The Psychological Corporation.

[17] Wade, SL; Monroe, SM; Michelson, LK. Chronic life stress and treatment outcome in agoraphobia with panic attacks. *Am J Psychiatry*, 1993, 150(10), p. 1491-5.

[18] Lteif, GN; Mavissakalian, MR. Life events and panic disorder/agoraphobia. *Compr Psychiatry*, 1995, 36(2), p. 118-22.

[19] Black, DW; et al., A comparison of fluvoxamine, cognitive therapy, and placebo in the treatment of panic disorder. *Arch Gen Psychiatry*, 1993, 50(1), p. 44-50.

[20] Barlow, DH; et al., Cognitive-behavioral therapy, imipramine, or their combination for panic disorder: A randomized controlled trial. *JAMA*, 2000, 283(19), p. 2529-36.

[21] Klosko, JS; et al., A comparison of alprazolam and behavior therapy in treatment of panic disorder. *J Consult Clin Psychol*, 1990, 58(1), p. 77-84.

[22] Beck, AT; et al., A crossover study of focused cognitive therapy for panic disorder. *Am J Psychiatry*, 1992, 149(6), p. 778-83.

[23] Telch, MJ; et al., Group cognitive-behavioral treatment of panic disorder. *Behav Res Ther*, 1993, 31(3), p. 279-87.

[24] Clark, DM; et al., A comparison of cognitive therapy, applied relaxation and imipramine in the treatment of panic disorder. *Br J Psychiatry*, 1994, 164(6), p. 759-69.

[25] Kenardy, JA; et al., A comparison of delivery methods of cognitive-behavioral therapy for panic disorder: an international multicenter trial. *J Consult Clin Psychol*, 2003, 71(6), p. 1068-75.

[26] Ost, LG; Thulin, U; Ramnero, J. Cognitive behavior therapy vs exposure *in vivo* in the treatment of panic disorder with agoraphobia (corrected from agrophobia). *Behav Res Ther*, 2004, 42(10), p. 1105-27.

[27] Ost, LG; Westling, BE. Applied relaxation vs cognitive behavior therapy in the treatment of panic disorder. *Behav Res Ther*, 1995, 33(2), p. 145-58.

[28] Craske, MG; et al., Interoceptive exposure versus breathing retraining within cognitive-behavioural therapy for panic disorder with agoraphobia. *Br J Clin Psychol*, 1997, 36 (Pt 1), p. 85-99.

[29] Means-Christensen, A; et al., The Composite International Diagnostic Interview (CIDI-Auto): problems and remedies for diagnosing panic disorder and social phobia. *Int J Methods Psychiatr Res*, 2003, 12(4), p. 167-81.

[30] Clum, GA; Clum, GA; Surls, R. A meta-analysis of treatments for panic disorder. *J Consult Clin Psychol*, 1993, 61(2), p. 317-26.

[31] Butler, AC; et al., The empirical status of cognitive-behavioral therapy: a review of meta-analyses. *Clin Psychol Rev*, 2006, 26(1), p. 17-31.

[32] Mitte, K. A meta-analysis of the efficacy of psycho- and pharmacotherapy in panic disorder with and without agoraphobia. *J Affect Disord*, 2005, 88(1), p. 27-45.

[33] Westen, D; Morrison, K. A multidimensional meta-analysis of treatments for depression, panic, and generalized anxiety disorder: an empirical examination of the status of empirically supported therapies. *J Consult Clin Psychol*, 2001, 69(6), p. 875-99.

[34] McHugh, RK; et al., Cost-efficacy of individual and combined treatments for panic disorder. *J Clin Psychiatry*, 2007, 68(7), p. 1038-44.

[35] Heldt, E; et al., Quality of life and treatment outcome in panic disorder: cognitive behavior group therapy effects in patients refractory to medication treatment. *Psychother Psychosom*, 2006, 75(3), p. 183-6.

[36] Heldt, E; et al., One-year follow-up of pharmacotherapy-resistant patients with panic disorder treated with cognitive-behavior therapy: Outcome and predictors of remission. *Behav Res Ther*, 2006, 44(5), p. 657-65.

[37] de Beurs, E; et al., Treatment of panic disorder with agoraphobia: comparison of fluvoxamine, placebo, and psychological panic management combined with exposure and of exposure *in vivo* alone. *Am J Psychiatry*, 1995, 152(5), p. 683-91.

[38] Otto, MW; Hong, JJ; Safren, SA. Benzodiazepine discontinuation difficulties in panic disorder: conceptual model and outcome for cognitive-behavior therapy. *Curr Pharm Des*, 2002, 8(1), p. 75-80.

[39] Whittal, ML; Otto, MW; Hong, JJ. Cognitive-behavior therapy for discontinuation of SSRI treatment of panic disorder: a case series. *Behav Res Ther*, 2001, 39(8), p. 939-45.

[40] Davis, M. Role of NMDA receptors and MAP kinase in the amygdala in extinction of fear: clinical implications for exposure therapy. *Eur J Neurosci*, 2002, 16(3), p. 395-8.

[41] Richardson, R; Ledgerwood, L; Cranney, J. Facilitation of fear extinction by D-cycloserine: theoretical and clinical implications. *Learn Mem*, 2004, 11(5), p. 510-6.

[42] Siegmund, A; et al., D-cycloserine does not improve but might slightly speed up the outcome of in-vivo exposure therapy in patients with severe agoraphobia and panic disorder in a randomized double blind clinical trial. *J Psychiatr Res*, 2011, 45(8), p. 1042-7.

[43] Otto, MW; et al., Randomized Trial of D-Cycloserine Enhancement of Cognitive-Behavioral Therapy for Panic Disorder. *Depress Anxiety*, 2016, 33(8), p. 737-45.

[44] Klein, B; Richards, JC; Austin, DW. Efficacy of internet therapy for panic disorder. *J Behav Ther Exp Psychiatry*, 2006, 37(3), p. 213-38.

[45] Kiropoulos, LA; et al., Is internet-based CBT for panic disorder and agoraphobia as effective as face-to-face CBT? *J Anxiety Disord*, 2008, 22(8), p. 1273-84.

[46] Deacon, B; Abramowitz, J. A pilot study of two-day cognitive-behavioral therapy for panic disorder. *Behav Res Ther*, 2006, 44(6), p. 807-17.

[47] El Alaoui, S; et al., Predictors and moderators of internet- and group-based cognitive behaviour therapy for panic disorder. *PLoS One*, 2013, 8(11), p. e79024.

[48] Gabbard, GO. Long-term psychodynamic psychotherapy: a basic text. 2nd ed. *Core competencies in psychotherapy*., 2010, Washington, DC: American Psychiatric Pub. x, 223 p.

[49] Roy-Byrne, PP; Geraci, M; Uhde, TW. Life events and the onset of panic disorder. *Am J Psychiatry*, 1986, 143(11), p. 1424-7.

[50] Last, CG; Barlow, DH; O'Brien, GT. Precipitants of agoraphobia: role of stressful life events. *Psychol Rep*, 1984, 54(2), p. 567-70.

[51] Faravelli, C. Life events preceding the onset of panic disorder. *J Affect Disord*, 1985, 9(1), p. 103-5.

[52] Compton, A. The psychoanalytic view of phobias. Part III: Agoraphobia and other phobias of adults. *Psychoanal Q*, 1992, 61(3), p. 400-25.

[53] Compton, A. The psychoanalytic view of phobias. Part IV: General theory of phobias and anxiety. *Psychoanal Q*, 1992, 61(3), p. 426-46.

[54] Busch, FN; Milrod, BL; Singer, MB. Theory and technique in psychodynamic treatment of panic disorder. *J Psychother Pract Res*, 1999, 8(3), p. 234-42.

[55] Murray, B; Stein, MKG; Mark, H. Pollack; Peter, Roy-Byrne; Jitender, Sareen; Naomi, M. Simon, *Practice guideline for the treatment of patients with panic disorder.*, 2nd ed. 2010, American Psychiatric Association.

[56] Beutel, ME; et al., Implementing panic-focused psychodynamic psychotherapy into clinical practice. *Can J Psychiatry*, 2013, 58(6), p. 326-34.

[57] Milrod, BBF; Cooper, A; Shapiro, T. *Manual of Panic-Focused Psychodynamic Psychotherapy.*, 1997, Washington, DC: American Psychiatric Press.

[58] Sandberg, L., et al., Panic-focused psychodynamic psychotherapy in a woman with panic disorder and generalized anxiety disorder. *Harv Rev Psychiatry*, 2012, 20(5), p. 268-76.

[59] Milrod, B; et al., A randomized controlled clinical trial of psychoanalytic psychotherapy for panic disorder. *Am J Psychiatry*, 2007, 164(2), p. 265-72.

[60] Milrod, B; et al., Psychotherapies for Panic Disorder: A Tale of Two Sites. *J Clin Psychiatry*, 2016, 77(7), p. 927-35.

[61] Milrod, BL; et al., Do comorbid personality disorders moderate panic-focused psychotherapy? An exploratory examination of the American Psychiatric Association practice guideline. *J Clin Psychiatry*, 2007, 68(6), p. 885-91.

[62] Shear, MK; Weiner, K. Psychotherapy for panic disorder. *J Clin Psychiatry*, 1997, 58 Suppl 2, p. 38-43, discussion 44-5.

[63] Gabbard, GO. Long-term psychodynamic psychotherapy : a basic text. *Core competencies in psychotherapy.*, 2004, Washington, DC: American Psychiatric Pub. xiii, 210 p.

[64] Shapiro, F. Eye movement desensitization: a new treatment for post-traumatic stress disorder. *J Behav Ther Exp Psychiatry*, 1989, 20(3), p. 211-7.

[65] McNally, RJ; Lukach, BM. Are panic attacks traumatic stressors? *Am J Psychiatry*, 1992, 149(6), p. 824-6.

[66] Feske, U; Goldstein, AJ. Eye movement desensitization and reprocessing treatment for panic disorder: a controlled outcome and partial dismantling study. *J Consult Clin Psychol*, 1997, 65(6), p. 1026-35.

[67] Faretta, E. [EMDR and Cognitive-Behavioural Therapy in the treatment of Panic Disorder: a comparison]. *Riv Psichiatr*, 2012, 47(2 Suppl), p. 19-25.

[68] Rice, LN; Saperina, EP. *Task analysis of the resolution of problematic reactions* Patterns of Change: Intensive Analysis of Psychotherapy Process, ed. Rice LN and Greenberg LS. 1984, New York: Guilfore press.

[69] Shear, MK; et al., Emotion-focused psychotherapy for patients with panic disorder. *Am J Psychiatry*, 2001, 158(12), p. 1993-8.

[70] López, FSS. Acceptance and Commitment Therapy (ACT) in the Treatment of Panic Disorder: Some Considerations from the Research on Basic Processes. *International Journal of Psychology and Psychological Therapy*, 2009, p. 299-315.

[71] Zettle, RD. The Evolution of a Contextual Approach to Therapy: From Comprehensive Distancing to ACT. *International Journal of Behavioral Consultation and Therapy*, 2005(2), p. 77-89.

[72] Harris, R. Embracing your demons: an overview of Acceptance and Commitment Therapy. *Psychotherapy in Australia*, 2006, 12(4), p. 2-8.

[73] Hayes, SCSKD; Wilson, KG. *Acceptance and Commitment Therapy. An experiential approach to behavior change*, 1999, New York: Guilford Press.

[74] Hayes, SC; Gifford, WKEV; Follette, VM; Strosahl, KD. Experiential avoidance and behavior disorder: A functional dimensional approach to

diagnosis and treatment. *Journal of Consulting and Clinical Psychology*, 1996, 64, p. 1152-1168.

[75] Luciano, MCHS. Trastorno de evitación experiencial. *Internacional Journal of Clinical and Health Psychology*, 2001, 1, p. 109-157.

[76] Hayes, SC; Gifford, EV; Hayes, GJ. Moral behavior and the development of verbal regulation. *Behav Anal*, 1998, 21(2), p. 253-79.

[77] JG, AT; et al., A meta-analysis of the efficacy of acceptance and commitment therapy for clinically relevant mental and physical health problems. *Psychother Psychosom*, 2015, 84(1), p. 30-6.

[78] Piet, J; Hougaard, E. The effect of mindfulness-based cognitive therapy for prevention of relapse in recurrent major depressive disorder: a systematic review and meta-analysis. *Clin Psychol Rev*, 2011, 31(6), p. 1032-40.

[79] Kim, YW; et al., Effectiveness of mindfulness-based cognitive therapy as an adjuvant to pharmacotherapy in patients with panic disorder or generalized anxiety disorder. *Depress Anxiety*, 2009, 26(7), p. 601-6.

[80] Hofmann, SG; Sawyer, AT; Fang, A. The empirical status of the "new wave" of cognitive behavioral therapy. *Psychiatr Clin North Am*, 2010, 33(3), p. 701-10.

[81] Hayes, SC; et al., Open, aware, and active: contextual approaches as an emerging trend in the behavioral and cognitive therapies. *Annu Rev Clin Psychol*, 2011, 7, p. 141-68.

[82] Brown, LA; et al., A randomized controlled trial of acceptance-based behavior therapy and cognitive therapy for test anxiety: a pilot study. *Behav Modif*, 2011, 35(1), p. 31-53.

[83] Segal, Z; Teasdale, J; Williams, M. *Mindfulness-Based Cognitive Therapy for Depression.*, 2002, New York: Guilford Press.

[84] Casey, LM; Oei, TP; Newcombe, PA. An integrated cognitive model of panic disorder: the role of positive and negative cognitions. *Clin Psychol Rev*, 2004, 24(5), p. 529-55.

[85] Fava, L; Morton, J. Causal modeling of panic disorder theories. *Clin Psychol Rev*, 2009, 29(7), p. 623-37.

[86] Segal, ZV; Dinh-Williams, LA. Mindfulness-based cognitive therapy for relapse prophylaxis in mood disorders. *World Psychiatry*, 2016, 15(3), p. 289-291.

[87] Kim, B; et al., Factors associated with treatment outcomes in mindfulness-based cognitive therapy for panic disorder. *Yonsei Med J*, 2013, 54(6), p. 1454-62.

[88] Lidren, DM; et al., A comparison of bibliotherapy and group therapy in the treatment of panic disorder. *J Consult Clin Psychol*, 1994, 62(4), p. 865-9.

[89] Kabat-Zinn, J; et al., Effectiveness of a meditation-based stress reduction program in the treatment of anxiety disorders. *Am J Psychiatry*, 1992, 149(7), p. 936-43.

[90] Miller, JJ; Fletcher, K; Kabat-Zinn, J. Three-year follow-up and clinical implications of a mindfulness meditation-based stress reduction intervention in the treatment of anxiety disorders. *Gen Hosp Psychiatry*, 1995, 17(3), p. 192-200.

In: Panic Disorder
Editor: Yong-Ku Kim
ISBN: 978-1-53613-001-0

Chapter 12

INTERNET-BASED COGNITIVE BEHAVIORAL THERAPY AND ONLINE MINDFULNESS TRAINING FOR PANIC DISORDER

Jennifer Apolinário-Hagen* and Christel Salewski
Department of Health Psychology, University of Hagen, Germany

ABSTRACT

Anxiety disorders such as panic disorder with or without agoraphobia are a huge burden for individuals and societies with a relatively high lifetime prevalence [1] of up to 33.7 percent of the population. Estimates for the lifetime prevalence of panic disorder without agoraphobia mount up to 22.7% [2]. In panic disorder, the highest prevalence is found in younger adults, while other anxiety disorders such as generalized anxiety disorder (GAD) are more common across different later stages of adulthood [3].

In general, panic disorder can be effectively treated with pharmacological and psychological treatments such as cognitive behavioral therapy (CBT) and mindfulness interventions [4], the latter being applied to develop and increase the individual's ability to be

* Corresponding author. E-mail: jennifer.apolinario-hagen@fernuni-hagen.de.

mindful in the present moment [5]. There is some evidence that psychological treatment approaches are crucial for the improvement of panic-related symptoms. Although pharmacological treatments have proven to be potent in panic disorder therapy, their potential side effects can turn out as obstacles for the adherence to treatment and the long-term maintenance of achieved treatment outcomes [4]. Thus, it is important to provide effective psychological interventions for panic disorder either as adjunctive or stand-alone treatment [4]. However, despite the existence of evidence-based psychological therapy programs, the availability of treatment places is limited in conventional face-to-face mental health care [6]. This drawback termed as "treatment gaps in mental healthcare" was declared as a global key issue by the World Health Organization [7].

The dissemination and implementation of Internet-delivered computerized or electronic mental health (eMental health) services have been proposed to overcome barriers to access to professional help services [6]. Internet-based CBT (iCBT) and online mindfulness interventions (OMI) are examples of such eMental health services. The accessibility of eMental health services is facilitated by the increasing distribution of smartphone devices with mobile Internet access. The Internet has affected health behavior in daily life, such as health information-seeking behavior, and has provided novel options for self-help activities. Mobile health applications (mHealth apps) related to cognitive therapy and mindfulness practice have increasingly become popular as they are conveniently accessible through app stores [8]. Given the acceptance of "Dr. Google" as an informal health advisor and the growing number of publicly accessible online self-help services, patients with panic disorder face countless options with more or less sound evidence base for their usefulness. In contrast to other anxiety disorders, persons suffering from panic disorder show increased help-seeking behavior to get repeated reassurance that their physiological symptoms are not related to medical problem [3]. By identifying and communicating criteria for helpful and adequate evidence-based online self-help programs for panic disorder, health professionals could expand treatment options for young adults – the group with the highest prevalence of panic disorder and a high preference for the Internet and electronic devices - that are better suited for their daily routines than conventional face-to-face interventions.

Therefore, this chapter aims to identify the evidence base for the effectiveness of iCBT and OMI in the treatment of panic disorder with and without agoraphobia. Another purpose is to explore determinants of the effectiveness and adherence in Internet-based interventions, such as professional guidance, and to derive evidence-based recommendations for health professionals regarding the quality assessment of self-help options for panic disorder.

1. Determinants of Self-Help in Panic Disorder

Panic disorder evolves from recurrent panic attacks and worries that negatively affect subjective well-being, quality of life and psychosocial functioning in mostly young adults. Per Diagnostic and Statistical Manual (DSM) IV, panic disorder with or without agoraphobia is characterized by (A) recurrent unexpected panic attacks that (B) occur frequently (at least once per month) with persistent worries about impending panic attacks and their personal consequences, and/or involve substantial maladaptive behavior change that are not limited to (C) medical conditions or direct biological responses and/or (D) symptoms of other mental disorders [9]. Panic disorder usually has its onset in adolescence and early adulthood and is the most frequent type of anxiety disorders during this earlier life stages, whereas other types of anxiety disorders can be found across later stages of adulthood [3]. The development of maladaptive behavior changes is a specific risk factor in young adults: If not treated appropriately, panic disorder can impede the socioemotional development over the life span, considering that early adulthood is a critical phase with important transitions, life events, increased physiological vulnerability and higher reactivity to stress [4].

By addressing the key factors in panic disorder, patients can gain back perceived control over their life. Psychoeducational interventions are an important starting point for therapeutic support of panic patients. To understand how emotional reactivity, core beliefs and coping strategies interrelate, the widely-used *ABC-model* by Ellis [10] can be applied for a better understanding of cognitive and behavioral mechanisms involved in panic disorder. The ABC-model classifies a variety of triggering events, situations or stimuli that can result in responses at the levels of *(A) alarm* sensations, *(B) beliefs*, and associated *(C) coping* strategies and behaviors [4]. In the alarm phase, the initial panic attack is triggered through a stimulus, sensation, situation or event that activates the alarm networks in the brain with subsequent physiological and acutely severe stress responses. Such a trigger can also function as an indicator of an impending panic attack. Information processes related to the feared threat become associated with subjective beliefs about the threat to one's health and safety. Persons with panic disorder become hypervigilant of contextual details related to their panic attacks. As a coping strategy to minimize worries, persons with panic disorder try to reduce the perceived danger by seeking reassurance through medical consultations. Because there is no definitive guarantee of the absence of danger, repeated medical consultations may result in constituting rather than reducing irrational beliefs about the causes of their complaints. These evaluation patterns contribute to persistent worries, anxiety and distress preserving the vicious cycle of recurrent panic attacks [4]. Consequently, patients with panic disorder tend to initially misinterpret panic attacks as a medical problem rather than a psychiatric condition, which increases the likelihood of repeatedly seeking medical help in internal medicine practices and emergency divisions [3]. Hence, in contrast to reduced help-seeking behavior identified in specific phobias and social anxiety disorder (SAD), panic disorder was found to be associated with substantially higher health care utilization rates. These variable help-seeking patterns result from the distinctive features of panic disorder compared to other anxiety disorders: In specific phobias, coping with anxiety can be obtained through the mere avoidance of the stimulus. This characteristic makes coping in specific phobia in daily life often less demanding as in panic disorder with agoraphobia when public places are the conditional stimulus [4]. Especially agoraphobia can involve severe forms of symptoms and substantial impairment, as well as comorbidity with other mental disorders [2]. A significant feature of panic disorder is the symptom overlap with other mental health problems and the high prevalence of comorbidities across the life span. After the successful treatment of an initial panic disorder in adolescence or early adulthood, symptoms of other anxiety disorders can emerge years later. For instance, maladaptive coping behavior in panic disorder and agoraphobia with avoiding triggers for panic attacks can result in the manifestation of SAD [4]. A US-American epidemiological study [2] has shown that the percentage of comorbidity (one or more comorbid conditions) mounts up to 71.9% in patients with panic attacks, and up to 83.1% of patients with panic disorder and 100% in patients diagnosed with panic disorder and agoraphobia. The presence of combordities in panic disorder is considered in CBT manuals for the simultaneously transdiagnostic treatment of anxiety disorders [11].

2. From Cognitive Therapy to Mindfulness Interventions for Panic Disorder: The "Third Wave of CBT"

Both pharmacotherapy and psychotherapy are effective in the treatment of panic attacks and other symptoms of anxiety [4, 12]. Considering the potential side effects of pharmacotherapy for panic disorder, it appears reasonable that numerous patients and professionals indicate overall positive attitudes toward psychological interventions as an adjunctive or stand-alone treatment option. As one of the best studied psychological technique, CBT has been shown to be highly effective in the treatment of panic disorder and agoraphobia [13]. Though CBT programs for the different anxiety disorders share core methods, such as cognitive restructuring, extinction, habituation, exposure, psychoeducation, and relaxation exercises, manuals usually scope on single diagnoses, such as CBT for either panic disorder or SAD, but not both [11, 14]. Given the high proportion of comorbidity in panic disorder with other anxiety disorders [2], the development of tailored transdiagnostic CBT programs for different anxiety disorders is considered as an important advance in providing therapeutic options [11]. Advances in CBT have been described by the metaphor of waves. While the First Wave of CBT was dominated by behavioristic paradigms scoping on stimulus-response-reinforcement processes (classical and operant conditioning) and only observable behavior changes, the Second Wave of CBT added the cognitive perspective to shed light on the "black box" – a synonym for the human mind. To change dysfunctional behavior and emotional appraisals, the Third Wave of CBT has taken one step further to the meta-level emphasizing the relevance of changing the function and context of maladaptive psychological processes, such as negative automated thoughts [15, 16]. Interventions related to the Third Wave of CBT focus on the positive concepts of mindfulness and acceptance. According to Kabat-Zinn [16], mindfulness is widely defined as "...the awareness that emerges through paying attention on purpose, in the present moment, and nonjudgmentally to the unfolding of experience moment by moment." ([16], p. 145). Accordingly, Bishop et al. [17], conceptualize "... mindfulness as a process or regulating attention in order to bring a quality of nonelaborative awareness to current experience and a quality of relating to one´s experience within an orientation of curiosity, experiential openness, and acceptance" ([17], p. 234).

In panic disorder, mindfulness interventions are mostly used as an additional self-help option to "first line" treatments, such as CBT in combination with pharmacotherapy [4]. Per Shapiro et al. [18], multiple mechanisms may enable behavior changes in mindfulness interventions, namely self-regulation, values clarification, cognitive-behavioral flexibility, and exposure. To systematically develop and promote mindfulness, regular practice in daily life is mandatory [16]. Formal mindfulness meditation exercises can be systematically trained and include sitting or walking or loving-kindness meditation, mindful yoga, body scan. The formal practices are complemented by informal mindfulness practices that aim to bring back awareness to automated daily activities, such as breathing, eating, or teeth brushing [19]. Mindfulness skills are usually trained in 8-week programs within the three major concepts of mindfulness interventions: Mindfulness-Based Stress Reduction (MBSR), Mindfulness Based Cognitive Therapy (MBCT), and Acceptance and Commitment Therapy (ACT) are the most popular mindfulness programs [16]. Based on mindfulness meditation practice adapted from Buddhist tradition, Kabat-

Zinn developed MBSR as the first Western mindfulness program in the late 1970s. MSBR was initially designed as an adjunctive therapeutic option for patients with chronic pain undergoing medical treatments [16]. As a combination of MBSR and CBT principles, MBCT was developed as disorder-specific mindfulness intervention for the relapse prevention of major depressive disorder (MDD) [20]. Another derivate of MSBR and CBT is ACT that is grounded on the premise that the suppression of negative perceptions result in increased frequency and severity of aversive experiences; ACT emphasizes the importance of accepting these negative aspects as a precondition to change [21].

Most clinical studies related to face-to-face mindfulness interventions are based on MBSR targeting coping with somatic conditions, depression, distress, and anxiety. In face-to-face settings, mindfulness programs have demonstrated their effectiveness in reducing the symptoms of anxiety [22-24]. Accordingly, the evidence base for the feasibility of MBCT is scarce for panic disorder, except for a few studies targeting comorbidity with MDD and personality disorders (e.g., [25]). The literature further suggests that the individual success of mindfulness-based trainings depend on the active participant engagement and regular exercises of acquired mindfulness techniques in daily life [26]. However, regularly attending a face-to-face 8-week MSBR course and implementing mindfulness practice into daily life can be challenging for persons with mental health problems. A potential solution to expand the access to mindfulness interventions could be the provision of OMI [27]. As mentioned before, panic patients are predominantly younger persons that can be best reached for psychological services through the Internet. In this population, the coverage with smartphones is very high and using mHealth apps appears to match their habits [28]. The same applies to persons who are familiar with using the Internet for health purposes. In line with this, an online survey [29] demonstrated that most of the 500 respondents preferred the Internet (42%) as a first choice for mindfulness-based courses, followed by individual (38%) and group formats (20%). In addition, 11% of the sample reported that they would refuse traditional group formats [29]. This study points to the necessity of matching the preferences and habits of participants of therapeutic interventions, especially of those with panic attacks and agoraphobia, through providing mindfulness interventions via the Internet. The same can be applied to CBT delivered online.

3. Online Self-Help Programs for Panic Disorder

Concerning the scarce resources for public mental healthcare, Internet-delivered therapy approaches have been suggested as a means to bridge treatment gaps in primary care [6]. Indeed, the Internet has a high potential to provide additional opportunities for the dissemination of evidence-based psychological interventions for a broader range of individuals [5]. In general, eMental health services include the usage of new media and modern technologies in screening, monitoring, prevention, health promotion, counselling, self-help, recovery and therapy [30]. Most Internet-delivered therapy programs are based on the principles of CBT. Other distinctive features of Internet-delivered therapies involve the categorization as unguided or self-guided vs. therapist-guided digital interventions. Self-guided Internet-delivered interventions include the provision of treatment information, such as bibliotherapy, whereas patients work through structured online self-help program on their own, without the assistance of a professional or peer [31]. Self-guided Internet interventions can also involve automated feedback or support provided through online activities and interactive programming, whereas clinician-supported online interventions commonly consist of a combination of both structured iCBT exercises and therapist-assistance, such as personalized feedback provided via email [31]. The contents of programs, number of modules, and the provision of professional assistance vary largely across iCBT programs for panic disorder: Minimal guidance in iCBT programs usually consists of personalized communication with online therapists via email, chat, or SMS, telephone contacts, discussion forums with peers or a combination of different modes [32]. Examples for clinician-assisted iCBT self-help programs for panic disorder are "Panic Online" [31], FearFighter®" [33], "velibra®" [14], "PaxOnline" [34], and the "Panic Program" by the "VirtualClinic" [35]. For instance, "Panic Online" (PO) from Australia is a self-administered iCBT program for panic disorder and agoraphobia is a 12-week e-therapy program that is available in different versions varying in assistance: as unguided self-help program and as program with guidance from a psychologist or a general practitioner [36]. PO consists of a five-module open-access psychoeducational intervention, an optional six-module stress management program, and a password-protected four-module iCBT program for panic disorder. The contents of the latter include self-monitoring, progressive muscle relaxation, controlled breathing, cognitive restructuring, and two gradual exposures [31].

Like iCBT programs, OMI are suggested as a further opportunity to enlarge self-help options for patients per individual preferences [37]. Most of clinically tested OMI follow the structure of 8-week MSBR courses and many provide at least a minimal professional support, including therapist-assistance, individualized feedback or coaching [37]. Although 8 weeks are proposed as optimal duration time for MSBR and MBCT [16], a review with 15 OMI has shown that the actual time span ranged from 2 to 12 weeks [37]. As an example, the British program "Mindfulness online" [38] consists of 10 sessions of guided meditation presented by experienced MSBR instructors, including 3-minute breathing meditation, mindful movement, sitting meditation, body scan, and interactive sessions with minimal guidance through automated emails. However, only few mindfulness programs have been tested in patients with panic disorder (see [25]). Given the high proportion of comorbidity in panic disorder [2], transdiagnostic tailored iCBT programs turn out as a promising option. Transdiagnostic manuals provide the option of simultaneous therapy of different anxiety disorders [39]. Tailoring and personalization can be obtained by adjusting the contents of transdiagnostic treatments with preferences of patients, including choices regarding device types, the amount of background information, or optional sections [14].

Table 1. Two exemplary Internet-based tailored programs for the transdiagnostic treatment of panic disorder

Program	Main features of the program	Number and contents of the modules
iCBT program "velibra" [14]. Switzerland	**Program**: 9-week unguided iCBT intervention "velibra" for the transdiagnostic treatment of (comorbid) anxiety disorders (panic disorder, agoraphobia, SAD, GAD), including panic attacks. **Grounding**: iCBT program "deprexis". **Delivery mode**: Internet-delivered via smartphone, computer or tablet, with minimal therapist assistance provided mostly by email and/or telephone, and daily automated messages via email or SMS; self-monitoring of changes in symptom severity (symptom tracking questionnaires).	**Contents**: 6 tailored modules with psychoeducation, stimulus exposure, cognitive restructuring, self-monitoring, mindfulness exercises, relaxation, relapse prevention, as well as stress reduction techniques. **Sessions**: 1. Introduction, 2. Coping with anxiety, 3. Learning mindfulness and relaxation exercises, 4. Understanding and practicing exposure, 5. Social skills, social support, and interpersonal relationships, and 6. Summary and relapse prevention.
Online mindfulness intervention [39]. Sweden	**Program**: 8-week unguided Internet-delivered mindfulness intervention for the transdiagnostic treatment of (comorbid) anxiety disorders, including panic disorder and agoraphobia. **Grounding**: MBSR [16] **Delivery mode**: Internet-delivered, self-administered sessions with audio files, provided without therapeutic assistance (ten minutes of training, twice a day)	**Contents**: 8 tailored modules with 96 audio files with instructions for mindfulness mediation, body scan, and psychoeducation. **Sessions**: 1. Stopping and Getting Started, 2. Knowing Your Body, 3. Increasing Your Concentration, 4. Managing Your Thought Noise, 5. Stretching Your Borders, 6. SOAL: Stop, Observe, Accept, and Let Go, 7. It Is What It Is, and 8. Sitting with Whatever Comes Up.

Note. Both Internet-based interventions include adaptive tests for disease-specific treatment modules for anxiety disorders (i.e., tailored transdiagnostic programs). Pilot studies confirmed the feasibility of both programs in panic disorder [14, 39].

In summary, the Internet can improve the availability of evidence-based interventions for adolescents and adults. Both CBT and mindfulness interventions share a common grounding and are established methods for the treatment of anxiety in face-to-face setting [4]. Online self-help programs appear to be a suitable option, especially for young persons suffering from panic disorder with or without agoraphobia.

4. Evidence Base for the Effectiveness of Online Interventions for Panic Disorder

In recent years, several randomized controlled trials (RCTs) have demonstrated the effectiveness of iCBT programs in reducing the symptoms of anxiety disorders, including panic attacks [40-42]. Most iCBT studies stem from Australia or Sweden and targeted a specific diagnosis within the spectrum of anxiety disorders [12]. For instance, a meta-analytic review [43] with 23 RCTs on computer-assisted iCBT programs (n = 10 targeting panic disorder and agoraphobia) showed that their effectiveness did not differ significantly from face-to-face CBT. The effects of iCBT did not differ in terms of type of anxiety disorder and delivery modes of programs, either. However, therapeutic effects decreased once therapist time was replaced by computer [43]. In line with this, another systematic review of 101 studies [44] suggested that online self-help for anxiety can be appropriate for individuals who are not able or willing to seek professional help from face-to-face services. Nonetheless, this review [44] also indicated a clinical superiority of face-to-face CBT in reducing anxiety-related symptoms, but only a few studies compared iCBT with face-to-face CBT so far to provide deeper insights into the comparability of delivery formats. Regarding the "Panic Online" program, both previous pilot studies with or without support from GPs via face-to-face counselling yielded comparable outcomes in reducing the symptoms of panic disorder [31]. In a RCT on the treatment of agoraphobia and panic disorder, both patient groups attending the "Panic Online" program (n = 68) and the face-to-face CBT group (n = 40) showed significant levels of symptom reduction [45]. In another RCT with 55 patients diagnosed with panic disorder with or without agoraphobia [46], both iCBT with assistance via email contacts and therapist-assisted CBT manual were more effective than information-only control group in reducing anxiety. Calbring et al. [47] found evidence for the effectiveness of a 10-week iCBT self-help bibliotherapy program for panic disorder and agoraphobia with assistance provided via brief telephone contacts and email. Results further showed that the weekly expenditure of time amounted to 3.9 hours on average. At the nine months' post-treatment follow-up, 77% of participants in the treatment group did not meet the DSM-criteria for panic disorder anymore [47]. An emerging trend is the implementation of tailored transdiagnostic treatment of comorbid anxiety disorders. For example, Berger et al. [14] conducted a RCT on the transdiagnostic treatment program "velibra®" with 139 anxiety patients.47.5% of the 70 patients in the treatment group had panic disorder as primary diagnosis (further 21.4% as secondary diagnosis). The program was found to be effective compared to the control group. In addition, 38.5% of participants in this RCT did not fulfil the criteria of panic disorder at the 6-months follow-up [14]. Transdiagnostic iCBT was also shown to be effective in longer-term follow-up examinations. A RCT with 24 patients diagnosed with panic disorder [48] demonstrated longer-term effects: both the disease-specific and the transdiagnostic iCBT were effective with large reductions of panic symptoms at the 24-months follow-up. Moreover, the assumption that young adults with panic disorder may benefit especially well from iCBT programs was confirmed by a meta-analysis [49]. Nevertheless, to make definite conclusions about the helpfulness of iCBT for patients in primary care, further research is needed [49]. In addition, it should be also noted that some studies reported non-significant results of iCBT programs. For instance, in a RCT [33] with 67 patients diagnosed with social phobia or panic disorder, the iCBT program "FearFighter®" was not effective compared to a waiting-list control group – despite therapist-support via telephone.

Contrary to iCBT, the evidence base for the effectiveness of OMI in panic disorder is considerably smaller. Studies on OMI for different populations revealed small to medium effect sizes [37]. In a review [37] with 11 of 15 RCTs on Internet-delivered MSBR and ACT, effect sizes for the reduction of symptoms of different anxiety disorders were significant, but relatively small. However, there are only few studies and thus limited evidence for the effectiveness of online ACT in reducing symptoms of anxiety according [50]. As an example, for an effective OMI for panic disorder, a RCT [39] on a transdiagnostic treatment of anxiety disorders with 91 patients revealed large effect sizes in the treatment group compared to an active control group. This indicated the feasibility of this stand-alone OMI in the transdiagnostic treatment of anxiety. Participants assigned to the mindfulness group completed 44 of the 96 exercises (standard deviation = 33.7) on average, with a mean of 7.3 hours of mindfulness practice during the 8-week course [39]. This and other studies [26] showed that the average practice time in effective OMI can be briefer than recommended in conventional MBSR programs pointing to their potential for anxiety disorders. Conversely, as mentioned above, the evidence base for OMI adapted for panic disorder is very small. One review identified only 11 eligible OMI studies, with 4 studies on anxiety [51], while another review [37] found 15 eligible RCTs (n = 11 studies targeting anxiety) and revealed that most included RCTs (n = 10) were of medium quality. Taken together, the quality of studies investigating the effectiveness of OMI is often poor due to lack of control groups or follow-up assessments [51].

5. Quality Assessment of Panic Disorder Apps

Smartphone-delivered mHealth apps probably provide the most efficient way to reach young patients suffering from panic disorder on a large scale. However, most interventions provided via app stores are not developed in clinical contexts and thus quality indicators are needed to assess their usefulness for persons with panic disorder. Given the scarce evidence base on this topic, we describe the findings of two reviews targeting distinct app types.

To investigate the quality of Android apps related to panic disorder, van Singer et al. [52] applied the self-help model for panic disorder, according to treatment guidelines of the American Psychiatric Association to identify their helpfulness in daily life, and used the brief DISCERN instrument [53] and the "Health on the Net" (HON) quality label [54]. Quality indicators included the self-help score, interactivity, accountability, and evidence-based content quality. Most of the 52 Android apps included in this review were based on the principles of CBT. Overall, this review evaluated the quality of evidence-based information and the self-help score as poor in both paid and free apps for panic disorder. In addition, neither the payment grade (paid or free) nor the quantity of downloads were associated with the contents-related quality of these apps [52]. Although smartphone apps provide a popular delivery mode for OMI, the helpfulness of the high number of such interventions in app stores can be considered as questionable. Mani et al. [8] performed a systematic review on the quality of iPhone apps using the Mobile Application Rating Scale (MARS; [55]). This review showed an acceptable median MARS score of 3.2 of max. 5 points across the 23 included apps with the highest average score found for the *Headspace app*, followed by *Smiling Mind*, *mindfulness*, and *Mindfulness Daily*. Mani et al. [8] mentioned further that the claim of many apps to be related to mindfulness approaches was misleading, because most were guided meditation apps, timers or reminders. In addition, only few apps scored high on information quality. There was also poor evidence regarding the usefulness of apps to help consumers to develop mindfulness skills [8]. Hence, further clarification about the quality of apps for panic disorder is required.

6. The Role of Guidance in Internet-Based Therapies

The provision of minimal guidance was suggested as key factor of effective Internet-delivered treatments for panic disorder. Generally, guided iCBT interventions for anxiety disorders achieve higher effect sizes for therapeutic outcomes than unguided programs, as well as higher acceptability in terms of adherence and participant satisfaction [56]. Adherence rates in iCBT were found to be comparable to those in face-to-face CBT in various RCTs [43]. However, a systematic review [57] of 13 studies (n = 3 targeting panic disorder) also revealed large variations of drop-out rates in iCBT trials, scaling up to 55% in a RCT on social anxiety (see [58]). The variations in drop-outs in iCBT trials for panic disorder identified in this review [57] were quite small, ranging from 0% [45], to 12% [59] and up to 18% [60]. Other studies on iCBT for panic disorder conducted in primary care showed moderate to relatively high attrition rates, including 21% [35], 28.6% [14], 30% [33], and 43.9% [61]. Potentially, guidance in iCBT is relevant for completion rates. Currently, there is no consensus about the necessity or the optimal form of support in iCBT, and the degree or type of guidance varies broadly across RCTs [32]. According to a systematic review [12] with 37 RCTs on the efficacy of iCBT in different anxiety disorders, moderate to large between-group effect sizes were achieved that were comparable to face-to-face CBT. In line with this, another review [32] on the impact of guidance in e-mental health treatments (n = 14 studies) confirmed that guided interventions were significantly more effective than unguided programs, but several questions for instance regarding the dose-dependency of guidance remained open. In a study [62] on a guided iCBT program for panic disorder provided either with one or three email contacts per week, no significant difference in therapeutic outcomes was identified between both guidance groups. Furthermore, based on the findings of a study on a clinician-supervised five-lesson iCBT program for panic disorder with 330 primary care patients, Allen et al. [60] stated that adherence increased once therapist contact was provided. Mewton et al. [12] concluded that guidance was not needed for the immediate effects of iCBT, but appeared to be relevant for the long-term maintenance of symptom improvements and increasing adherence. Additionally, there are inconsistent results concerning the impact of the therapeutic relationship in iCBT. Some studies indicated that the therapeutic working alliance appears to be less essential for treatment outcomes in iCBT compared to face-to-face psychotherapy [63]. In OMI, the impact of guidance on the effectiveness and adherence is less well studied compared to iCBT research though many OMI provide at least minimal guidance. According to a review [37], adherence rates for the included iMSBR and iACT studies on anxiety and distress ranged between 39.5% and 92% in 6 to 8-week programs. However, due to the limited evidence on the impact of guidance in OMI for anxiety disorders, this aspect needs to be examined in future studies. To improve adherence in OMI, theory-driven strategies to generate meaningful contents of motivational messages can be obtained from health behavior change models, such as the Health Action Process Approach (HAPA) by Schwarzer [64]. For instance, HAPA-enhanced messages and online support groups in tailored online MSBR interventions were suggested as a strategy to decrease attrition rates and improve adherence in non-clinical populations [27]. Interestingly, despite the provision of guidance, high attrition rates in OMI studies were found especially in non-clinical populations (e.g., [5, 27]). This suggests the need for research to determine effective motivational features in online self-help, such as the application of persuasive design [65].

7. Drawbacks in the Current Application of Online Interventions for Panic Disorder

The evidence base for the usefulness of media-assisted psychological self-help interventions for persons suffering from panic disorder grows steadily. Media-delivered self-help interventions have been widely endorsed as an initial step in the treatment of anxiety, although it should be also considered that there is a deficiency of studies on their long-term effectiveness investigated in large pragmatic trials as well as publication bias as a further confounding factor [44]. Furthermore, there is a scarcity of RCTs on OMI in clinical populations [51]. In addition, it should also be considered that evidence-based e-mental health treatment services are currently not available for the public outside the context of clinical trials in many countries [5]. The novelty of these self-help options and unclear conditions for health professionals may have contributed to the rising number of market-driven apps that are mostly not regulated by healthcare policies. To provide support for informed decisions about mHealth apps, health professionals can assist patients to find appropriate online self-help programs for panic disorder [52]. Concerning the effects of professional guidance, research data indicate that guided iCBT programs are associated with larger effect sizes and reduced attrition rates in comparison to unguided program [56]. Nonetheless, there is uncertainty regarding effective features of guidance in e-mental health interventions [32]. Moreover, high-quality RCTs comparing the effects of guided iCBT and face-to-face CBT in the treatment of anxiety disorders are also rare [41]. Unguided programs are rather recommended for mild problems, subclinical symptoms and the prevention of mental disorders [32]. Therefore, it appears vital to identify options to prevent panic disorder. OMI could be a convenient alternative for hard-to-reach nonclinical populations such as young adults who are unlikely to attend traditional course settings [23, 24, 66]. However, given the inflationary customization of mindfulness approaches, Kabat-Zinn [16] cautioned about too much professional enthusiasm resulting in decontextualization and a reductionistic understanding of MSBR as another CBT technique.

SUMMARY AND OUTLOOK

In this chapter, we evaluated the current evidence base on the effectiveness of iCBT and OMI for panic disorder to derive recommendations for health professionals in practice and research. Overall, the evidence base suggests that guided iCBT programs are superior to unguided iCBT programs regarding their effectiveness, acceptability and adherence [32]. Moreover, tailored transdiagnostic Internet-delivered programs for comorbid anxiety disorders appear to have some potential for the adjunctive therapy of panic disorder, even as unguided formats [14, 39]. Nonetheless, several questions remain open, such as the required level of professional support and individual predictors of treatment outcomes [32, 56]. In addition, the assumption that OMI could be used to reach otherwise (face-to-face) hard-to-reach populations [66] needs further clarification. To achieve a large-scale dissemination, more information about the facilitators and barriers to access Internet-based psychological treatments in patients with panic disorder are also required. Although the evidence base for web-delivered MSBR for panic disorder and comorbid anxiety disorders appears promising, it should be noted that the development of OMI is still in its infancy [37]. Thus, a global issue in research on OMI is the scarcity of high-quality studies [51, 66]. Due to the small evidence base, it remains largely unclear whether or under which conditions both iCBT and mindfulness interventions are a useful long-term complement to face-to-face interventions for panic disorder. Furthermore, little is known about individual facilitators and barriers to using Internet-delivered intervention, such as technology acceptance in primary care patients and clinicians [67]. Pathways of change in mindfulness interventions need further clarification [18]. For instance, the transdiagnostic construct intolerance of uncertainty in patients with panic disorder has been proposed as a potential factor in reducing the severity of symptoms in panic disorder in MBCT interventions [68]. Future research should target specific mechanisms of change in OMI in comparison to face-to-face MSBR [38]. Taken together, the fragmentary evidence base for online self-help options for panic disorder makes it necessary for health professionals to keep up with the newest developments and provide guidance for informed decisions.

References

[1] Baxter AJ, Vos T, Scott KM, Ferrari AJ, Whiteford HA. The global burden of anxiety disorders in 2010. *Psychol Med* 2014; 44(11):2363–74.

[2] Kessler RC, Chiu WT, Jin R, Ruscio AM, Shear K, Walters EE. The Epidemiology of Panic Attacks, Panic Disorder, and Agoraphobia in

the National Comorbidity Survey Replication. *Arch Gen Psychiatry* 2006; 63(4):415-424.

[3] Bandelow B, Michaelis S. Epidemiology of anxiety disorders in the 21st century. *Dialogues in Clinical Neuroscience* 2015;17(3):327-335.

[4] Bystritsky A, Khalsa SS, Cameron ME, Schiffman J. Current Diagnosis and Treatment of Anxiety Disorders. *Pharmacy and Therapeutics* 2013; 38(1):30–57.

[5] Kvillemo P, Brandberg Y, Bränström R. Feasibility and Outcomes of an Internet-Based Mindfulness Training Program: A Pilot Randomized Controlled Trial. *JMIR Mental Health* 2016; 3(3):e33.

[6] Musiat P; Tarrier N. Collateral outcomes in e-mental health: a systematic review of the evidence for added benefits of computerized cognitive behavior therapy interventions for mental health. *Psychol Med* 2014; 44(15):3137-3150.

[7] Collins KA, Westra HA, Dozois DJA, Burns DD. Gaps in accessing treatment for anxiety and depression: challenges for the delivery of care. *Clin Psychol Rev* 2004; 24(5):583–616.

[8] Mani M, Kavanagh DJ, Hides L, Stoyanov SR. Review and Evaluation of Mindfulness-Based iPhone Apps. *JMIR Mhealth Uhealth* 2015; 3(3):e82.

[9] Craske MG, Kircanski K, Epstein A, Wittchen H-U, Pine DS, Lewis-Fernandez R et al. Panic disorder: a review of DSM-IV panic disorder and proposals for DSM-V. *Depress Anxiety* 2010; 27(2):93–112.

[10] Ellis A. Rational Psychotherapy and Individual Psychology. *Journal of Individual Psychology* 1957; 13:38-44.

[11] Berger T, Boettcher J, Caspar F. Internet-based guided self-help for several anxiety disorders: a randomized controlled trial comparing a tailored with a standardized disorder-specific approach. *Psychotherapy (Chic)* 2014; 51(2):207–19.

[12] Mewton L, Smith J, Rossouw P, Andrews G. Current perspectives on Internet-delivered cognitive behavioral therapy for adults with

anxiety and related disorders. *Psychol Res Behav Manag* 2014; 7:37–46.

[13] Pompoli A, Furukawa TA, Imai H, Tajika A, Efthimiou O, Salanti G. Psychological therapies for panic disorder with or without agoraphobia in adults: a network meta-analysis. *Cochrane Database Syst Rev* 2016; 4:CD011004.

[14] Berger T, Urech A, Krieger T, Stolz T, Schulz A, Vincent A et al. Effects of a transdiagnostic unguided Internet intervention ('velibra') for anxiety disorders in primary care: results of a randomized controlled trial. *Psychol Med* 2017; 47(1):67–80.

[15] Hofmann SG, Sawyer AT, Fang A. The empirical status of the "new wave" of cognitive behavioral therapy. *Psychiatr Clin North Am* 2010; 33(3):701–10.

[16] Kabat-Zinn J. Mindfulness-Based Interventions in Context: Past, Present, and Future. *Clinical Psychology: Science and Practice* 2003;10(2):144-156.

[17] Bishop M, Lau S, Shapiro L, Carlson ND, Anderson J, Carmody Segal ZV, Abbey S, Speca M, Velting D, Devins G. Mindfulness: A proposed operational definition. *Clinical Psychology: Science and Practice* 2004; 11:230–241.

[18] Shapiro SL, Carlson LE, Astin JA, Freedman B. Mechanisms of mindfulness. *J Clin Psychol* 2006; 62:373–386.

[19] Fulwiler C, de Torrijos F. Mindfulness and health. *Psychiatry Issue Brief* 2011; 8(2):1-3.

[20] Teasdale JD, Segal ZV, Williams JM, Ridgeway VA, Soulsby JM, Lau MA. Prevention of relapse/recurrence in major depression by mindfulness-based cognitive therapy. *J Consult Clin Psychol* 2000; 68:615-623.

[21] Hayes SC, Luoma JB, Bond FW, Masuda A, Lillis J. Acceptance and commitment therapy: Model, processes and outcomes. *Behav Res Ther* 2006; 44:1-25.

[22] Hofmann SG, Sawyer AT, Witt AA, Oh D. The effect of mindfulness-based therapy on anxiety and depression: A meta-analytic review. *J Consult Clin Psychol* 2010; 78(2):169–83.

[23] Khoury B, Lecomte T, Fortin G, Masse M, Therien P, Bouchard V et al. Mindfulness-based therapy: a comprehensive meta-analysis. *Clin Psychol Rev* 2013; 33(6):763–71.

[24] Khoury B, Sharma M, Rush SE, Fournier C. Mindfulness-based stress reduction for healthy individuals: A meta-analysis. *J Psychosom Res 2015*; 78(6):519–28.

[25] Kim B, Cho SJ, Lee KS, et al. Factors Associated with Treatment Outcomes in Mindfulness-Based Cognitive Therapy for Panic Disorder. *Yonsei Med J* 2013; 54(6):1454-1462.

[26] Cavanagh K, Strauss C, Cicconi F, Griffiths N, Wyper A, Jones F. A randomised controlled trial of a brief online mindfulness-based intervention. *Behav Res Ther* 2013; 51(9):573–8.

[27] Mak WW, Chan AT, Cheung EY, Lin CL, Ngai KC. Enhancing Web-Based Mindfulness Training for Mental Health Promotion With the Health Action Process Approach: Randomized Controlled Trial. *J Med Internet Res* 2015; 17(1):e8.

[28] Bakker D, Kazantzis N, Rickwood D, Rickard N. Mental Health Smartphone Apps: Review and Evidence-Based Recommendations for Future Developments. *JMIR Ment Health* 2016; 3(1):e7.

[29] Wahbeh H, Svalina MN, Oken BS. Group, One-on-One, or Internet? Preferences for Mindfulness Meditation Delivery Format and their Predictors. *Open Med J* 2014; 1:66-74.

[30] Riper H, Andersson G, Christensen H, Cuijpers P, Lange A, Eysenbach G. Theme issue on e-mental health: a growing field in Internet research. *J Med Internet Res* 2010; 12(5):e74.

[31] Klein, B., Shandley, K., Austin, D., & Nordin, S. Pilot trial of Panic Online self-guided version: Internet-based treatment for panic disorder. *E-Journal of Applied Psychology;* 2008; 4(2):25-30.

[32] Baumeister H, Reichler L, Munzinger M, Lin J. The impact of guidance on Internet-based mental health interventions: A systematic review. *Internet Interventions* 2014; 1(4):205-215.

[33] Mathiasen K, Riper H, Ehlers LH, Valentin JB, Rosenberg NK. Internet-based CBT for social phobia and panic disorder in a

specialised anxiety clinic in routine care: Results of a pilot randomised controlled trial. *Internet Interventions* 2016; 4:92-98.

[34] Ciuca AM, Berger T, Crisan LG, Miclea M. Internet-based treatment for Romanian adults with panic disorder: protocol of a randomized controlled trial comparing a Skype-guided with an unguided self-help intervention (the PAXPD study). *BMC Psychiatry* 2016; 16:6.

[35] Wims E, Titov N, Andrews G, Choi I. Clinician-assisted Internet-based treatment is effective for panic: A randomized controlled trial. *Aust N Z J Psychiatry* 2010; 44(7):599–607.

[36] Shandley K, Austin DW, Klein B, Pier C, Schattner P, Pierce D et al. Therapist-assisted, Internet-based treatment for panic disorder: can general practitioners achieve comparable patient outcomes to psychologists? *J Med Internet Res* 2008; 10(2):e14.

[37] Spijkerman MPJ, Pots WTM, Bohlmeijer ET. Effectiveness of online mindfulness-based interventions in improving mental health: A review and meta-analysis of randomised controlled trials. *Clin Psychol Rev* 2016; 45:102–14.

[38] Krusche A, Cyhlarova E, Williams JMG. Mindfulness online: an evaluation of the feasibility of a web-based mindfulness course for stress, anxiety and depression. *BMJ Open* 2013; 3(11):e003498.

[39] Boettcher J, Astrom V, Pahlsson D, Schenstrom O, Andersson G, Carlbring P. Internet-based mindfulness treatment for anxiety disorders: a randomized controlled trial. *Behav Ther* 2014; 45(2):241-253.

[40] Arnberg FK, Linton SJ, Hultcrantz M, Heintz E, Jonsson U. Internet-delivered psychological treatments for mood and anxiety disorders: a systematic review of their efficacy, safety, and cost-effectiveness. *PLoS One* 2014; 9(5):e98118.

[41] Olthuis JV, Watt MC, Bailey K, Hayden JA, Stewart SH. Therapist-supported Internet cognitive behavioural therapy for anxiety disorders in adults. *Cochrane Database Syst Rev* 2016; 3:CD011565.

[42] Penate W, Fumero A. A meta-review of Internet computer-based psychological treatments for anxiety disorders. *J Telemed Telecare.* 2016;22:3–11.

[43] Cuijpers P, Marks IM, van Straten A, Cavanagh K, Gega L, Andersson G. Computer-aided psychotherapy for anxiety disorders: a meta-analytic review. *Cogn Behav Ther* 2009; 38(2):66–82.

[44] Mayo-Wilson E, Montgomery P. Media-delivered cognitive behavioural therapy and behavioural therapy (self-help) for anxiety disorders in adults. Cochrane Database *Syst Rev* 2013; (9):CD005330.

[45] Kiropoulos LA, Klein B, Austin DW, Gilson K, Pier C, Mitchell J et al. Is internet-based CBT for panic disorder and agoraphobia as effective as face-to-face CBT? *J Anxiety Disord* 2008; 22(8):1273–84.

[46] Klein B, Richards JC, Austin DW. Efficacy of Internet therapy for panic disorder. *J Behav Ther Exp Psychiatry* 2006; 37(3):213-238.

[47] Carlbring P. Remote Treatment of Panic Disorder: A Randomized Trial of Internet-Based Cognitive Behavior Therapy Supplemented With Telephone Calls. *Am J Psychiatry* 2006; 163(12):2119.

[48] Fogliati VJ, Dear BF, Staples LG, Terides MD, Sheehan J, Johnston L et al. Disorder-specific versus transdiagnostic and clinician-guided versus self-guided internet-delivered treatment for panic disorder and comorbid disorders: A randomized controlled trial. *J Anxiety Disord* 2016; 39:88–102.

[49] Barak A, Hen L, Boniel-Nissim M, Shapira N. A Comprehensive Review and a Meta-Analysis of the Effectiveness of Internet-Based Psychotherapeutic Interventions. *Journal of Technology in Human Services* 2008; 26(2-4):109–60.

[50] Brown M, Glendenning A, Hoon AE, John A. Effectiveness of Web-Delivered Acceptance and Commitment Therapy in Relation to Mental Health and Well-Being: A Systematic Review and Meta-Analysis. *J Med Internet Res* 2016; 18(8):e221.

[51] Fish J, Brimson J, Lynch S. Mindfulness Interventions Delivered by Technology Without Facilitator Involvement: What Research Exists and What Are the Clinical Outcomes? *Mindfulness* 2016; 7(5):1011-1023.

[52] Van Singer M, Chatton A, Khazaal Y. Quality of Smartphone Apps Related to Panic Disorder. *Frontiers in Psychiatry* 2015; 6:96.

[53] Khazaal Y, Chatton A, Cochand S, Coquard O, Fernandez S, Khan R, et al. Brief DISCERN, six questions for the evaluation of evidence-based content of health-related websites. *Patient Educ Couns* 2009; 77(1):33–7.

[54] Boyer C, Selby M, Scherrer JR, Appel RD.. The health on the net code of conduct for medical and health websites. *Comput Biol Med* 1998; 28(5):603–10.

[55] Stoyanov S, Hides L, Kavanagh D, Tjondronegoro D, Zelenko O, Mani M. Mobile App Rating Scale: A new tool for assessing the quality of health-related mobile apps. *JMIR mhealth and uhealth* 2015; 3(1):e27.

[56] Andrews G, Cuijpers P, Craske MG, McEvoy P, Titov N. Computer therapy for the anxiety and depressive disorders is effective, acceptable and practical health care: a meta-analysis. *PLoS One* 2010; 5(10):e13196.

[57] Andersson G, Cuijpers P, Carlbring P, Riper H, Hedman E. Guided Internet-based vs. face-to-face cognitive behavior therapy for psychiatric and somatic disorders: a systematic review and meta-analysis. *World Psychiatry* 2014; 13(3):288-295.

[58] Botella C, Gallego MJ, Garcia-Palacios A, et al. An Internet-based self-help treatment for fear of public speaking: a controlled trial. *Cyberpsychol Behav Soc Netw* 2010; 13:407–21.

[59] Carlbring P, Nilsson-Ihrfelt E, Waara J, et al. Treatment of panic disorder: live therapy vs. self-help via Internet. *Behav Res Ther* 2005; 43:1321–33.

[60] Allen AR, Newby JM, Mackenzie A, Smith J, Boulton M, Loughnan SA et al. Internet cognitive-behavioural treatment for panic disorder: randomised controlled trial and evidence of effectiveness in primary care. *BJPsych Open* 2016; 2(2):154–62.

[61] Bergström J, Andersson G, Ljótsson B, et al. Internet-versus group-administered cognitive behaviour therapy for panic disorder in a psychiatric setting: a randomised trial. *BMC Psychiatry* 2010; 10:54.

[62] Klein, B., Austin, D., Pier, C., Kiropoulos, L, Shandley, K, Mitchell, J., Gilson, K., & Ciechomski, L. (2009). Frequency of email therapist contact and internet-based treatment for panic disorder: Does it make a difference? *Cognitive Behaviour Therapy*, 38, 100-13.

[63] Berger T. The therapeutic alliance in internet interventions: A narrative review and suggestions for future research. *Psychother Res* 2016:1-op14.

[64] Schwarzer R. Modeling Health Behavior Change: How to Predict and Modify the Adoption and Maintenance of Health Behaviors. *Applied Psychology* 2008; 57(1):1–29.

[65] Kelders SM, Kok RN, Ossebaard HC, van Gemert-Pijnen JEWC. Persuasive system design does matter: a systematic review of adherence to web-based interventions. *J Med Internet Res* 2012; 14(6):e152.

[66] Jayewardene WP, Lohrmann DK, Erbe RG, Torabi MR. Effects of preventive online mindfulness interventions on stress and mindfulness: A meta-analysis of randomized controlled trials. *Prev Med Rep* 2017; 5:150–9.

[67] Hennemann S, Beutel ME, Zwerenz R. Drivers and Barriers to Acceptance of Web-Based Aftercare of Patients in Inpatient Routine Care: A Cross-Sectional Survey. *J Med Internet Res* 2016; 18(12):e337.

[68] Kim MK, Lee KS, Kim B, Choi TK, Lee S-H. Impact of Mindfulness-Based Cognitive Therapy on Intolerance of Uncertainty in Patients with Panic Disorder. *Psychiatry Investig* 2016; 13(2):196–202.

About the Editor

Yong-Ku Kim
Department of Psychiatry,
Korea University Ansan Hospital, Gojan-Dong,
Danwon-Gu, 516, Kyunggido, Republic of Korea
yongku@korea.ac.kr

INDEX

A

B

C

D

E

F

G

H

I

L

M

N

O

P

R

S